Modernism and Performance

with warm ~~regards~~.
pleasure to meet you.

V. ////

Modernism and Performance

Jarry to Brecht

Olga Taxidou

palgrave
macmillan

First published 2007 by
PALGRAVE MACMILLAN
Houndmills, Basingstoke, Hampshire RG21 6XS and
175 Fifth Avenue, New York, N.Y. 10010
Companies and representatives throughout the world

PALGRAVE MACMILLAN is the global academic imprint of the Palgrave Macmillan division of St. Martin's Press, LLC and of Palgrave Macmillan Ltd. Macmillan® is a registered trademark in the United States, United Kingdom and other countries. Palgrave is a registered trademark in the European Union and other countries.

ISBN-13: 978–1–4039–4100–8 hardback
ISBN-10: 1–4039–4100–9   hardback
ISBN-13: 978–1–4039–4101–5 paperback
ISBN-10: 1–4039–4101–7   paperback

This book is printed on paper suitable for recycling and made from fully managed and sustained forest sources. Logging, pulping and manufacturing processes are expected to conform to the environmental regulations of the country of origin.

A catalogue record for this book is available from the British Library.

A catalog record for this book is available from the Library of Congress.

10 9 8 7 6 5 4 3 2 1
16 15 14 13 12 11 10 09 08 07

Printed and bound in Great Britain by
Antony Rowe Ltd, Chippenham and Eastbourne

For Katerina

and for

Roger Savage

Contents

List of Illustrations   ix

Acknowledgements   xi

Preface   xiv

1   Introduction: Savages, Gods, Robots and Revolutionaries: Modernist Performance   **1**

2   Puppets and Actors   **10**
     'Gentlemen: the Marionette'   16
     The Ghost in the Machine   34
     'When the Puppets Come to Town': Wooden Characters   40

3   The Director, the Playwright and the Actress   **43**
     'A Slice of Life'   46
     'The Woman Question'   54
     Naturalism and its Discontents   58

4   '… as if the words themselves could sing and shine': Poetic Drama and Theatricality   **69**
     W. B. Yeats: Poetry, Philosophy and Nationality   80
     T. S. Eliot: 'He do the police in different voices'   86
     Gertrude Stein: The Landscape Play   92
     'Solely because of the increasing disorder':
       Poetic Drama and Epic Theatre   99
     Stages for Dancers   103

5   Sada Yakko, Michio Ito and Mei Lan-fang: Orientalism, Interculturalism and the Performance Event   **118**
     The European Tour   127
     Mei Lan-fang in Moscow   137

6   Greeks and Other Savages: Neo-Hellenism, Primitivism and Performance   **148**

7 **'The Revolution said to the theatre ...': Performance
and Engagement** **181**
    The Futurist *Serate* 184
    'First International Dada Fair' 187
    The Blue Blouse (1923–28) 193
    The Federal Theatre Project (1935–39) 201

Notes 214

Name Index 234

Subject Index 241

List of Illustrations

1 Alfred Jarry, Ubu Roi (Frontispiece for *Ubu Roi*).
   Paris: Mercure de France, 1896.   21
2 Alfred Jarry, Ubu Roi (Programme for *Ubu Roi*).   22
3 *The Magnanimous Cuckold* by Fernand Crommelynck,
   designed by Lyubov Popova, directed by Vsevolod
   Meyerhold, 1922.   32
4 *The Magnanimous Cuckold*, 1922.   33
5 *The Bathhouse*, by Mayakovsky, directed by Meyerhold,
   1930.   62
6 *The Bedbug*, by Mayakovsky, designed by Aleksandr
   Rodchenko, directed by Meyerhold, 1930.   63
7 Zinaida Reikh as Vera in *The Second Commander* by
   I. L. Selvinsky, directed by V. E. Meyerhold, 24 July 1929,
   Kharkov. Photo by A. A. Temerin.   65
8 Edward Gordon Craig, *Photograph of a model stage
   setting for a scene in Hamlet*, 1912.   67
9 Edward Gordon Craig, Mask of the Fool in *The Hour Glass*
   by W. B. Yeats, *The Mask*, Vol. 3, Nos. 10–12, p. 147a, 1911.   83
10 Natalia Goncharova, Drawing for *Les Noces*, 1923.   110
11 'The Pyramid of Heads', Igor Stranvinsky/Bronislava
   Nijinska, *Les Noces* [1923], from the 1966 revival
   directed by Bronislava Nijinska, The Royal Ballet,
   Covent Garden.   112
12 Jean Cocteau, Design for *Les mariés de la
   Tour Eiffel*, 1922.   114
13 Sada Yakko, circa 1900.   130
14 Michio Ito as the hawk in W. B. Yeats, *At the
   Hawk's Well*, 1916. Photo: A. L. Coburn.   132
15 Michio Ito. Photo A. L. Coburn.   134
16 Mei Lan-fang as the fisherman's daughter in
   The Fisherman's Revenge, 1930s.   139
17 Edward Gordon Craig, *Isadora Duncan Dancing*,
   The Mask, Vol. 1, No. 6 (1908), p. 126b.   163

18–21   Brecht-Neher, *Antigone-Model 1948*, photos Ruth Berlau.
Source: Brecht-Neher, *Antigone-Model 1948*, Berlin:
Herausgegeben von der Deutschen Akademie der Künste,
1955. Helene Weigel as Antigone and Hans Gaugler
as Kreon.   177–9

22–24   The Blue Blouse, A Skit in the Interest of
Industrialization; A Poster Composition: New and
Old Holidays; A Dance of the Machine: 'Ford and Us'.
Source: *The Drama Review*, Vol. 17, No. 1 (March),
1971 (Russian Issue), pp. 35–46.   195–6

25   Poster for the Federal Theatre Project production
of the Living Newspaper *One Third of a Nation*,
Adelphi Theatre, New York, 1938.   207

26   *One Third of a Nation*, opening scene of the
above production.   208

27   Design for *Dr Faustus*, directed by Orson Welles.   209

28   From the production of T. S. Eliot, *Murder in the
Cathedral*, directed by Halsted Welles, with Harry
Irvine as the Archbishop.   210

Acknowledgements

Many friends and colleagues have contributed to the making of this book through insightful discussion and careful commentary on earlier versions. I am especially thankful to: Claire Altree, David Bradby, Clare Brennan, Douglas Cairns, Quentin Daniel, Jane Goldman, Ourania Karoula, Nikki Kekos, Vassiliki Kolocotroni, Maria Panoutsou, Tassos Petris, Roger Savage, Randall Stevenson, Liana Theodoratou, Panos Tsakalogiannis and J. Michael Walton; to Robert Leach for the use of his photographic archive and for all his ground-breaking work on the Russian and Soviet avant-garde. Elke Pfeil of the Brecht Archive at the Akademie der Künste in Berlin, Mrs Hilda Hoffmann of the Ruth Berlau Estate, Marie J. Taylor of the Edward Gordon Craig Estate and Veronica Fletcher of the Special Collections Archive at George Mason University were all extremely generous with their time and the materials in their collection; I am grateful to be able to reproduce some of them in this study. Anne Mason, Rachel Evans and Adam Budd helped with the final for-matting of the typescript and I am thankful for their patience and technologi-cal acumen. At Palgrave Macmillan, Kate Wallis and Felicity Noble have been extremely supportive throughout all the work on this project, and Kitty Van Boxel and Brian Morrison have been particularly attentive to detail during the production process. My thanks, also, to the anonymous readers of this book whose comments I have tried to address, I fear not always successfully.

A final draft of this book was completed during a research leave funded by the AHRC (Arts and Humanities Research Council) for which I am grateful. Sabbatical time and a research grant awarded by the School of Literatures, Languages and Cultures at the University of Edinburgh allowed me to bring this project to completion.

This book could not have been written without Roger Savage; his generosity – with his ideas, his magnificent library and his time – is evident on every page. It also could not have been written without Katerina Taxidou; she has helped in more ways than she will ever know.

The author and publishers wish to thank the following for permission to use copyright material:

Spencer Research Library, University of Kansas Libraries for the frontispiece of Alfred Jarry, *Ubu Roi*, Paris: Mercure de France (1896);

Spencer Museum of Art, The University of Kansas for the programme insert for the 1896 performance at Théâtre de l'Oeuvre of Alfred Jarry, *Ubu Roi*, (Museum Purchase: Letha Churchill Walker Memorial Art Fund);

The Robert Leach Archive for the following images:

Two photographs from *The Magnanimous Cuckold*, by Fernand Crommelynck, designed by Lyubov Popova, directed by Vsevolod Meyerhold, 1922.
The Bathhouse, by Mayakovsky, directed by Meyerhold, 1930.
The Bedbug, by Mayakovsky, designed by Alesandr Rodchenko, directed by Meyerhold, 1930.
Zinaida Reikh as Vera in *The Second Commander* by I. L. Selvinsky, directed by V. E. Meyerhold, 24 July 1929, Kharkov. Photo by A. A. Temerin;

The Edward Gordon Craig Estate for the following images:

Edward Gordon Craig, *Photograph of a model stage setting for a scene in Hamlet*, 1912.
Edward Gordon Craig, Mask of the Fool in *The Hour Glass* by W. B. Yeats, *The Mask*, Vol. 3, Nos. 10–12, p. 147a, 1911.
Edward Gordon Craig, *Isadora Duncan Dancing*, *The Mask*, Vol. 1, No. 6 (1908), p. 126b;

Bill Cooper for photo 'The Pyramid of Heads' taken of the revival of Igor Stravinsky/Bronislav Nijinska, *Les Noces* (1923) by The Royal Ballet, Covent Garden, (2001);

George Eastman House for the following images:
Michio Ito as the hawk in W. B. Yeats, *At the Hawk's Well*, 1916. Photo: A. L. Coburn.
Michio Ito. Photo A. L. Coburn;

The Archive of the Akademie der Künste, Bertolt Brecht Archive/Hilda Hoffmann, Berlin, for the use of four photographs by Ruth Berlau from Brecht-Neher, *Antigone-Model 1948*;

The Federal Theatre Project Collection, Special Collections & Archives, George Mason University, USA, for the following images:

Poster for the Federal Theatre Project production of the Living Newspaper, *One Third of a Nation*, Adelphi Theatre, New York, 1938.
Photograph, *One Third of a Nation*, opening scene from New York production.
Photograph, Set design for *Dr. Faustus*, directed by Orson Welles.
Photograph from the production of T. S. Eliot's *Murder in the Cathedral*, directed by Halsted Welles, with Harry Irvine as the Archbishop.

Faber and Faber Limited for reproducing extracts from *Poetry and Drama* by T. S. Eliot, *Selected Essays* by T. S. Eliot, *Women of Trachis* by Ezra Pound and *Ten Principal Upanishads*, translated by Shree Purohit and W. B. Yeats. Reprinted by permission of Faber and Faber Limited;

New Directions Publishing Corporation for reproducing extracts from *Women of Trachis* and from the Preface of *Women of Trachis*, by Ezra Pound, from SOPHOKLES/WOMEN OF TRACHIS, copyright © 1957 by Ezra Pound. Reprinted by permission of New Directions Publishing Corp.

Every effort has been made to trace the copyright holders but if any have been inadvertently overlooked the publishers will be pleased to make the necessary arrangement at the first opportunity.

Preface

This book is largely a continuation of the work carried out with Vassiliki Kolocotroni and Jane Goldman in our *Modernism: An Anthology of Sources and Documents*, which presented the historical avant-garde side-by-side with the exponents of literary Modernism. Like that project, it attempts to read through the concept of performance the moments of interaction, over-lap and influence between these two strands of Modernism. This perform-ance imperative, the analysis claims, is matched by an equally passionate attachment to the workings of the word. Rather than read these two strands as independent, each signalling a different 'school' of Modernism – where the performance-inflected avant-garde comes to stand in for formal and political radicalism and literary 'high', predominantly Anglophone Modernism is seen as conservative, at best formally aestheticist – this study concentrates on moments of performance that are at once literary and the-atrical, textual and discursive. In each case the interdependence of these categories is highlighted, where the experiments in performance of the historical avant-garde are seen to be underpinned by equally experimental attitudes towards the literary/poetic word (and not simply by a negation of it). In turn literary modernist drama constantly negotiates notions of embodiment and spatialisation. The term 'modernist performance' used throughout this study is located in the interface between these two domi-nant, but not mutually exclusive strands of Modernism.

Equally this study results from my experience of teaching theatre studies and performance theory within a Department of English Literature. Admittedly the profile of performance studies has been considerably raised within the general study of literature over the past twenty years. The gen-eral 'spilling out' of the category of the performative into every aspect of cultural production has called for a radical reconceptualisation of how we understand and critically appreciate literary production. This study hopes to stress the particular significance of performance for our general under-standing of the workings of Modernism. My understanding of performance and its relationships to literary drama has been greatly influenced by my first teaching appointment at the University of Exeter's Drama Department, then as now committed to exploring the relationships between practice and theory in the making of theatre. This was a formative and creative period and I am grateful to the staff and students I worked with, as I am grateful to all the performance studies students I have worked with over the past ten years at Edinburgh University's Department of English Literature. This book is an attempt to bridge the two traditions in theatre studies in a way that hopefully stresses the significance of performance in general studies of the literature of the period; in turn the literary dimension is not approached as that which needs to be overcome, negated, surpassed but forms a constituent component of the projects examined.

The two texts that frame this study are admittedly 'literary', or rather they at once 'advertise' their literary inheritance while also proposing notions of avant-garde performance. Alfred Jarry's *Ubu Roi* (1896) and Bertolt Brecht's *The Antigone of Sophocles* (1947) both rework canonical texts (*Macbeth* and Sophocles) in terms of a classical literary inheritance and in terms of the modes of theatre proposed by each play-text. In many ways the issues that the *Ubu* phenomenon raises are addressed and somewhat formalised by Brecht. It may appear somewhat incongruous to have Brecht at the end of a trajectory that starts with Jarry's blasphemous endeavours and then proceeds through the radical experiments of the avant-garde. However, Brecht's work is seen to derive from the experiments in modernist performance, including the historical avant-garde. This positioning of Brecht within the workings of the historical avant-garde is in line with Peter Bürger's significant assessment of the avant-garde in the 1960s, and with Fredric Jameson's more recent work on Brecht (*Brecht and Method*), which views his work in terms of a 'method'; one that brings together radical experimentation of the historical avant-garde, the philosophical underpinning of the so-called project of modernity, and distils everything into a working model. Indeed, the *ANTIGONEMODELL 1948*, with which this book ends, could be seen as such a proposal for the engaged work of avant-garde art; one that rewrites the past (in terms of form and content) for the purposes of the future.

This analysis highlights significant moments across this notional spectrum where the notion of performance is rigorously experimented with and begins to emerge as an independent aesthetic activity. Within this framework, the works of T. S. Eliot, W. B. Yeats, Gertrude Stein, W. H. Auden – amongst others – are read to highlight the ways in which their literary and theatrical projects are interdependent. In this sense the concerns of literary Modernism are filtered and sometimes mediated through notions of performance. Indeed, the phrase 'modernist performance' could be located between the more literary innovations of a predominantly Anglophone Modernism – in many ways obsessed with the word – and the Continental experiments of the avant-garde, seen to be obsessed with the performing body. As this analysis hints, however, this binary is often blurred not least by the workings of performance itself, which displays a strong attachment to the word, albeit in most cases the 'word as flesh'.

The various sections of this book attempt to tease out ways in which this notion of modernist performance begins to be conceptualised and given form. The radical reworking of the 'professions' of the theatre (the rise of the director; the conspicuous presence of the female performer; the actor or marionette debate; the reworking of the roles of the designer, and so on) under Modernism are now part of received theatre history and are approached here to the extent that they impact on this new notion of performance. In this context, this study treats Naturalism – so crucial for all the above categories – as an integral part of modernist theatre and not simply as the movement against which Modernism and the avant-garde are reacting. Despite its proclamations of 'newness', the theatre of this period, like Modernism in general, exhibits a profound and complex relationship with the workings of tradition, particularly the classical European tradition against which it appears to be rebelling. The canonical European models of theatre from the Greeks to the Renaissance to German Romanticism are constantly evoked throughout the period as signifiers of the failures of the European project of the Enlightenment and its economies of representation. However, this love/hate relationship itself fuels much of the experimentation in performance at the time, from Jarry's *Ubu* plays to the later Dadaist reworking of Greek tragedies to Brecht's version of *Antigone*. In particular the revival of interest in ritual and primitivism through the influence of Modernist anthropological schools, particularly those inspired by the work of James Frazer and the Cambridge Ritualists, proposes a reading of the 'classics' that is located, physicalised and embodied. In turn this anthropological take on performance presents new ways of reading the theatres both of the past and the present.

This difficult relationship with the past is also mirrored in the ways European modernist performance approaches the theatres of China, Japan and South East Asia. More than a search for 'rejuvenation' or a straightforward case of Orientalist appropriation, the encounter with the theatres of the 'Orient' is formative for many schools of modernist performance and impinges on both their aesthetics and politics.

Modernist performance features conspicuously in the political debates of the period, where the issues of autonomy or engagement are usually enacted and debated through models that are predominantly theatrical (Walter Benjamin's championing of Brecht's Epic Theatre, for example). In turn, much of the politics of the period is mediated through performance and performative discourses, not least in the form of the manifesto. The performance events analysed in this book tease out some of the ways the relationships between aesthetics and politics are reconfigured through the radical and sometimes utopian aspirations of the historical avant-garde. These aspirations are somewhat incongruously also read into the phenomenon of the Federal Theatre Project (FTP) in the USA, presented here as a transatlantic example of the impact of the avant-garde. The FTP appears much earlier (1929) than the mass exodus of avant-garde artists from Europe to the US after World War II and presents a fascinating example of the transposition of avant-garde politics and aesthetics into the context of US liberalism and existing American theatrical experimentation and tradition. It also presents ways of reading the debates about autonomy and commitment – so crucial for the European avant-garde – not strictly in total and sometimes totalising terms, and possibly foreshadows the routes that these debates would follow until they are partly overtaken by the discourses of the Cold War and postmodernism.

This book does not claim to present a general account of the historical avant-garde; the instances of avant-garde performance mentioned and briefly analysed are there to help draw the connecting links between the Continental avant-garde and literary Modernism. The term 'historical avant-garde' is here used in the manner applied by Günter Berghaus in his recent, illuminating and comprehensive study on the topic, *Theatre, Performance and the Historical Avant-Garde*, to cover the movements of Expressionism, Futurism, Dadaism and Constructivism. Also, and despite the emphasis placed on the body of the performer, this book does not present detailed accounts of theories of acting (or indeed dance) but, again, mostly reads these in conjunction with debates about the use of poetry on the stage. Jane Milling's and Graham Ley's study *Modern Theories of Performance* covers such theories with insight and rigour. This book aspires to be read alongside these (both published by Palgrave Macmillan) and hopefully offer ways of further integrating modernist performance into the general study of Modernism.

1

Introduction: Savages, Gods, Robots and Revolutionaries: Modernist Performance

> I go to the first performance of Alfred Jarry's Ubu Roi, at the Théâtre de L'Oeuvre, ... and he [my friend] explains to me what is happening on the stage. The players are supposed to be dolls, toys, marionettes, and now they are all hopping like wooden frogs, and I can see for myself that the chief personage, who is some kind of King, carries for sceptre a brush of the kind we use to clean a closet. Feeling bound to support the most spirited party, we have shouted for the play, but that night at the Hôtel Corneille I am very sad, for comedy, objectivity, has displayed its growing power once more. I say: 'After Stéphane Mallarmé, after Paul Verlaine, after Gustave Moreau, after Puvis de Chavannes, after our own verse, after all our subtle and nervous rhythm, after the faint mixed tints of Conder, what more is possible? After us the Savage God'.
>
> (W. B. Yeats, 'The Tragic Generation', 1914)[1]

Yeats's famous, aphoristic response to the first public dress rehearsal of Jarry's *Ubu Roi*, in 1896, manages to touch upon all the experimental elements at the time that come to form the hallmark of schools of performance within Modernism. This highly staged and densely intertextual response (written in hindsight) manages to combine aspects of disgust and wonder, fear and awe, distance and familiarity; all soon to be theorised by the Russian Formalists as 'estrangement' and a little later by Bertolt Brecht as the *Verfremdungseffect*. It was not so much that Yeats disliked the performance as that he was simply shocked by it. And the reverberations of that shock lead him to pronounce, 'After us the Savage God'. This, however, he does assuming a dramatic, or rather melodramatic, pose himself. It is as if

1

he cannot resist the theatrical and so lashes out with a performative *gestus*. Before he reaches his final apocalyptic pronouncement he provides us with a detailed formal analysis of the production, explaining what it is that he found so uncanny as to resort to a type of inarticulate primitivism.

This strangeness is initially created by the fact that his French is not good enough and he has to be guided through the performance – perhaps not very explicitly – by his friend. At once he is forced to decode the stage business through means besides language. His discomfort is further compounded by the fact that the live actors are imitating marionettes. The protagonist in turn appears to be holding a toilet brush. By now his desperation is about to overflow. However, in the spirit of cosmopolitanism he is compelled to support the play ('we have shouted for the play'). This betrayal only breeds melancholy and in the end he bursts out with a fully blown dramatic gesture himself. This he presents as both a diagnosis and a cure (a *pharmakon*) to the 'barbarism' he has just experienced. This is particularly apt as it comes as the final paragraph in a chapter of autobiography entitled 'The Tragic Generation', which charts and exemplifies the great symbolist and aestheticist traditions of the late nineteenth century. The savage tragedy (and indeed Jarry, at Lugné-Poë's instigation, toyed with the idea of staging *Ubu Roi* as a tragedy) is what remains of a grand tradition once it has been put through the modernist shredder. Indeed it is no longer a tragedy at all in the classical sense but a kind of objective comedy: anti-humanist, godless, decadent and blasphemous. And, more disconcertingly, for Yeats it also appears to be formally primitive.

Yeats's aphorism usefully summarises much of the experiment that was to mark the theatres of Modernism, and help to define the notion of performance as an autonomous aesthetic activity. The difficult relationship between language and the stage; the attempt to create a stage for a 'total' experience, sometimes synaesthetic, sometimes fragmentary; the relationships between the sacred and the profane; the actor or marionette debate; the relationships between tradition, Hellenism in particular, and a concept of the uniquely demanding modern; the eschatological urgency highlighted by the use of 'After'. Probably not since the Athenian model of classical Greece has western theatre undergone such a major refurbishment; hence the fascination with that classical model that much of modernist performance exhibits (from the concept of tragedy in Yeats's 'Tragic Generation' to Brecht's vehement anti-Aristotelianism). And through all these experiments the notion of performance develops with its own epistemology, politics and aesthetics. Although dramatic theory, particularly theories of tragedy, has since Aristotle always been central to general theories of aesthetics, the attempt to create a distinct language of performance – one that differentiates itself from the dramatic text – needs to be read within the context of modernity.

This book sets out to trace this trajectory through its main debates from the first public performance of *Ubu Roi* in 1896 to the publication of Bertolt Brecht's *Short Organum for the Theatre* in 1949 and his first *model*, *The Antigone-Model*. The choice of playwrights/directors to mark the spectrum covered is significant, as Lugné-Poë's stagings of Jarry's plays sparked off a series of debates about the relationships between theatre and life, the aesthetic and the political, tradition and innovation, the sacred and the profane that can be seen as formulated and somewhat schematised with Brecht's Epic Theatre. The year 1949 is equally significant as it is the year Brecht established the Berliner Ensemble, having returned in 1948 to East Berlin after exile in Europe and the USA: a gesture that raises issues about engagement, critique and autonomy. In the interim this study looks at a number of charismatic figures, from W. B. Yeats himself, T. S. Eliot, Edward Gordon Craig, W. H. Auden, Christopher Isherwood and Gertrude Stein in the Anglophone tradition of poetic drama through Vsevolod Meyerhold, the theatre of the Bauhaus, F. T. Marinetti, Jean Cocteau and the pioneers of modern drama in the legacies of the European avant-garde. This process is not as random as it may appear to be, for, like Yeats's quotation above, this book attempts to reinstate the binding link between Anglophone Modernism (primarily literary) and the historical, European avant-garde of the Continent.[2]

In some respects the idea of performance as specific practice and theory transpires as a way of bridging or unlocking the impasse created by a critical tradition that views textuality (literary or otherwise) and materiality (stage, bodily or otherwise) as mutually exclusive discourses. Conceiving performance as in part autonomous acknowledges both 'the poetry *in* the theatre' and 'the poetry *of* theatre' (to borrow Cocteau's phrase).[3] The dramatic dimension of many of the 'literary modernists' needs to be read as formative of their projects and not simply as analogy or metaphor. The experiments on the stage and the experiments on the page inform each other during this period. Indeed (as this study hints) and in as much as Modernism has been read as a 'revolution of the word', the emphasis it puts on language itself is material and spatial, always in search of modes for staging, enactment and embodiment. The encounter with the European theatrical avant-garde, as exemplified by Yeats's response above, highlights the theatricality of much of the modernist literary experiment as well. In turn that avant-garde, as many scholars have shown, and despite its protestations, has a very strong attachment to the word, nowhere staged more emphatically than in its favourite mode: the manifesto.[4]

The manifesto itself could be read as a mode that acts out the difficult relationship between theatre and philosophy, presenting an enacted form of the word. In as much as the word is 'estranged' and presented as a material object, the manifesto presents an embodied, situated, *theatricalised* form for it to occupy. The quest for a language of performance is strangely doubled by modernist theatre's 'fascination for theory'.[5] And this fascination permeates most schools of performance, from the Anglophone 'high modernist' experiments of Yeats, Eliot and Pound to the more radical strands of the historical avant-garde. The journal that Brecht co-edited while in exile in Moscow was called *Das Wort* (1936–39). Viktor Shklovsky's ideal of bringing out the 'literariness' in literature ('How I want simply to describe objects as if literature had never existed; that way one could write literarily'[6]) translates into the search for theatricality on the stage. However, this theatricality displays a deep attachment to the word. John E. Bowlt and Olga Matich make a similar point about the Russian avant-garde:

> The radical writers and artists of the 1910s and 1920s were reiterating the Symbolist concern with the physical vitality that the word, when purified of its nonessentiality, could engender – the word made flesh. Almost every avant-garde production ... relies on the word as declaration, prediction, or affirmation and as an element that supersedes and transcends the pictorial or musical component.[7]

'The word made flesh' suggests connections with Christianity and the transcendental tradition, and it may not be accidental that Christian iconography features heavily in many modernist plays. In another sense, however, modernist performance revisits that crucial encounter between Christianity and Hellenism, as a result of which (in the fourth century C.E.), theatre was officially outlawed in the European tradition.[8] Ironically Christianity also offers a formidable instance of 'the word made flesh' with its very own performance conventions and rituals, deriving from the presence – in the incarnation and in the transubstantiation – of the 'corpus Christi'. The Athenian model of tragedy and Christianity (both with beguiling elements of ritual) transpire as the two main historical/aesthetic sites that modernist theatre encounters on its quest for languages of performance. These are, more often than not, filtered through an Orientalist and/or primitivist perspective. Modernist schools of performance display a keen interest in the theatres of South East Asia, China and Japan, while also exploring oral and popular forms in their own cultures. These usually come together in a sometimes opaque, but heady cocktail of Orientalism, Hellenism and modernist experiment.

The quest for theories of acting, the most systematic and inspired in theatre history, provides the main context for the agon between the word and the flesh. This battle between the word and the body is primarily fought through and on the body of the modernist performer. The apparent bankruptcy of the European project of the Enlightenment and its economies of representation created the need for a non-humanist, non-anthropomorphic, non-mimetic art form: one that relies on abstraction and distance rather than empathy and identification. This becomes particularly pertinent (and particularly demanding) when dealing with the human body. The body of the actor, according to Martin Puchner, becomes the 'scape-goat' of modernist performance,[9] which is why arts of the body – spiritual gymnastics (Dalcroze) and avant-garde ballet (Diaghilev) – become suddenly central. In another sense, however, from Heinrich von Kleist's influential essay, *On the Marionette Theatre* (c.1810) to the Futurist Robot plays, via Meyerhold's biomechanics, the body of the performer is called upon not only to filter and mediate ideas but crucially also to create them, physically and materially.

The body of the performer begins to be historicised but also gendered. The 'woman question', central to Modernism more generally, also informs theories of acting.[10] The specific histories of actresses from the period and their contribution to these experiments constitute a growing area of research. These need to be read with an awareness of those schools of performance where the notion of the actress appears almost obscene (Craig, Marinetti) and of the many technophobic renditions of 'evil' female robots. For many of these schools the classical theatres of the 'Orient' and of the Graeco-Roman tradition are made more attractive by their all-male productions involving female impersonators. Every encounter with the representational efficacy of the human form stumbles across the particular representation of the female. Again the historically difficult relationship between the female performer and the stage is constantly revisited by modernist performance, inflecting most theories. In many cases, the work of the performers themselves (Eleonora Duse, Isadora Duncan, Zinaida Reikh) addresses this challenge. Speaking for 'The Tragic Generation', Yeats almost accidentally stresses the centrality of gender in the quest for a new art form (which he was later to find in the form of his own 'Plays for Dancers'):

> Yet I am certain that there was something in myself compelling me to attempt creation of an art as separate from everything heterogeneous and casual, from all character and circumstance, as some Herodiade of our theatre, dancing seemingly alone in her narrow moving luminous circle.[11]

Yeats does not 'create' this new art form; he embodies it. Interestingly, this quest for a language of performance compels him, yet again, to utilise dramatic modes of representation, only this time he does it in drag. And it is not Salome he identifies with (he refers to Oscar Wilde's play in the same essay) but the previous generation, her mother. In a sense this is his generation – the Symbolists and the Aestheticists – who have to come to terms with the modernist Salome's frenzied dance. His is the 'tragic generation' that is in search of a 'sacred' art form in a godless world. Instead, all he encounters is the 'Savage God'. In doing so he too engages in discourses of gender.

The manner in which these discourses are engaged, however, points towards what Martin Puchner has called 'closet drama',[12] referring not solely to gender, but to the fraught relationships between modernist drama and the legacies of anti-theatricality. His study of modernist drama charts the ways in which the legacies of anti-theatricality are employed in forging the aesthetics of modernist performance. In this sense, he calls modernist drama a Platonic drama. The founding philosopher of anti-theatricalism, indeed possibly of the original rift between theatre and philosophy, is readdressed in the search for an art form that is at once embodied *and* philosophical, flesh and word. And this process is further problematised by the issues of gender, which according to theories of performativity, are crucial in any understanding of the word *as* flesh (or vice versa).

Modernist performance also takes part in the Platonic tradition in its sheer utopian aspirations. Eliot's quest for Christian Tragedy, Yeats's attempts at creating a national Irish drama, the world-building (and destroying) fervour of the historical avant-garde, Brecht's search of 'models' for the future, all re-establish the link between theatre and philosophy, while, importantly, proposing new ways of living, utopian worlds. This is theatre not as one amongst the arts; it is drama as *the* foundational art form. However, in this instance the utopia proposed is not merely a philosophical utopia; it is a theatrical one. Or rather it is located between the two, enacting the shortcomings in the representational economies of both. It is a utopia located in the word and the body, and, significantly, in the body politic. This is not so much a continuation of a Platonic legacy as a radical critique of it. If, as G. S. Morgan suggests, 'all utopias are Platonic',[13] relying on an idealist opposition of 'real' and 'imagined' worlds, then modernist performance – or so I hope to show – proposes an anti-Platonic utopia. This notion of utopia does not simply propose a new vision of the world but critically engages the discourses that make such visions possible. It is visionary, metaphysical but also material and practical, offering 'models' and 'methods' for a new art form, for a new notion of the subject and, finally, for a new world. In other words it is both Artaudian and Brechtian. Indeed, this concept of 'utopia' helps to bridge these two high priests of modernist performance, usually read in opposition. Drawing on the recent approaches to Brecht by Fredric Jameson and Antony Tatlow, this study reads Artaud and Brecht in tandem (particularly in relation to the theatres of East Asia and Japan), highlighting a melancholy sensibility in Brecht, and also politicising Artaud.

It is a similar Platonically inflected critical tradition that sees the Anglophone legacy primarily in the so-called school of 'poetic drama' as inherently anti-theatrical, somatophobic and conservative, while the Continental avant-garde is read as revelling in a pure theatricality often punctuated by its radical politics. To a certain extent this formulation may be true, but the relationships between the two camps are more intricate and fraught than it may suggest. The work of Yeats and Gordon Craig, Eliot and the influential group of scholars called the Cambridge Ritualists, Auden and Isherwood and Berlin Cabaret are all areas of recent research that exhibit the deep attachment that literary Modernism displays towards the workings of performance. In this context the plays of T. S. Eliot are read not only in relation to Christian iconography and aesthetics, but also in relation to the new Hellenism and to similar experiments in the plays of Gertrude Stein. Similarly, the bleaker, more misogynist and technophobic (even fascist) aspects of the Continental avant-garde problematise the direct relationships between formal experiment and radical politics. Indeed, the political efficacy of formal experiment is much debated from the early discussions of expressionism between Ernst Bloch and Walter Benjamin to the Stalinist purges of the 1930s. And these discussions, which evolve into full-blown theses on the relationships between politics and aesthetics (commitment versus autonomy), are in most cases animated through examples from performance. It is no coincidence that for Walter Benjamin, Brecht's Epic Theatre becomes the emblem of the modernist work of art, at once formally experimental and politically committed, while for Theodor W. Adorno such a co-existence is almost impossible, and the same example becomes the emblem of a compromised art. It is significant that performance features heavily in these discussions. Its emphasis on embodied and collective experience, at once personal/public and historical, makes it an appropriate forum to test out 'models' for all modernist art forms.

The work of Gertrude Stein features as an example of the avant-garde but also as the work of an 'American in Paris', adding a transatlantic strand to this analysis. The links between Continental literary Modernism and the USA (between Apollinaire and e.e. cummings for example) have been extensively charted and have come to shape significantly our overall understanding of Modernism. The relationships, however, between the historical European avant-garde and theatrical experiments in the USA have received less attention. The USA is usually read as the *locus* of refuge of the avant-garde after the Stalinist and fascist purges on the Continent of Europe. Through an analysis of the Federal Theatre Project of the late 1930s, this study hopes to show that the relationships between the USA and the historical avant-garde are more intricate, and go beyond the reading that sees that avant-garde as simply providing a historical precedent for later more 'American' movements like Pop Art or postmodernism. In some respects the fascination with 'Americana' can be viewed as constitutive of the avant-garde itself, particularly – and incongruously – in its Russian/Soviet articulations. Brecht's early work, particularly the Leustrucke and the operas (*The Lindberg Flight*, *The Seven Deadly Sins*) exhibit an equal fascination with the possibilities offered by 'America' as a utopian site. The Federal Theatre Project, probably the closest the USA has ever been to establishing a 'national theatre', was directly influenced by the Soviet experiment, transplanting the radical politics of the avant-garde into the more liberal context of the Roosevelt government and within the existing theatrical tradition. Significantly this migration brings with it all the debates about political efficacy, commitment and autonomy, as the Federal Theatre is at once the privileged liberal site that rewrites the sometimes extreme positions of its European counterparts, but, in turn, becomes the first victim of the newly formed House Un-American Activities Committee (HUAC) in 1939. Through the paradigmatic position that performance occupies, the modernist debates about autonomy or commitment come to inflect the discourses of the Cold War. Or indeed, the Cold War itself, fought mainly through culture and technology, may be seen as continuing the debates initiated by the historical avant-garde. This moment in 1930s USA is crucial for the later establishment of the Cold War discourses on the arts, but also for what was to be even later termed postmodernism.

In the meantime, however, the concept of performance remained singularly connected to the critical legacies of the historical avant-garde and stubbornly ignored in canonical readings of literary Modernism. Literary Modernism itself became the champion of the newly formed school of New Criticism with its emphasis on readings divorced from context and on formal experimentation. Crucially, in the process the radical politics of both the historical avant-garde and of literary Modernism is rewritten as formal experimentation.

It is the same concept of performance, however, that might help to link the critical legacies that have separated Modernism *from* the avant-garde, emphasising as it does embodied philosophical experience, while always reading that body in relation to the body politic. As actor/philosopher/director, the modernist performer emerges as the privileged site on and through whom modernist experimentation takes form. What he or she is gesturing towards, as savage, prophet, robot or revolutionary, is the centrality of performance for the modernist project.

2
Puppets and Actors

'... Grace appears most purely in that human form which either has no consciousness or an infinite consciousness. That is, in the puppet or in the god.'

'Does that mean', I said in some bewilderment, 'we must eat again of the tree of knowledge in order to return to the state of innocence?'

'Of course,' he said, 'but that's the final chapter in the history of the world.'

(Heinrich von Kleist, *Über das Marionettentheater*, c.1810)[1]

Although published as early as 1810, Kleists's essay, 'On the Marionette Theatre', was to have a huge impact on modernist thinking about puppets and their relationships to the human actor. Eschatological and apocalyptic in tone, this short essay manages to engage all the issues surrounding the man/marionette debate that were to help shape theories of acting within Modernism. The relationships between anthropomorphism and abstraction, between the sacred use of puppets and the profane, between orality and high – mostly textual – culture, between identification and estrangement on the level of reception, were all played out through these sometimes blasphemous, sometimes holy figures. With its total artificiality on the one hand, and its seeming humanism on the other, the ambiguous half-life of the puppet becomes an appropriate *topos*, that allows modernist theatremakers – playwrights, actors and directors – to experiment with the possibilities and the limitations of anthropomorphic and psychological representation. Although the thinking surrounding puppets, marionettes, automata and robots at first appears to be about inanimate creatures, it is, at the same time, contributing to the growing fascination that Modernism exhibits with the human body. In this sense modernist performance theories about the relationships between actors and puppets form part of the ongoing reconfiguration of the human

10

form – its expressive efficacy as aesthetic medium and agent – within the broader philosophical contours of modernity.

In another sense, however, this can be read as an inflection on the most classical of debates: that of the power and impact that mimesis – read as enactment – may have. This is one of the original aesthetic debates, that of Aristotle contra Plato. For Plato,[2] mimesis could only bring about decadence and corruption as the body of the actor would always carry within it the miasma of the 'role' that he, the male actor in this instance, was enacting and would encourage a concentration on appearances rather than realities in the audience. Whereas for Aristotle (unconcerned with actor-psychology) such an enactment would have therapeutic, cathartic qualities for the community at large, for Plato it always contained the danger of a social epidemic, a disease that would spill out into the audience, causing great damage to the Body Politic, and always invariably bringing with it the fear of effeminacy, as enactment is identified with the feminine. In fact through his attack on mimesis as enactment Plato initiates the great tradition of anti-theatrical philosophical thinking which would later manifest itself in the Church Fathers, seventeenth-century Puritanism and so on. Aristotle, in an attempt to render theatre socially useful and beneficial for the workings of a democratic city, bases his poetics on the notion of catharsis and purgation, on both an individual and social level. Interestingly enough, Plato himself in the famous 'Image of the Cave' (*Republic* 514A–519A)[3] also draws on the image of the marionette (*andriantes, skeuasta*) to help explicate his allegory about truth and its representation. The reflection on the wall of the cave – a pale shadow of the ideal world – is mediated not through live 'actors', as it were, but through *andriantes*, dummies, androids, as he calls them. These *skeuasta* (constructed, containers) in a sense protect the human actors from the distorting effects of enactment itself, while at the same time, their ability to mediate the sun (and project the world of shadow play) affords them a privileged position in relation to the truth. And this ambivalent aspect of the marionette as both distorting/debasing and potentially sacred/elevating object informs most of the experimentation taking place throughout the late-Romantic early modernist period. It is in this sense that the propagation of the marionette *in the place of* the human actor may be said to form part of the great anti-theatrical tradition initiated by Plato. Recent scholarship sometimes reads Kleist himself as a Platonist in some sense.[4] The human emerges as inadequate, prone to narcissism and excess and totally unsuitable for the grand art of acting. The puppet, on the other hand, with its affinities to God, as Kleist claims, can help restore to theatre not only its lost grandeur, but also its lost metaphysical dimension.

However, not all the experiments with marionettes, from Kleist, through Edward Gordon Craig to the Futurist and the Bauhaus movements, follow such a trajectory. It is true that aspects of this legacy flirt with Plato's anti-theatrical idealism and use the emblem of the marionette as a way of validating a wholly philosophical theatre, where the very theatrical nature of enactment is symbolically transferred to the puppet in an attempt to maintain the power of the literary and the philosophical. According to this view, only through the puppet can the author maintain full control of the transference from text to stage: a philosophical view of theatre where the physical, the bodily and the civic are not determining discourses, and where the theatrical act is relegated to a mere 'enactment' of philosophical debate, such as are Plato's own dialogues; a form that Kleist himself utilises. But despite the impact of this legacy – one which will be sketched out further on – the puppet is also used as part of Modernism's attempt to theatricalise theatre. The ability of the puppet and marionette to offer schematised and non-anthropomorphic representations of the human form feeds very neatly into the preoccupation with abstraction, stylisation and estrangement.

In this way, the puppet, rather than reverberating with the age-old idealist anti-theatricalism of Plato, becomes the most apt site for modernist experimentation in the theatre. It is championed by the most radical of theatremakers and theorists of the period and is drafted into the search for a performance language that does not rely on the power of the literary text. Not only does it involve reconfigurations regarding the representation of the human form, it also sets up modes of reception, which rely on distance and estrangement rather than identification and empathy. As such it helps shape the anti-humanist strand in much of the art of the period with obvious political dimensions, and inspires the radical spirit of both the Russian/Soviet avant-garde and the Italian Futurists. It is aligned with the experiments that see form and content as constitutive elements. In this sense, the puppet, despite its ancient past, becomes of the emblem of modernist, anti-humanist experimentation in form. And this formal experiment is usually situated in an equally radical context. The puppet as a physical object, and as carrier of meaning, seems to elide the form/content divide in ways that make it particularly attractive to modernist theatrical projects that also seek to align themselves with radical political projects. It is thus a leading figure within the revolutionary impetus of Modernism and the avant-garde.

This revolutionary aspect of the puppet is further inflected by the debates surrounding the power and efficacy of technology. Whereas the human form seems to present a seamless unification of form and content, of the inner-organic world and its expression, the puppet very clearly relies on a mechanics of production. This 'mechanics of production' itself, rather than being seen as an innocent means to an end (as it had in some traditional nineteenth-century European puppetry), comes to be foregrounded as part of the artistic practice. From the theatres of the Russian/Soviet construct-ivists to Futurism, Dada and the Bauhaus, the emphasis is placed on process and modes of production rather than finished products. The technology debate, eloquently articulated by Walter Benjamin in 'The Work of Art in the Age of Mechanical Reproduction' (1936), although quintessentially modern, could also be read as involving figures like Wagner and his quest for the *Gesamtkunstwerk*. This total, synaesthetic view of theatre is both enacted and facilitated by the figure of the puppet. This aspiration for totality is further enabled by the faith in technology. For the stage this debate proves crucial as its total physiognomy changes with the advent of elec-tricity and the development of sophisticated stage technologies. The puppet forms part of this technological apparatus of the modernist stage.

The allure of the puppet works both ways. On the one hand it represents the utter utopian faith in technology as the emancipatory force of modern-ity, as seen in the Futurist robot plays or in Vsevolod Meyerhold's appro-priation of puppetry in the formation of his biomechanics, while on the other it can also represent the bleakest, most technophobic aspects of the same project, as seen in Karel Čapek's *R.U.R.* (*Rossum's Universal Robots*), published in 1920. The utopian and somewhat uncritical accept-ance of technology as almost inherently emancipatory and critical by the constructivists is matched by the utterly dystopian and apocalyptic tone of the Czech work, where the robots take over and apocalypse is imminent. *R.U.R.* does end on a somewhat Kleistian note, where the robots after revolting against the humans and killing all of them except Alquist – a builder, hence like a robot – finally turn into 'better' versions of their origin-al human creators. The last robots/new humans go forth into the world to the tune of, 'Go, Adam. Go, Eve – be a wife to him. Be a husband to her, Primus'.[5] This technophobic use of puppets, marionettes and robots can be read as a direct descendant of the Romantic, even Gothic tradition of the monstrous machine. Like *Frankenstein*, this narrative is fully equipped with uncontrollable reason gone wild, anxieties about gender and reproduction and dubious relationships with parent figures.

Although the puppet inhabits the modern world with its anxieties about mechanisation and its fears about an ever-decreasing humanism, it also firmly resides within the oral and popular tradition. The puppets such as Punch and Judy deriving from the *Commedia dell'Arte*, popular shadow puppets like Karagiozis from the Balkans, Turkey and Greece, the Petrushka tradition in Russia, all attract interest and inspire imitation. This is a tradition that is seen as having somehow escaped the all-encompassing and humanising impact of the Enlightenment. It is viewed cheerfully as blasphemous and anti-theological, offering modernist artists, like Kandinsky and Picasso, paradigms for imitation and homage. The attitude that most theatre practitioners and theorists of the period share towards the oral tradition of puppetry in some ways mirrors a similar attitude towards the so-called Theatres of the Orient. This is almost invariably permeated with Romantic undertones about its authenticity, its naivety, its uniqueness and its unquestionable anti-authoritarianism. It is this view of orality and the popular tradition as almost inherently radical that inspires Mikhail Bakhtin's *Rabelais and his World* (c.1935).[6] It is a somewhat uncritical attitude to all things oral, popular and folk, and the puppet seems to successfully represent all three. The puppets deriving from the *Commedia dell'Arte* or from the Petrushka tradition come to represent the defiant body of the people, against the overwhelming impact of Christianity, the Church and the State. As such they can become either the actors or the models of the actors for the new societies, envisaged by their puppet-masters/directors.

This fascination with popular entertainment in general is paralleled by an equal fascination in the period with the figure of the child. Interestingly enough this fascination is in turn paralleled by an equal shift in the audience for puppet theatres, who are no longer children but adults. While the puppet leaves his nineteenth-century home of the box of dolls and toys to enter the theatrical stages of the period, childhood itself attracts much philosophical speculation; it becomes theorised in new and innovative ways. Harold B. Segel writes:

> If childhood had had little prior impact on artistic consciousness, except in the most superficial ways, the situation changed radically in the late nineteenth century ... Put as simply as possible, the world of the child became newly attractive to artists as a source of opposition, and an antidote, to the conservatism and traditionalism of bourgeois culture. In its resistance to change, to new ideas, the old order, which was understood to be the guarantor of bourgeois values, came to be regarded as old in more ways than just the chronological sense. It was a geriatric case, suffering from crippling arthritis and poor circulation; its joints were numb, its mental capacity diminished, and its vision declining.[7]

Childhood is not merely seen as a preparatory stage for adulthood and subjectivity, but is viewed as an alternative way of inhabiting the world. The Surrealists, the Dadaists and most schools of the avant-garde give childhood a privileged position in their manifestos. The principle of rejuvenation, together with the emphasis placed on the unconscious make the child and his or her dolls, the puppets, appropriate models for the artwork and for the artist. Freud's writings on childhood and Walter Benjamin's fascination with the figure of the child share a similar trajectory. As early as 1853, Charles Baudelaire projects a theory of childhood that echoes Benjamin's in his essay 'The Philosophy of Toys':

> The facility for gratifying one's imagination is evidence of the spirituality of childhood in its artistic conceptions. The toy is the child's earliest initiation into art, or rather it is the first concrete example of art; and when maturity intervenes, the most rarefied example will not satisfy his mind with the same enthusiasm, nor the same fervent conviction.[8]

The immediate, almost 'primitive' access to art remains unencumbered until the advent of adulthood. It is this immediacy that modernist theatre practitioners felt the need to regain. And it is a direct, vital connection that is doubled by the ability of the puppet and the doll to bring out the uncanny and ultimately strange quality of objects and people. Rainer Maria Rilke wrote a wonderful essay on dolls after viewing an exhibition of dolls for adults by Lotte Pritzel in Munich in 1913. These dolls that venture into the uncanny seem to Rilke to be in exile from childhood:

> To determine the realm in which these dolls have their existence, we have to conclude from their appearance that there are no children in their lives, that the precondition for their origin would be that the world of childhood is past. In them the doll has finally outgrown the understanding, the involvement, the joy and sorrow of the child; it is independent, grown up, prematurely old; it has entered into all the unrealities of its own life.[9]

The puppet, like the doll, has the ability to conjure that magical, unmediated (one could say narcissistic) relationship with the world, but crucially, can also draw attention to the strange, the uncanny, to the fact that humans, in Nietzsche's words, are the only creatures who can be 'strangers to themselves'. Rilke's closing lines underline the melancholy power of the doll to estrange us:

> They swarm and fade out at the uttermost limit of our vision. Sexless like our childhood dolls themselves, they experience no decline in their permanent sensuality, into which nothing flows and from which nothing escapes. It is as if they yearned for a beautiful flame, to throw themselves into it like moths (and then the momentary reek of burning would fill us with limitless unfamiliar sensations). Thinking these thoughts and raising our eyes, we stand unnerved as we contemplate their waxen nature.[10]

This 'unnerved' sensation is doubled by the feelings of vitality and rejuvenation conjured up by the image of the child. Childhood in the period carries with it the fresh, new vision of Modernism but also breeds melancholy for a lost wholeness that can never be regained.

At once modern and ancient, carrying within it the wisdom of the people but also making itself available to the wonders of technology, the puppet emerges as a model not only for the art of the actor but also as a paradigm of the work of art itself. It shares in the vital and organic nature of the oral tradition while also celebrating the artificiality of its mechanics of production. Both organic and inorganic, human-like and mechanical it becomes one of Modernism's best vehicles for experimentation with the limits of representation itself. In both its quest for the new, and in its fraught relationship with tradition, modernist theatre finds an apt emblem in the puppet.

'Gentlemen: the Marionette'[11]

The cult of the puppet is particularly evident in the anglophone tradition of late nineteenth-century aestheticism and symbolism. Arthur Symons, Walter Pater and Oscar Wilde all write passionate tracts exalting the puppet as the ultimate art form, as the expression of Nietzsche's *aesthetic will*. And this was a legacy continued by many modernist writers whom we do not normally associate with ideas of theatre and performance. The aura of awe and wonder that surrounds the puppet is expressed by Joseph Conrad, who sets its strength against the inadequacy of mere human actors:

> The actors appear to me like a lot of wrong-headed lunatics pretending to be sane. Their malice is stitched with white threads. They are disguised and ugly. To look at them breeded [sic] in my melancholy soul thoughts of murder and suicide, – such is my anger and my loathing of their transparent pretences. There is a taint of subtle corruption in their blank voices, in their blinking eyes, in their grimacing faces, in their light false passion, in their words that have been learned by heart. But I love a marionette-show. Marionettes are beautiful, – especially those of the old kind with wires, thick as my little finger, coming out of the top of the head. Their impassibility in love, in crime, in mirth, in sorrow, – is heroic, superhuman, fascinating. Their rigid violence when they fall upon one another to embrace or to fight is simply a joy to behold. I never listen to the text mouthed somewhere out of sight by invisible men who are here today and rotten tomorrow. I love the marionettes that are without life, and that come so near to being immortal![12]

Kleist could not have put it better himself. And yet this reading of marionettes that Conrad proposes, apocalyptic and metaphysical as it is, may bear some relevance to the narrative paths he chooses to follow in the construction of character/persona in his own literary works. Indeed, Conrad had expressed his admiration for puppets as early as 1890 when the above quotation initially appears. Conrad's reference to murder and suicide is not totally inappropriate either as he, together with many of his contemporaries, is propagating the total banishment of the human form from the stage. It is interesting to note that in the process he should involve the *Übermensch*. Craig's *Übermarionette* is only a few years away.

The high priest of aestheticism himself, Walter Pater, also contributes to the 'man or marionette' debate, reiterating the Platonic strand of the argument. The actor, corrupted and weakened by the act of mimesis itself, subsequently becomes unsuitable material for art. The power of the stage to act as a contaminating agent, spreading social and moral disease, is elaborated on by Pater:

> The stage in these volumes presents itself indeed not merely as a mirror of life, but as an illustration of the utmost intensity of life, in the fortunes and characters of players. Ups and downs, generosity, dark fates, the most delicate goodness, have nowhere been more prominent than in the private existence of those devoted to the public mimicry of men and women. Contact with the stage, almost throughout its history presents itself as a kind of touchstone, to bring out the bizzarrerie, the theatrical tricks and contrasts of the actual world.[13]

Like any body or object that has been ordained with the power to *stand in for* somebody or something else, the stage and the actor acquire magical, almost totemic qualities. It is this ritualistic power of acting (as both poison and cure, a *pharmakon*) that makes it unsuitable for humans. The puppets, on the other hand, seem ideal. On a lighter note Oscar Wilde comments on a similar matter:

> There are many advantages in puppets. They never argue. They have no crude views about art. They have no private lives. We are never bothered by accounts of their virtues, or bored by recitals of their vices; and when they are out of an engagement they never do good in public or save people from drowning; nor do they speak more than is set down for them. They recognise the presiding intellect of the dramatist, and have never been known to ask for their parts to be written up. They are admirably docile, and have no personalities at all.[14]

The lack of personality is a huge attraction in puppets and is again echoed in much of the writing of the time. As the stage is trying within Modernism to articulate a language distinct from its own modes of production, the puppet is conscripted into the argument that tries to maintain the power of the playwright. It becomes the purest form of mediation for the playwright's voice. It encapsulates all the synaesthetic qualities of the stage while still maintaining the stronghold of the representational efficacy of the written word. This, of course, is not the sole interpretation of the role of the puppet. As we shall examine further on, it is also enlisted on the side of a democratic use of the stage. As it is, however, in the Anglophone tradition, puppet theatres present a kind of absolute aesthetic totality that is linked directly to the power of the artist's aesthetic will. They acquire a very special aura, as they are seen as propagating this role. In particular, the Petit Théâtre des Marionettes in Paris, with Maurice Bouchor as its director at the Galérie Vivienne from 1889 to 1894, becomes one of those modernist sites, like the Cabaret Voltaire later on, to attract many visitors and much attention. Oscar Wilde writes in a letter from the same period (the same letter as the one quoted above):

> I saw lately, in Paris, a performance by certain puppets of Shakespeare's *Tempest*, in M. Maurice Bouchor's translation. Miranda was the image of Miranda, because an artist had so fashioned her; and Ariel was true Ariel, because so had she been made. Their gestures were quite sufficient, and the words that seemed to come from their lips were spoken by poets who had beautiful voices. It was a delightful performance, and I remember it still with delight, though Miranda took no notice of the flowers I sent her after the curtain fell.[15]

Many such puppet theatres throughout Europe became the centre of aesthetic and sometimes political experimentation. They managed to act as magnets for the cosmopolitan and sometimes internationalist outlook of much of the modernist experiment in the theatre. Arthur Symons writes of such a visit to a theatre in Rome:

> After seeing a ballet, a farce, and the fragment of an opera performed by the marionettes at the Costanzi Theatre in Rome I am inclined to ask myself why we require the intervention of any less perfect medium between the meaning of a piece, as the author conceived it, and that other meaning which it derives from our reception of it.[16]

Most of the puppet theatres of Italy, however, were of the traditional kind. Maurice Bouchor's Petit Théâtre des Marionettes was already a specific reading of puppet theatre. Inspired by symbolism, Bouchor wrote a number of original plays for his puppets (*Tobias, Noël, or The Mystery of the Nativity, The Story of Christmas, The Legend of Saint Cecile, Devotion to Saint Andrew, The Dream of Kheyam, The Mysteries of Eleusis in Four Acts and Verse*) that were inspired by biblical or mythological themes and staged mediaeval mysteries and plays by Hrostwitha. These were all very successful and caused a stir despite the short life of the Petit Théâtre (1889–93).

Bouchor himself transpires as a major theorist of puppetry of the period.
He writes:

> Marionettes – I have had the opportunity of observing – are above all lyrical, and
> the ideal place of their action cannot be other than poetry; all the gates of dream
> open before them; the highest speculations are naturally familiar to them, and
> these strange figures move comfortably within the systems, beliefs, and symbols
> of all times and all peoples; everything that is distant, fairylike, mysterious, is
> particularly suited to them. Moreover, emotion, even the most profound, the most
> human, is not inaccessible to them; they can excel in tenderness and grace, freely
> mixing delicate irony, humour, fantasy, and comic lyricism.[17]

Bouchor's conception of marionettes and their expressive abilities is in line
with the slightly mystical and heightened use proposed of them by symbolism. Indeed, Maeterlinck's first collection of plays for marionettes
appears in 1894. Like Bouchor's adaptations, alongside which they were
staged, these are highly stylised pieces with metaphysical undertones. And
the Belgian's experiments with the use of marionettes were to be hugely
influential all over Europe and Russia. During the same time, however,
another experiment was taking place that was to undermine all the basic
premises of the European stage, particularly the legacies inherited from the
Renaissance.

Alfred Jarry's *Ubu Roi* burst onto the European stage in 1896, directed by
the charismatic Aurélien Lugné-Poë for his newly founded Théâtre de
l'Oeuvre (a company that was to have a huge impact on the history of the
modernist stage). Before this entry into the public domain, the Ubu triptych
cycle of plays had already enjoyed an interesting life of performance. Jarry
started work on these plays while he was still at the Rennes lycée between
the ages of fifteen and seventeen. They had been performed at his school,
and Jarry with his 'Théâtre des Phynances' performed them in his home for
a private audience. Possibly one of the most interesting aspects of the Ubu
plays is that they were written with marionettes in mind. Jarry's use of marionettes, however, could not be further removed from the strict and slightly
pious use proposed by Maeterlinck. Jarry's puppets were part of the irreverent, blasphemous and carnivalesque tradition. His youthfulness punctuates
this quality and draws attention to the primacy accorded to youth during this
period. The plays, however, were not simply the inarticulate ramblings of an
angry young man. This anger and irreverence – as is the case with many
angry young men of the European avant-garde – is framed by a knowledge
of classicism and tradition. Like the Dadaists and the Futurists who were to
follow in Ubu's footsteps, Jarry had had the benefit of a classical European

education. *Ubu Roi* itself can be read as a reworking of *Macbeth*. Rewriting the classics of the European stage later becomes a trope of the modernist stage. It is fascinating to note that in his attack on the Renaissance stage and the notions of humanism it entails, Jarry employs marionettes.

It is, however, a vulgar and blasphemous reworking of the European classical tradition. The play opens with the word *merdre* and unfolds to tell a tale of empire, battles, usurpation and absolute power through violence and dismemberment on stage. Père Ubu, formerly the king of Aragon, is urged by his wife Mère Ubu to overthrow King Venceslas of Poland. After Ubu takes over as King of Poland, he mounts a reign of pure and absolute terror. In turn his throne is usurped in a monumental battle scene between the Russian and the Polish armies, allowing Jarry to utilise the ability of marionettes to act out extreme violence on the stage. Pursued by the forces of the Czar, Ubu ends up in a cave in Lithuania where Mère Ubu finds him, only to be greeted by yet more versions of extreme violence as Père Ubu starts to tear her apart (echoing that other violent pair of spouses, Punch and Judy). Miraculously Mère Ubu survives and the unruly couple seek refuge in the Baltic in flight from their enemy Bougrelas. However, this is clearly not a tragedy, as the closing lines of the play confirm:

PA UBU: Wild and inhospitable ocean which laps the shores of the land called Germany, so named because it's exactly half way to Jermyn Street as the blow flies.

MA UBU: Now that's what I call erudition. It's a beautiful country, I'm told.

PA UBU: Beautiful though it may be, it's not a patch on Poland. Ah gentlemen, there'll always be a Poland. Otherwise there wouldn't be any Poles![18]

Wild and absurd an ending as this may be, it still relies on Jarry's philological education. And it is this uneasy co-existence of high and low cultures, of the intellectual and the boldly physical, of the sacred and the profane that makes the play deeply unsettling. It is the same unease that prompted W. B. Yeats to pronounce the aphorism quoted at the head of the previous chapter: 'After us the Savage God' after watching the first public dress rehearsal on 9 December 1896. This important production was mounted for an audience mainly of artists and writers, and was greeted with tremendous interest and support: one of those performances that has created its own mythology within the history of modernist theatre.

This early production used actors and not marionettes. However, the actors themselves were directed to behave 'like marionettes', to borrow the

Véritable portrait de Monſieur Ubu,

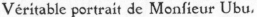

1   Alfred Jarry, Ubu Roi (Frontispiece for *Ubu Roi*)

style and expressive qualities of the wooden forms (Yeats remembers that the 'players are supposed to be dolls, toys, marionettes, and now they are all hopping like wooden frogs').[19] Harold Segel writes of this performance:

> This was very much in accord with Jarry's wishes. Besides imitating the typical jerkiness of marionettes' movements, the actors also wore masks; Firmin Gémie, who played the part of Ubu Roi, wore a heavy, pear-shaped or triangular mask,

designed for him by Jarry, as well as a huge cardboard belly. The whole idea was to distance setting and costuming as much as possible from anything even suggestive of historical accuracy ... In a touch foreshadowing future Expressionist theatre, an old man in a long white beard, in evening dress, tiptoed across the boards and hung placards on a nail at the side of the stage to indicate the scene.[20]

It is not simply the expressionist tradition that this use of actors foreshadows. It in many ways initiates one of the greatest experiments of the modernist stage: that of the marionette or puppet as a model for human acting (Jarry initially wanted to attach strings to the actors' bodies).[21] In its quest for stylised modes of acting that do not rely on psychological expression but rather tend towards abstraction, modernist theatre finds in the puppet a highly appropriate model. Coupled with its irreverent nature and its anti-humanist ideology, it proposes a way of representing the human form that proves particularly attractive to its anti-naturalist and quasi-epic project, from Craig, then to Meyerhold and finally to Brecht himself. The interaction proposed between puppet and human

2   Alfred Jarry, Ubu Roi (Programme for *Ubu Roi*). A special edition on salmon-coloured paper inserted in the deluxe programmes for the 1896 performance of the play at the Théâtre de l'Oeuvre, Paris.

actor at that first public performance of *Ubu Roi* in some ways makes the occasion even more significant. Rather than opting for the simple and extreme banishment of the human form from the stage, the space created by Lugné-Poë's staging is the one most modernist theatre practitioners and theorists inhabit.

This might seem obvious in the case of the charismatic Englishman Edward Gordon Craig, who has acquired a dubious place in the history of modernist theatre for supposedly promulgating the banishment of actors and their substitution by the *Übermarionette*. Craig's theoretical works and experiments comprise by far the most articulate and adventurous Anglophone experiment on the stage at the time. However, as the trajectory of his life clearly exhibits, that experiment needs to be read in conjunction with similar ones on the Continent. The son of the actress Ellen Terry and the architect E. W. Godwin, Craig transpires as one of the leading figures in this debate. When Craig abandoned England in 1907, taking charge of the Arena Goldoni in Florence, he had already made a significant contribution to the Arts and Crafts movement, to the revival of the 'Book Beautiful' (through the publication of the little magazine, *The Page*, in 1898), and most importantly, through the publication of his book *The Art of the Theatre* (1905), was already heralded as a prophet of the 'new movement' in the theatre. Craig realised very early on, though, that his project needed to be transported to the Continent, where it would benefit from the creative interactions with other innovators in the field. Although not the most congenial of collaborators throughout the first two decades of the twentieth century, Craig managed to at least initiate theatrical and other projects with figures as diverse as Max Reinhardt, Count Harry Kessler (the famous 'red count'), Konstantin Stanislavsky, Eleonore Duse and Isadora Duncan amongst others. His main project, however, upon moving to Italy was the publication of the long-running and extremely influential periodical, *The Mask* (1908–29).[22] Blending the legacies of the 'Book Beautiful' and the radical spirit of the 'little magazine' movement that was flourishing at the time, *The Mask* emerges as one of the first magazines to be wholly devoted to the 'art of the theatre' as living performance. Indeed, it is one of the most systematic attempts to theorise performance itself, as something other than the extension of the literary text; and concern for the puppet leads the redefinition of the art of the actor into a new dimension. Craig's essay 'The Actor and the *Übermarionette*' appears in 1908 in the very first volume of *The Mask*, the newly coined word in its title being a semi-serious play on a word very much in vogue at the time, the Nietzschean 'superman' or *Übermensch*. Here he sets out his ideas on the relationships between actors and puppets. In the slightly aphoristic tone of the manifesto that *The Mask* borrows from similar publications of the time, Craig proclaims:

> Acting is not an art. It is therefore incorrect to speak of the actor as an artist. For accident is an enemy of the artistic. Art is the exact antithesis of Pandimonium [sic], and Pandimonium is created by the tumbling together of many accidents; Art arrives only by design. Therefore in order to make any work of art it is clear we may work in those materials with which we can calculate. Man is not one of these materials.[23]

This essay caused a stir at the time and in some ways also defines the image of Craig today as a somewhat arrogant but visionary theatre theorist who wanted to banish actors from the stage. Read in context and in conjunction with Kleist's essay, which Craig published in one of its earliest English translations,[24] it appears as neither particularly original nor extreme. Craig is simply fusing the high Romanticism of Kleist with the radical potential of the avant-garde manifesto in a style that is both original and intertextual.

Both essays derive a 'grand theory' of art from the theatre and especially from marionettes. Taking this aestheticising logic to its extreme, the marionette is seen as the new idol of this quasi-religious art form, endowed not only with artistic qualities but also with metaphysical ones. It comes to represent a total, eschatological theory that may redeem not only the art of the theatre but life itself. Craig writes of this all-encompassing view of the marionette, which can even create a bridge between the living and the dead:

> I pray earnestly for the return of the Image, the Übermarionette, to the Theatre; and when he comes again and is but seen, he will be loved so well that once more will it be possible for people to return to their ancient ... homage rendered to existence ... and divine and happy intercession made to Death.[25]

This echoes Kleist's 'relapse into the state of Innocence', and bears all the signs of a Platonic anti-theatricalism, of which Craig is often accused in some form or another. On the other hand, both essays could be read as applying varying degrees of literary licence. Yes, they are both manifestos but they are also both literary works, not meant to be taken literally. Craig's seeming anti-theatricalism and his tracts against the actor also need to be read in the context of an attempt at defining the rapidly mutating role of the director around 1900. The actor can find role-models in puppets but the role of the director cannot be reduced to either that of the playwright or the stage-manager or prompter or impresario or actor-manager (which seemed to be the available models). The art of the actor needs to be redefined so that a new art for the director can emerge. Many of the totalising and absolute statements pronounced in Craig's essay express this very anxiety. Nor did he refrain from working with actors. Although he probably had the best collection of puppets (European and Eastern) for his time, he never actually built an *Übermarionette*. Indeed, we can speculate as to whether he ever intended to construct one. The *Übermarionette*, like Yeats's 'Savage God', might represent yet another *phantasmic* modernist notion of an ideal performer; one that is more likely to be embodied by physical actors themselves rather than being a totally mechanical construction. At the same time, Craig praised actors who were renowned for their particular 'star' quality, like Eleonora Duse and Henry Irving. He writes of Irving, with whom he had worked as an actor at the Lyceum:

> I consider him to have been the greatest actor I have ever seen, and I have seen the best in Italy, France, Russia, Germany, Holland and America. They were all imitable, and yet he was unique. By Irving, the Mask and the Marionette were better understood than by all other actors … and it is because of his trust in these two ancient traditions … the two unshakeable traditions … that he stood unique. Some of you know this … I need hardly remind you of it. But you who are younger, and who never saw Irving, will see him now … a figure solemn and beautiful like an immense thought in motion … If you will be an Actor in such a day as this, and if you are an English man, take but one model, … the masked marionette.[26]

This is truly a fascinating assessment of acting, as Irving in many ways represents the type of acting that modernist performers are defining themselves *against*. Modernist experimentation in acting (from the naturalism of Stanislavsky to the biomechanics of Meyerhold) sees the Romantic tradition of acting as fostering all the evils of the 'old theatre', as it is seen as wholly 'star' driven and vacuous. It is the tradition that compels Eleonora Duse herself to proclaim:

> To save the theatre the theatre must be destroyed; the actors and actresses must die of the plague. They poison the air, they make art impossible.[27]

Not completely impossible, as one thinks of Duse herself as inextricably linked to the legacy that she throws into the fire. Craig makes designs for her and plans to work with her. As collaboration, with women particularly, is not his strong point, all these plans prove disastrous. It is important to stress that we need to read his polemical essay within its own context, taking account of its literary dimension.

For Craig the evocation of the *Übermarionette* as the solution to the problems of modernist Theatre functioned on many levels. Initially it connects him to the visionary and somewhat idealist Romanticism of Kleist. At the same time, it provides a homage to the great theatrical paradigms of the past. He spent years studying the puppets from the *Commedia dell'Arte* but also from the Wayang and Bunraku traditions. The *Übermarionette* also allows him to begin to theorise the newly emerging role of the director. However, he seemed to be more interested in sketching out the imaginative and aesthetic potential of such a 'creature' rather than actually exploring the mechanics of its production. The *Übermarionette*, for Craig, as is the case for many early experiments with puppets/marionettes/automata in modernist theatre, acquires a *phantasmic* quality. In many ways, it was never meant to be constructed. It was always meant to provide the 'ghost in the machine', where the machine itself was of little or no interest.

This attitude might be better understood if it is read as part of the general attitude towards technology at the time. Craig belongs to the school of thought that saw technology as a threat. The *Übermarionette* remains an unrealisable vision as it lacks the necessary mechanics of production. Technophobic and in the final analysis anti-modern as this approach may be, it nevertheless animates much of the discussion about puppets and marionettes at the time. Indeed, it fuels many of the dystopian uses of marionettes and automata in much of the literature of the period as well. As in *R.U.R.*, there is always the fear that the robots may rebel. Instead of embracing modernity itself, the marionette in this instance is seen as the link that can connect the demoralised and dilapidated modern stage with the grand theatrical traditions of the past. It does not provide a model for the theatre of the future, one that ideally embraces technology. And it does not in any sustained way provide models of acting that can then be transferred to the body of the human actor. At most it can provide an enactment of a collective technophobic nightmare that many robots and automata embody at the time.

While this tradition in modernist performance views technology as a threat and uses the inanimate figure of the marionette and/or robot to express that very fear and loathing, at the other extreme of this trajectory there is a legacy that embraces modernity, technology and progress and wishes to express this aspiration through the same inanimate but 'animated' figure. In order to sketch out this notional schema it may be helpful to touch upon the work of another visionary and theorist, working at roughly the same time. Oskar Schlemmer's work on the Theatre of the Bauhaus may provide yet another way of reading this interaction between theatre and technology.

For Schlemmer and the Bauhaus, the engagement with the puppet becomes a way of redefining the human body on the stage. He writes in his manifesto for 'The Theatre of the Bauhaus':

> The history of the theatre is the history of the transformation of the human form. It is the history of man as actor of physical and spiritual events, ranging from naïveté to reflection, from naturalism to artifice.[28]

Schlemmer proceeds to enlist the categories of 'abstraction, mechanization and technology' in his new reconfiguration of the human form on the stage. Unlike Craig and the symbolist legacy of the marionette, which sees technology as the modern blight, he claims that technology may 'give promise of the boldest fantasies'. This, sometimes uncritical, embrace of technology is also manifested in some of the Italian Futurist robot plays. Rather than banishing the human form and substituting it with the marionette, the latter becomes a model to be emulated with the assistance of modern technology. What Craig exalted as the 'masked/marionette' – supposedly embodied by Irving – Maholy-Nagy, Schlemmer's collaborator, formulated as the 'Mechanized Eccentric':

> The effect of this body mechanism (Körpermechanik) (in circus performance and athletic events, for example) arises essentially from the spectator's astonishment or shock at the potentialities of his own organism as demonstrated to him by others. This is a subjective effect. Here the human body is the sole medium of configuration (Gestaltung). For the purpose of an objective Gestaltung of movement this medium is limited, the more so since it has constant reference to sensible and perceptive (i.e. again literary) elements. The inadequacy of the 'human Exzentrik' led to the demand for a precise and fully controlled organization of form and motion, intended to be a synthesis of dynamically contrasting phenomena (space, form, motion, sound and light). This is the Mechanized Eccentric.[29]

For Schlemmer and Nagy, like Craig, the human form is not the most appropriate material for art. Rather than banish it, however, he proceeds to mechanise it. The puppet in this scheme is a model and not a substitute. Technology is seen as means of providing the all-desirable abstraction which is hailed as the most appropriate mode of art for modernity. This is a strand in the German tradition, which was initially formulated by Wilhelm Worringer in his book-length manifesto, *Abstraction and Empathy*, published in 1908.[30] The appropriate reception of such a work would not be empathy but distance and estrangement. The Mechanized Eccentric is enlisted not only in terms of its ability to restructure the representation of the human form but also as a way of creating the very desirable and very modern response of estrangement. However, through the application of modern technology, Schlemmer also 'corrects' the radical idealism of Worringer, which resorts to pure aestheticism. Worringer writes:

> In the urge to abstraction the intensity of the self-alienative impulse is incomparably greater and more consistent. Here it is not characterised, as in the need for empathy, by an urge to alienate oneself from individual being, but as an urge to seek deliverance from the fortuitousness of humanity as a whole, from the seeming arbitrariness of organic existence in general, in the contemplation of something necessary and irrefragable. Life as such is felt to be a disturbance of aesthetic enjoyment.[31]

Although the 'urge to abstraction' and the estrangement it requires have traditionally been read as almost inherently critical, from Russian Formalism to Brecht's appropriation of the term, Worringer's clearly aestheticist view, coupled with the objectionable politics of his book, bears witness to the fact that form is not somehow 'inherently' radical and emancipatory. It may rely on the principles of 'shock and astonishment', and it may be 'a slap in the face of public taste'; but nevertheless, it can derive its politics from a variety of sources and traditions. I would claim that Craig's lack of confidence in the human form and his fascination with the *Übermarionette* possibly occupies a similar Radical Idealist trajectory to Worringer's. Schlemmer, while possibly continuing this, is certainly 'correcting' and inflecting it with his infusion of technology. The Mechanized Eccentric is not a marionette but a human figure emulating a marionette with the application of modern technology. Rather than aesthetisation, yearned for by Worringer and in many respects by Craig, Schlemmer yearns for a synthesis of art and life through theatre, expressing one of the main axioms of the European avant-garde. He says with a nod to Kleist:

> The medium of every art is artificial and every art gains from recognition and acceptance of its medium. Heinrich Kleist's essay 'Über das Marionetten theater' offers a convincing reminder of this artificiality ...

And he continues with a comment on the application of 'the new mathematics of relativity':

> Both these modes of consciousness – the sense of man as a machine, and the insight into the deepest walls of creativity – are symptoms of one and the same yearning. A yearning for synthesis dominates today's art ... This yearning also reaches out for the theatre, because the theatre offers the promise of total art.[32]

The fascination with science, something that Brecht was to follow as well, coupled with the very psycho-physical act of yearning, make for a very interesting reading of the Mechanized Eccentric, less as a programmatic emotionless piece of metal, and more as a desiring machine, there to channel the hopes and aspirations for a total theatre.

As in Oskar Schlemmer, the work of the Russian visionary theatre director Vsevolod Meyerhold may be said to be characterised by a similar yearning of marrying the modern and the technological with the traditional and the organic. This is clear in the coinage of the term 'biomechanics', the technique for training actors that he formulated. Meyerhold's work and life can be read as comprising one of the boldest and most utopian projects of the historical avant-garde.[33] His biomechanics occupies a central position as it brings together, in an inspired fusion, the Symbolist legacy, the oral tradition of puppetry and the modernist fascination with technology. Although this formed a heady cocktail of 'high' and 'low' traditions, precise technology and Symbolist stylisation, it did culminate in a series of concrete applications: *études* as Meyerhold called them. The object of the exercise for Meyerhold, however, was different from that of Craig, as Meyerhold's aim was to redefine the actor, not to find a substitute for him. In many ways both men start from the same position: the arbitrariness of the human form and its inappropriateness as raw material for the art of the theatre. This is a concern that permeates much Russian Symbolist writing on theatre. Fyodor Sologub writes in his influential essay of 1908, 'The Theatre of a Single Will':

> I think the first obstacle to be overcome on this trail is the performing actor. The performing actor draws too much attention to himself, and obfuscates both drama and author. The more talented the actor, the more insufferable his tyranny over the author and the more baneful his tyranny over the play. To depose this attractive but nonetheless baneful tyranny, two possible remedies exist: either transfer the central focus of the theatrical presentation to the spectator in the pit or transfer it to the author backstage.[34]

In Craigian terms, the solution is provided by the 'author backstage' in his newly created guise of the all-powerful director. Meyerhold, on the other hand, transfers the action to 'the spectator in the pit' through a reconfiguration of the art of the actor. Although this is indeed a radical difference and foreshadows the different political shades of these respective projects (Craig's fellow-travelling Fascism and Meyerhold's utopian Marxism), it is important to underline the fact that both men were trying to provide solutions to similar problems and both initially work within similar theoretical frameworks. Craig's first dialogue had been pirated and published in Russia by 1906 and he was very influential within the group of 'decadent' Symbolists who published similar manifestos, mostly on acting. Sologub himself declared his debt to Craig and Meyerhold, writing in 1909:

> It is remarkable that in the very first year of this new century E.G. Craig flung a challenge to the naturalistic theatre ... therefore, this young Englishman is the first to set up initial guideposts on the new road of the Theatre.[35]

Despite the homage that Meyerhold respectfully pays to Craig, his own path would be considerably different. For Meyerhold the ultimate aim of all this experimentation with the human form would be the redefinition of the role of the spectators themselves. In ways that foreshadow Brecht's Epic Theatre, Meyerhold moved the 'man or marionette' debate considerably forward by making the spectator's engagement crucial. This engagement, however, was to be achieved not through empathy and identification, but through the Russian Formalist principle of *estrangement*. Through the application of biomechanics and the use of what Eisenstein later described as 'The Montage of Attractions' (1923), theatrical form, theatricality itself, would form part of the experience of the audience. Through shock, amazement and wonder the audience would be invited to reconsider the world and their place in it. This for Meyerhold was the ultimate destination of the theatrical act. Robert Leach writes:

> Biomechanics, with its Soviet-seeming orientation, helped to bring Meyerhold's somewhat self-indulgent approach into the present. It was 'tendentious', and brought an unexpected sharpness to the metaphorical and playful elements of a theatrical style that played with contradictions and shifted the audience's perspective in unexpected ways. By doing so, it reasserted the audience's vital function. The audience was the fourth and final point in 'the Theatre of the Straight Line', which began with the playwright and went through the director to the actors, who 'reveal their souls' to the spectators.[36]

This insistence on the spectator heavily inflects the decadent Symbolist legacy that Meyerhold inherits from Fyodor Sologub or Nikolai Evreinov. It also fully thrusts the debate into its modernist context and differentiates it from the Romantic Idealism of Kleist and Craig. As we have seen, Craig's *Übermarionette* smacks of Platonic anti-theatricalism, while Meyerhold's biomechanics sets out to celebrate the very theatricality of the stage. However neat and schematic this formulation may appear, it misses much of the overlap in all these projects and it somehow assumes that they were all successful. As mentioned earlier, Craig never actually constructed a supermarionette. The technology of production that he was searching for was formulated by Meyerhold through his embracing of technology and the popular tradition. Meyerhold's turn to popular puppetry, on the other hand, also involved levels of idealisation and romanticisation, where, as Catriona Kelly claims, local, Russian traditions were overlooked in favour of those traditions emanating from the Western European theatre:

> Many writers associated with Symbolism who praised the vitality of the folk the-atre ignored the native Russian tradition and turned instead to Italian or French street performers (the commedia dell'arte, or the medieval Passion Plays). Meyerhold's essay 'Balagan', despite using the Russian word for its title, is devoted exclusively to the Western European theatre.[37]

Meyerhold's fascination with the popular tradition was first put into practice in the production of Aleksandr Blok's *The Fairground Booth* in 1906. Harold B. Segel claims that this play, conceived originally as a puppet play, was meant to be a comment on the mystical symbolism of Maeterlinck. The use of puppets itself, despite the very lyrical language, is enlisted in this cause. As Segel writes, 'in his production of *The Fairground Booth* in 1906, Meyerhold accentuated the play's puppet theatre dimension'.[38] It is true also that various performance traditions, mostly Western European, morph into an undifferentiated whole. In relation to Meyerhold's project, however, it is important to stress that very early in his career as a director he starts experimenting with puppets. These will help provide him with a paradigm for the art of the actor.

The most famous adaptation of the Russian popular puppet tradition is the ballet *Petrushka*, the result of the now almost mythic collaboration between Igor Stravinsky, Aleksandr Benois and Michel Fokine. The ballet was premiered at the Théâtre du Châtelet in Paris on 13 June 1911 and was a sensation. It probably comprises the most consistent Symbolist reworking of the Petrushka tradition for the modernist stage. The text was reworked as a wordless drama, accentuating the puppet-like quality of the actors/dancers. According to Kelly, Benois's preference for 'the puppet play to other fairground genres is rooted in Symbolist contempt for the human actor'.[39] This is something that she rightly claims the Symbolists share with Craig. Meyerhold's involvement, how-ever, departs significantly from this tradition, both in its local and its broader Western European setting. In many ways, Meyerhold reinter-prets the 'man or marionette' debate within the broader concerns of the avant-garde.

Whereas Craig's *Übermarionette* is called upon to help create a ghost-like quality that de-materialises the human form, Meyerhold is in search of ways of making that very materiality conscious and vibrant on the stage. Following Schklovsky's Formalist slogan of 'making the stone stoney', Meyerhold sees in the puppet tradition ways of materialising the human form; ways of redefining it in terms of its basic materials. Again these concerns feed into the broader ones about the representation of the human body. Making the 'human, human again' for Meyerhold primarily entails exalting physicality, movement, energy and collectivity. Looking at the human body afresh, through the paradigm of the puppet, leads him to reinterpret the relationships between inner world and its expression. The body is not seen as the simple and direct medium that unproblematically expresses the psychic world. Through his biomechanics he forges a new relationship between the two that bears direct relevance to his theories of acting.

Where Kleist and Craig negate the human form and the art of acting, Meyerhold is primarily interested in examining the art of the actor. If Craig's *Übermarionette* was to connect the puppet with its lost totemic quality as an idol, Meyerhold's biomechanics was to establish a historical connection. The body of the actor was to be seen as resulting from a specific history of the human form and its representation. In this the popular

3   *The Magnanimous Cuckold* by Fernand Crommelynck

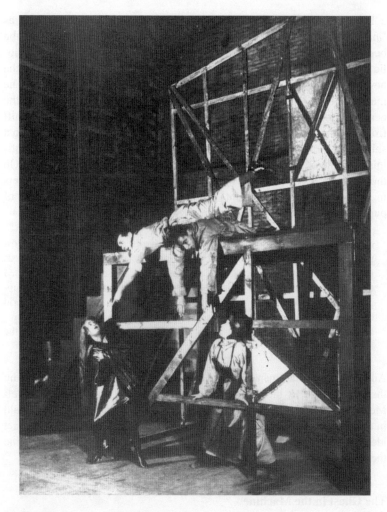

4   *The Magnanimous Cuckold*, 1922

tradition in puppetry, whether Russian or from the *Commedia dell'Arte*, proved vital. The idealistic tradition that identifies the puppet-idol with God is further inflected by the materialist legacy of the puppet-'machine' with history. Instead of replacing the human actor by the puppet-idol the goal was to *puppetise* the human form itself. Its materiality was no longer an obstacle but the very substance of the creative process. It was this materiality that would place the human form within history and help it find a language for the art of acting. No longer was the actor viewed as 'inappropriate' material for art. Against the Platonic legacy that sees the body of the actor as degenerate and corrupt, the locus of personal and public miasma, that same body is seen as the primal material for the art of the new theatre. 'Above all drama is the art of the actor,' wrote Meyerhold. The material of the human form was the very substance that was to create the new 'dialectic-actor', as Meyerhold put it. This is how he explains the shift from the inanimate and immaterial to the living and the human. It is also a shift from the decadent Symbolism of Sologub to the more critical optimism (some might say utopianism) of his own brand of the avant-garde. On the way, like Brecht, who was to follow in his footsteps, Meyerhold ushers in a wholly modernist concept of humanism. The director of one sort of puppet-show, he says in an exemplary fable:

> quickly realised that as soon as he tried to improve the puppet's mechanism it lost part of its charm. It was as though the puppet were resisting such barbarous improvements with all its being. The director came to his senses when he realised that there is a limit beyond which there is no alternative but to replace the puppet with a man. But how could he part with the puppet, which had created a world of enchantment with its incomparable movements, its expressive gestures achieved by some magic known to it alone, its angularity which reaches the heights of true plasticity?[40]

And in this way, the 'man or marionette' debate comes full circle. Replacing the human actor by the puppet was a process not without its merits: it left Meyerhold with a particular technique, with a method of training that could in turn puppetise the human actor. The marionette for him is not an abstract ideal but a specific mode of production, a process that could help to redefine the art of the actor and gesture towards a new humanism on the way.

The Ghost in the Machine

So far the discussion about puppets and their relevance to theories of acting has assumed, like much of the primary material covered, that the body of the marionette is a body that is either neutral in terms of gender or fluctuates between the body of the male and the female. However, as feminism has taught us, there is no such thing as a neutral body and, usually, when one is evoked it acts as a disguise for the male body. What kind of body, then, is being hailed either as a substitute or as a paradigm for the human actor? The various marionette traditions from the popular European tradition or from the theatres of the Orient form part of broader theatrical tropes that also have attitudes both towards the representation of women and towards the idea of the female actor. Interestingly enough, the so-called theatres of the Orient have no female performers but very intricate performing languages for female impersonators. On the other hand, the *commedia* tradition was one of the first in Europe to have female performers. The attraction to marionettes for some modernists, like Craig, was a way of neutralising the incongruity of women on the stage: something very pressing since, as he saw it:

> The introduction of women upon the stage is held by some to have caused the downfall of the European theatre.[41]

His *Übermarionette* presented a unique solution to the oxymoron, in Craigian terms, of the female actor. The marionette as a solution to the problem of the female actor comes with its own distinguished history: Ben Johnson in the famous puppet scene of *Bartholomew Fair* (1614) has the puppet-master demonstrate to the outraged Puritans that puppets were harmlessly sexless.

In an attempt to trace some kind of genealogy for this gender politics that informs many theories on acting of the period, I would like to digress slightly and mention two publications that proved extremely influential for the modernist life of puppets, elaborating on Victoria Nelson's analysis which was the first to group these two texts.[42] The first is the *The Adventures of Pinocchio: Story of a Puppet*[43] published in Naples in1883 and written by Carlo Lorenzini (under the pseudonym Carlo Collodi), the second is the French novel *The Future Eve* by Auguste Villiers de L'Isle-Adam (*L'Ève future*)[44] published in 1885–86. *The Adventures of Pinocchio* is well known (not least because of the Walt Disney movie) and its impact has been well documented. Harold Segel writes:

> If we look at Pinocchio … from the viewpoint of the transformation of values characteristic of Modernism, the work is remarkably compatible with its time. Apart from its elements of purely national concern, such as language and its reflection of the social and cultural needs of the new Italian political unity, the book is a celebration of puppetry, childhood, and the artistic potential of popular and folk tradition.[45]

It is also a celebration of a father–son relationship and the fantasy of a life without mothers. Pinocchio, however, is not happy as the mechanical son of Geppetto and his ultimate aim is to be transformed into a real boy. Pinocchio's rite of passage into adulthood, from an inanimate creature to a living boy, could also be read as a journey into masculinity proper. After having symbolically 'created' a son, with all the obvious symbols, the fantasy turns into real flesh and bones, as by the end of the story Pinocchio becomes a real boy. Once he becomes a real boy, Pinocchio asks Geppetto:

'And the old Pinocchio of wood, where could he have gone to hide?'
'There he is over there,' answered Geppetto; and he pointed to a large puppet propped against a chair, its head turned to one side, its arms dangling, and its legs crossed and folded in the middle so that it was a wonder that it stood up at all.
Pinocchio turned and looked at it; and after he had looked at it for a while, he said to himself with a great deal of satisfaction,
'How funny I was when I was a puppet! And how glad I am that I've become a proper boy!'[46]

Through the collaboration of the father and the son the new 'proper boy' is born. The puppet, having fulfilled its role as surrogate, no longer has a reason to 'live'. The newly born 'proper boy' is fully satisfied with his new identity and in the process 'theatricalises' and ridicules his former self. This new identity, which has been read as representing the modernist spirit of rebellion and unease, can also be read as a gendered identity, one that specifically results from a fantasy world with no mothers.

As in *Frankenstein* this narrative of 'creation' entails anxieties about the female body. In Villier's *The Future Eve*,[47] Thomas Edison (a reference to the historical T. A. Edison) invents a 'magneto-electric android' for his friend Lord Celian Ewald. This is a perfect mechanical replica of Alicia Clary, an unobtainable actress. He promises that 'the copy will be ... a thousand times more identical to herself ... than she is in her own person'. Interestingly enough, although the real Alicia Clary is beautiful, she is but a shallow actress. Through the use of photosculpture and with the Venus de Milo as a prototype, Edison creates a new and 'inner world' for Hadaly, the replica. This 'inner world', however, carries its own dynamics of gender. The female replicas, as is the case with Hadaly, are usually endowed with qualities of falseness, emotional vacuity coupled with rampant sexuality. The owners of these robots discover this at their own peril. As Thomas Edison says, 'knowing the mechanism of the puppet will never explain to you how it becomes the phantom'.[48] And it is a phantom that haunts most of the female puppets, robots and automata from Alicia Clary to the 'false Maria' in Fritz Lang's *Metropolis* (1927). Creating life from machine throws up all sorts of anxieties about reproduction and its association with the female body. Nowhere is this better expressed than in the words of Damon the Robot in *R.U.R.* (1920):

> We will give birth by machine. We will build a thousand steam-powered mothers. From them will pour forth a river of life. Nothing but life! Nothing but robots![49]

This is a very different notion of the puppet as inherited from the oral and popular traditions. It follows a narrative of creation picked up from Romanticism, Symbolism and the Gothic. The puppet as the voice and body of carnival culture, irreverent and blasphemous, is not the prototype for this approach. Rather it becomes the emblem of a 'total work of art', self-contained and utterly controllable. Of course, on the dystopian side of this narrative, these robots/puppets are not self-contained and controllable; they acquire lives of their own. Despite its fascination with technology, the narrative is couched in a deep technophobia and a dread of modernity, particularly of its emancipatory and democratic potential, and is able to blend with the period's fascination with the *femme fatale*. It is no coincidence that Craig, in some ways part of this tradition, is intrigued by Mussolini's fascism.

The Italian Futurists probably present the most intriguing case where the love of technology and the ambivalence about women come together in the use of the puppet. Filippo Tommaso Marinetti's early play *Electric Puppets (Poupées électriques)* (1909) was published in Paris and then produced in Italian under the title *La donna è mobile* (*Woman Is Fickle*) in the same year. The play involves a combination of living actors and puppets in a theme that could otherwise be read as a classic farce, complete with adultery, revolver-dangling and suicide; all part of Marinetti's scorn of the decadent bourgeoisie. The American engineer John Wilson is in charge of several electric works while also inventing a series of puppets that he uses primarily as an audience to liven up his sex life with his wife, Mary. They are staying at a health resort on the Côte d'Azur, where they meet another couple, Paul and Juliette, who are also having marital difficulties. Although the play caused a stir when it was first staged, it has been read as 'a rather trivial attempt to create drama out of the tangled relations of insubstantial characters'. Segel claims that:

> Apart from John himself, Mary is perhaps the most interesting figure, a typical Marinettian high-strung female. She is compared in the play to John's puppets in that both are animated by electricity, which may be the only other purpose the puppets serve in the work. In Mary's case (as in Juliette's) the current comes

from the atmosphere as much as from the hyper-sensitive female nervous system
to which Marinetti, as a Futurist, always felt strong attraction.[50]

The attraction to electricity is similar to that exerted by the 'high-strung'
female nervous system, and in this play the two merge in the figure of the
puppet. In this case the puppet conveniently brings together the fascination
with technology and the ambivalence about the female. For the Italian
Futurists, modernity was celebrated through the high energy of electricity
and the speed of the automobile. The only way that the female enters into
this scheme is through her 'hyper-sensitive' nervous system, which somehow correlates to the energy of technology. This quality, which was traditionally felt to make women bad actresses on the stage, ironically places
that very theatricality, histrionic tendency and falseness at the heart of their
existence. As 'pure and raw nervous' energy, however, the female also
becomes the appropriate ghost within the futurist robot/machine. This
reaches its classic fusion of modernist love/hate of technology doubled by
a similar attitude towards the female in Fritz Lang's 'False Maria' of
Metropolis (1927). Female robots of the period, in contrast to the male ones
(who either present innocence or the utopian potential of technology),
usually connote falseness, vacuity and trickery, all seething with a charged
sexual energy. In as much as the puppet/robot acts as a medium that channels fears, anxieties but also hopes about technology, the feminine enters
this schema as the medium of the false, the artificial and the sexually
deadly. The predominance of the name Maria for these vicious robots is
interesting in itself. If for the Italian Futurists the modern world should be
characterised by its 'scorn of women', for Craig this 'scorn' connects him
to more classical European legacies:

> Woman as a rule being the most material packet of goods on this earth, makes a
> good effort to kill desire for an Ideal ... and is trying to break the man of his wor-
> ship of King-monarch – Stars and Gods – that he may have no other gods than
> Her. And she will succeed until she reaches the artist, and then she will utter a
> shriek and like the sphinx will throw herself off the cliff ...[51]

Despite its classical allusions, this narrative is dangerously similar to 'the
robots taking over the laboratory' one. In many ways women are too much
like robots or puppets to be their creators. And like puppets they can be
either holy or profane, connecting the puppeteer (and the audience) either
with God or dregs of the material world. There is, however, no guarantee
which direction this flow will follow. And like many of the puppet/robot
plays of the period, it usually goes *both* ways. It is also fascinating to note

that Craig wrote the above in a letter to Isadora Duncan, a woman who had revolutionised dance and who had had a child with him, against the moral code of her time.

The debate about the representational efficacy of the human form is inevitably also a debate about the relationship between femininity and representation. The modernist imperative for the abolition of the human form also shares a deep ambivalence towards the feminine. This is not always the case, however, as in the projects that look towards the puppet for an *example* rather than a substitution. The case of Meyerhold's biomechanics again acts as the counter-argument to the above. Inspired by the popular tradition in puppetry, Meyerhold's emphasis was on the art of the actor. His actress wife, Zinaida Raikh, played an important role in the formulation of his aesthetics and politics. Although she did not follow the independent paths of other significant performers of her time like Duncan, Duse or Bernhardt, with Meyerhold she formed a formidable actor/director team for whom issues of gender where inextricably linked to their broader aspirations.

Marxism and feminism have not always made amicable bedfellows. Rather than follow the Stalinist dictum, however, that the revolution had solved the 'woman question', Meyerhold and Raikh were more inspired by Trotsky, who proclaimed that 'in order to change the conditions of life, we must see them through the eyes of women' (1924). Indeed, the 'woman question', so evident in much of the drama of the period, can be read as also informing the 'acting question' and the 'training question'. It is fair to say that throughout their long and sometimes fraught collaborations (1921–39) Meyerhold and Raikh's work engaged with the issues of gender thematically but also formally.[52] Towards the end of their lives they were planning a trilogy 'on women and their contribution to historical change, dealing with the pre-revolutionary, Bolshevik and Stalinist periods'.[53] After a brief period of very radical and sometimes controversial policies introduced by the social reforms of 1917, headed by such figures as Alexandra Kollontai,[54] in 1939 abortion was again criminalised and the nuclear family stressed. Talking to Harold Clurman, who was then visiting the USSR, Meyerhold said of this trilogy, which included *The Lady of the Camellias*:

> I am interested in the bad attitude of the bourgeoisie to women. Marguerite is treated like a slave or servant. Men bargain over her, throw money in her face, insult her – all because they say they love her. I was interested to show this because we, too, in the Soviet Union, have had a wrong conception of love and of women.[55]

This is a far cry from the statements about women pronounced by Marinetti or Craig. For Meyerhold and Raikh the 'woman question' was constitutive of the broader thinking about the democratic potential of modernity. Embracing it was similar to embracing the revolutionary potential of technology. It informed Meyerhold's pedagogy and his stage productions. Rather than seeing the puppet as a way of banishing the art of the actor and resolving the issue of female actors once and for all, perhaps for Meyerhold and Raikh it presented new ways of formally experimenting with gender.

Clearly many of the experiments with puppets during this period feed directly into theories of acting. In some cases there is a call for the abolition of the human actor and in others this engagement is seen to celebrate the art of the actor. Either way, whether in the aphoristic tones of Craig or in the manifestos of the Bauhaus, the human body on stage is being reconfigured. The relationships between inner expressiveness and outer stylisation inform these approaches and gesture towards new understandings of the body and of subjectivity. Stylisation and abstraction do not necessarily signal superficiality or lack of an inner life. Rather they propose a new relationship to the historical process and a new version of the individual. All this emphasis on the external life of puppets, on the distance they impose on the audience, on their shameless artificiality helps shape Meyerhold's notion of the *dialectical actor*, an actor that at once *is* and *demonstrates* character. Brecht's V-effect is just around the corner.

'When the Puppets Come to Town': Wooden Characters

This modernist fascination with puppets does not confine itself solely to theatrical projects. Many of the so-called 'high' modernists, as we saw in the Conrad's letter, that helps to frame this chapter, expressed an interest in puppets. Yeats experienced the shock effects of the early performances of *Ubu Roi* and, as we have mentioned, it made a huge impression on him. Much of his own thinking about the stage was influenced by figures like Craig. Moreover, the ways the puppet engages notions of the human body and the complex relationships of inner world and outer expression parallel much of the experimentation of the period with the notion of character.

In July 1917, Djuna Barnes wrote an article entitled 'When the Puppets Come to Town', for the *New York Morning Telegraph Sunday Magazine*.[56] It is an account of a visit to a puppet theatre punctuated with strokes of Kleistian dialogue. Indeed, for a writer preoccupied with poetry and the novel, she displays a sophisticated awareness of the debates surrounding puppets, their philosophical inheritance and their applicability to modernist aesthetics in general. She frames her account of her visit with the characteristic 'acute languor' that connects her with Charles Ricketts, Charles

Baudelaire, Oscar Wilde and a variety of 'decadent' aestheticists who were also drawn to marionettes:

> I am tired; my days are full of a vain yet pleasant sorrow. I perceive that I am happy without being able to grasp my happiness. I am full of an acute languor and I must be up and doing. I have speculated upon life until existence has become a network of plot and incident tangled hopelessly in the complexities of human emotion …
> It is well. I go off to twenty-eight Macdougal Street and watch Bufano's marionettes.[57]

This bears traces of the melancholy that 'real actors' with 'real emotions' breed in Joseph Conrad. Both turn towards marionettes and away from the psychologism of the internalised world of character. As Barnes claims, marionettes are 'so impartial' because they have never 'had a private life'. In particular it is their formal attributes that allow for a different perception and rendition of subjectivity. She writes:

> Having no sense of colour a tear means no more to them than a drop of water, a pool of blood, nothing more than a pool of rain. They are filled with a strange, charming angular fidelity to moments that we should have slurred by our roundness of perception and our more flexible motions.[58]

And it is this formal, 'angular fidelity' that releases Barnes from her previously felt 'acute languor', 'mourning' and boredom. In the course of this essay she also adds a Kleistian dialogue (or a Platonic one) with a certain Tony Sarg, who proclaims that he 'respects marionettes because they are capable of tragedy without annoying anyone by being capable of tragic emotions'. Appropriately Barnes responds, 'Quite true. It is with wood that we express so much of that which is the flesh.'[59] In this concise but philologically sophisticated essay Barnes at once pays homage to the Kleistian legacy and moves the debate forward to the modernist obsession with matter, form and raw material. On the way, she mentions that the drama of Shaw and Yeats is not congenial to puppets. Interestingly enough, her thinking almost directly mirrors the modernist theatrical discourses on the representational efficacy of the human form, and the possibilities presented by the marionette.

In her preface to the republication of Barnes's article, Rebecca Loncraine claims that Barnes's attitude towards puppets might 'help make sense of the characterisations in her later work, where the emphasis is on language as an external performance and not a sign of psychological interiority'.[60] Indeed, many narrative experiments in character at the time could be read in the context of this modernist fascination with puppets. The puppet presents new ways of reconfiguring the relationships between inner psychological worlds and their outer expressiveness. In many ways, it acts as an antidote to the 'psychologism' of Freud and the fascination with interiority. It offers ways of stylising the human body and making it a material as flexible as any tool in the hands of an artist. It presents a notion of the individual that can either be connected to the collective body of the people (as in the carnival/popular tradition) or to the body of God (as in the transcendental legacy). Whether sacred or profane the modernist life of puppets seems to have had a huge impact on the theatrical and broader literary experiments of the period.

3

The Director, the Playwright and the Actress

> ... the Art of the Theatre is neither acting nor the play, it is not scene nor dance, but consists of all the elements of which these things are composed: action, which is the very spirit of acting; words, which are the body of the play; line and colour, which are the very heart of the scene; rhythm, which is the very essence of the dance.
>
> (Edward Gordon Craig, 1905)[1]

> Away with the author! Theatre shouldn't be written in the study, but built on the stage.
>
> (Ilya Ehrenburg, 1922)[2]

The figure of the director as the creative force in the theatre is to an extent codified, experimented with and given some form of definition within the aesthetic concerns of Modernism and within the broader socio-political framework of modernity. Indeed, the director could be seen as one of the emblematic figures of modernity. In as much as modernity is seen as part of the ever-increasing democratic project, providing visibility and opportunity to sections of the population previously invisible (like the working classes and women), the appearance of the director may be seen as embracing the democratic potential of modernity and its impact on the art of the theatre. On the other hand, the director, in whom every creative aspect of making theatre is seen to converge, may also be read as the epitome of the totalising dimension of much of modernist aesthetics and of its flirtations, in varying degrees, with the totalising political discourses of the period: fascism and Stalinism, since from Wagner to Brecht the quest for a language of the stage can be read within that broader political project too.

It is primarily the figure of the director that acts as a channel for the 'new' art of the theatre; this 'new' form of theatre in turn helps to create a

43

space and a language that is seen to be particular to the stage. The emergence of performance as a distinct epistemological category, differentiating it from the art of the playwright, is debated, contested and finally formulated within the debates about the function and identity of the director. Preechoing what would later become, through the advent of cinema, the signatory utterance of the director – 'action' – Craig differentiates his art from that of the playwright and the actor. The art of the director lies in the act of composing an artistic spectacle. However, the elements that need such scenic composition are themselves contested and sometimes claim authorship as well. And this helps to forge some of the most contradictory but also creative forces that come together in the figure of the director. For instance, Ehrenburg's slogan, with its emphasis on 'production' and its manifesto-fervour, calls for an art that is indigenous to the stage, yet when Meyerhold staged an adaptation of his novel *The History of the Fall of Europe* in 1924, Ehrenburg the author objected. 'I'm not some classic but a real, live person,'[3] he made a claim in defence of his text and his right over it.

The debates about authorship, the claims to impersonality, the relationships between autobiography and art are all issues that are theorised, experimented with and contested throughout this period. In renegotiating the relationship between the actor and the playwright, the text and the stage, the rise of the director can also be read as a comment – or a proposal – on the more general thinking at the time about the concept of authorship. Indeed, the theatre might be seen as the most appropriate *locus* for such an exploration. Its synaesthetic quality, coupled with its civic/political dimension, makes it ideal for both the discourse that sees the director as the ultimate embodiment of individual genius in the theatre and the one that sees him as a channel through which the fusion of the aesthetic and the political is filtered.

Although the notion of a 'mediating' figure between the text and the stage has always been part of theatre history, and particularly significant for the history of opera,[4] the modernist reworking of these categories into a distinct function acquires a particular force and urgency. From the autocratic Duke George II of Saxe-Meiningen and his mass spectacles in the 1860s to the more artistic, studio-based, 'intimate' theatres of André Antoine and Aurélien Lugné-Poë, the role of this 'mediating' figure is drastically reconfigured and comes to acquire a distinctive modernist inflection. Stage-manager, producer, actor-manager, scriptor, prompter, impresario, were all structures that were already in place, with their own history and function. In this sense, this new distinctly 'modernist' director-figure can be read as the culmination of a long and sometimes fraught history; one that is located in the space between the theatre text and the dramatic performance. It is significant that this particular form of theatre practice, located between the textual and the performative, begins to acquire a new and distinct identity within the discourses of modernity.

The two quotations that preface this chapter help to frame some of our explorations into this new form of director. On the one extreme is Craig, who assumes total responsibility, in the tradition initiated by Wagner's *Gesamtkuntswerk*, and on the other extreme the director as a figure who oversees the 'production' of the work of theatre. Like a composer, the director brings together and shapes all the artistic energies that create a performance. And like Wagner the composer-conductor-director of his own later operas, he is a type of *Übermensch* whose artistic will permeates every aspect of the stage. Indeed, the significant contribution of Wagner to the experimentation regarding the role of the director has sometimes been overlooked. This is primarily due to the fact that the modernist 'rise' of the director has been read mainly through the naturalist legacy (as will be examined below). However, the Wagnerian tradition also helps to account for the versions of the director that see him as a guru, as a prophet, as a charismatic and hence potentially despotic figure. The quest for totality that Wagner initiates fits in well with both the aestheticism of the 1890s and the more modernist fascination with technology. The search for a complete autonomy of the stage creates its own technology, facilitated by the advent of electricity to the theatre. The works of Wagner can be seen as one of the earliest examples of an attempt to create a 'technology of the stage'. Theodor Adorno describes Wagner's works as 'among the earliest "wonders of technology" to gain admittance to great art'.[5] Adorno is critical of the phantasmagoria that this use of technology creates, aestheticising reality and concealing the modes of production that help to create such an absolute illusion. In this sense the quest for the autonomy of the stage is also inflected by the modernist debates about the power, emancipatory or otherwise, of technology. So when Craig calls for the autonomy of the stage he differentiates between the work of a mere 'producer', who simply 'interprets' the dramatist, and that of an 'artist', standing in for every aspect of the artistic process:

> When he interprets the plays of a dramatist by means of his actors, his scene-painters, and his other craftsmen, then he is a craftsman. When he will have mastered the uses of actions, words, light, colour and rhythm, then he may become an artist. Then he shall no longer need the assistance of the playwright, for our art will then be self-reliant.[6]

And it is a distinction that characterises many of the experiments of the period. Never as absolute as Craig defines it, the tension between the reading of the director as facilitating 'producer', as an extension of the actor-manager tradition or the tradition of the nineteenth-century grand-operatic *régisseur*, and that of him as a prophet of the 'new movement' in the theatre, one that heralds a new era, is one that informs the work of many charismatic directors of the period. This tension is resolved in some cases by collapsing the roles of playwright and director into one, as is the case with Brecht. Like Wagner before him – or indeed the late-Victorian tradition as seen in the case of G. B. Shaw – Brecht is not necessarily modernist in occupying both positions (Molière also staged his own plays). The role of the actor, however, is a crucial one in this new dynamic and possibly helps to define the role of this new director-figure. This emphasis placed on the art of acting helps to reposition the modernist director.

And it is a relationship, which is equally difficult to negotiate. The shifting definition of the director always parallels redefinitions of the art of the actor. Most directors of the period, from Craig, Stanislavsky and Meyerhold to Brecht, formulate new theories for the art of acting. Indeed, all their projects have a distinct pedagogic dimension. Most of their projects are accompanied by 'schools' of acting. Acting becomes theorised and taught, no longer relying on the categories of genius and inspiration alone or on grinding apprenticeship in a hierarchical company. The training of actors becomes central to their directorial projects. Although the art of the actor is given a status never before achieved in the history of theatre and the limelight of the modernist stage falls on the actor, it is an art form that is inextricably linked with the art of the director. Any definition of one inevitably leads to a re-examination of the other.

'A Slice of Life'

> It would be absurd to suppose that one can transfer nature to the stage: plant real trees and have real houses lit by a real sun. We are forced into conventions, and must accept a more or less complete illusion of reality.
>
> (Zola, *La Naturalisme au théâtre*, 1881)[7]

Zola's defence of illusion strikes at the heart of the pretensions of Naturalism. The great theorist of the movement (whose primary domain was admittedly the novel) points towards one of the most creative tensions in Naturalist theatre: the tension between the desire for verisimilitude and the ontological inevitability of illusion and theatricality. And this translates into a tension between two views of the stage: as an extension of life and as a comment on that life. It is a tension central to the Naturalist project, both delineating its limitations and pointing towards further experimentation. It is significant that most, if not all, Naturalist playwrights both helped to codify the movement and significantly tested its boundaries. It is common-place to see the great Naturalist playwrights, like Strindberg and Ibsen, as 'evolving' into expressionism and other forms of stylisation in the late stages of their careers, going beyond the limits of Naturalism itself. It is also historically accepted in most studies that a new role of the director emerges within the workings of Naturalism. Indeed, it is the director, now with a distinct artistic identity and remit, who helps to articulate some of the tensions inherent in the movement.

We sometimes forget, due to the onslaught of criticism that Naturalism has received over the years, starting with the modernist period itself, that in many respects it too was part of the modern movement. Naturalism has been identified with late-nineteenth-century positivism, empiricism and a general faith in science and theories of heredity and environment. With regard not so much to the straight-jacket aesthetics that this use of social theory may impose, but to the critical potential that this quintessentially Enlightenment thinking represents, Naturalism has to be read as part of the 'New Movement' in the theatre and as identifying itself with democratic movements of the period. For example, Brecht's search for a form of the-atre that strives to bring about change in people's lives can also be read as an extension of the Naturalist project and not simply in opposition to it. (Brecht's early 'Three Cheers for Shaw' is a testament to this).[8] Again, although Naturalism is primarily identified with the so-called playwrights' theatre and with the 'theatre of ideas', it provides fertile ground for the rise of the director. In demanding a radical reworking of the shift from text to stage, Naturalism also demands a figure with a vision that will be respon-sible for every aspect of production. The advent of electricity and more sophisticated stage technologies constitutes one of the factors which allow the director further formal experimentation, while also placing Naturalism within the late-nineteenth-century movements that see technology as eman-cipatory and enabling, a facilitator in the creative process. This fascination that Naturalism presents, through the figure of the director, is one of the aspects that the avant-garde picks up on and passionately elaborates. The theatrical avant-garde's experimentation with technology and investment in egalitarian troupes of performers led by a new-style director in some respects start with Naturalism, despite its vehement protestations of opposition to it.

André Antoine and Aurélien Lugné-Poë in France are usually cited as the first directors to emerge from the Naturalist movement. Antoine with the Théâtre Libre is read as epitomising a more Naturalist style, having staged works by Zola, while Lugné-Poë is more in the Symbolist tradition, having started his directorial career with plays by Maeterlinck. The encounter with the plays of Ibsen proved crucial for both men (Antoine staging *Ghosts* in 1890 and Lugné-Poë *The Lady from the Sea* in 1892). These two companies introduced not only a new aesthetic to the theatre but also a new ethos. The excesses of Romanticism were pared down and the everyday was centrestage. If Naturalism can be read as charting a crisis within the bourgeoisie, then the audience were asked to recognise the stage as an extension of their lives, both physically and psychologically. From their humble and amateur beginnings these two theatres went on to become iconic within theatre history, and primarily through the work of their directors. These men saw their role not simply as the mounters of entertainment: they were very aware that these works were representative of a new era of social change. Their productions were successful but also considered scandalous. They were training the audience not simply through the issues the 'problem plays' covered, but through the ways they were asked to interact with the work *as a piece of theatre*. For example, when Antoine produced *Miss Julie* (1893), he distributed Strindberg's now famous preface amongst the audience. The concern with audience response and reception that becomes very explicit in the more overtly political theatres of the avant-garde may also have its predecessor in Naturalism. These directors, despite their fascination with the workings of the stage, remained faithful to the playwright as dominant figure. Indeed, the critical outcry caused by Ibsen and Ibsenism only led them to believe that these playwrights were truly the heralds of a new liberated era. Antoine said in an interview during a visit to London in 1889:

> The aim of the Théâtre Libre is to encourage every writer for the stage, and above all, to write what he feels inclined to write and not what he thinks a manager will produce. I produce anything in which there is a grain of merit, quite irrespective of any opinion I may form of what the public will think of it, and anything a known writer brings me, and exactly as he hands it to me. If he writes a monologue of half-a-dozen pages word for word, the actor must speak those half-dozen pages word for word. His business is to write the play; mine to have it acted.[9]

When it came to Jarry, however, Antoine was not as generous. Again, the first productions of *Ubu Roi* prove crucial in helping to demarcate the differences between Naturalism and the more experimental anti-illusionist projects that came to run parallel in the later 1890s. At the first public dress rehearsal at the Nouveau Théâtre on 9 December 1896, to an audience of mostly writers and artists, Antoine is recorded as rising from his seat and shouting out in protest against the play, initiating what almost evolved into a fist-fight for the following fifteen minutes. Unlike the protests that the production of Ibsen's plays triggered, these objections were made mainly on formal grounds. The way *Ubu Roi* looked as a piece of theatre was offensive, or at least troubling to that first audience. Indeed, many accounts of the now legendary performance voice their praise or objection in such terms. Arthur Symons wrote:

> ... the scenery was painted to represent, by a child's conventions, indoors and out of doors, and even the torrid, temperate, and arctic zones at once. Opposite you, at the back of the stage, you saw apple trees in bloom, under a blue sky, and against the sky a small closed window and a fireplace ... A venerable gentleman in evening dress ... trotted across the stage on the points of his toes between every scene and hung the new placard on its nail.[10]

The group of artists involved in designing the set is itself very impressive: Toulouse-Lautrec, Bonnard and Vuillard. Jarry himself was involved with every aspect of the production. He gave detailed notes to Lugné-Poë, most of which dealt with matters of production and theatrical convention rather than interpretation of the play.

Jarry writes in a letter to Lugné-Poë:

(1) Mask for the principal character, Ubu; I could get this for you if necessary. And, in any case, I believe you yourself have been studying the whole question of masks in the theatre.

(2) A cardboard horse's head which he would hang round his neck, as they did on the medieval English stage, for the only two equestrian scenes; all these details fit in with the mood of the play, since my intention was, in any case to write a puppet play.

[...]

(6) Costumes divorced as far as possible from local colour or chronology (which will thus help to give the impression of something eternal): modern costumes preferable, since the satire is modern, and shoddy ones, too, to make the play even more wretched and horrible.[11]

And it is this disruption of theatrical convention, illusionism and the certainties regarding representation that the original audience responded to.

It is worth mentioning, once more, Yeats's famous response:

> The players are supposed to be dolls, toys, marionettes, and now they are all hop-ping like wooden frogs, and I can see for myself that the chief personage, who is some kind of king, carries for a sceptre a brush of the kind that we use to clean a closet.[12]

Yeats too seems to engage with the performance in terms both of theatrical convention and content. The overwhelming anti-humanism of the piece, highlighted by the references to puppetry and carnival, led Yeats as we have seen to pronounce his famous aphorism: 'After us the Savage God.' And, in many ways, this was an appropriate reaction. The play's scatology, buf-foonery and general carnival atmosphere entail nothing of the regenerative aspects of comedy; it remains a bleak but critical gesture towards the great anthropomorphic and humanist discourses of European theatre. When we compare Jarry's notes with Yeats's reaction they do not seem that incongruous:

> Really these are hardly the constituents for an amusing play, and the masks demonstrate that the comedy must at the most be the macabre comedy of an English clown, or of a Dance of Death. Before Gémier agreed to play the part, Lugné-Poë had learned Ubu's lines and wanted to rehearse the play as a tragedy. And what no one seems to have understood – it was made clear enough, though, and constantly recalled by Ma Ubu's continually repeated: 'What an idiotic man! ... What a sorry imbecile!' – is that Ubu's speeches were not meant to be full of witticisms, as various little ubuists claimed, but of stupid remarks, uttered with all the authority of the Ape.[13]

In this sense, that initial reaction was the appropriate, even desirable one. The audience interacted with the performance in terms of content but also, and significantly, in terms of form. And it is in these terms that it was most shocked. Unlike the Naturalist dramas that were shocking for the ideas they proposed, this play seemed to undermine the very possibility of a coherent idea on the stage. Furthermore, it did this through a total destruction – scatological and eschatological at the same time – of the history of 'staging ideas on the stage' and the humanism that this presupposes. The audience that night experienced what was to become the hallmark of the avant-garde and epic theatres that were to follow: the feeling and sense of estrangement and defamiliarisation. In many ways this was the ideal response, as *Ubu Roi* burst onto the European stage less as a specific performance of a literary text and more as a litany to the dead theatres of the past, and as a proposal – albeit one seeped in negativity – about the possibilities of theatre in general.

Ubu Roi in performance becomes mythologised almost immediately and has since occupied an iconic status in the history of modernist theatre. It is fascinating that this happened because as a piece of theatre it sets out to engage critically with its audience. Like Naturalistic drama, but in significantly different ways, Jarry's play also proposes a new mode of reception, a mode of audience-relating in which the role of the director is crucial. The theatres that are to follow, like Meyerhold's and Brecht's, begin to redefine the role of the audience completely and posit it as central to their projects. And at this point what begin to emerge are two dominant strands of audience response. Although not clearly articulated as yet, they can be schematically drawn as empathy and identification on the one hand, as proposed by Naturalism, and distance and estrangement on the other, taking form in the early productions of the Jarry plays. The Epic Theatre of Brecht, as we will examine further on, engages with both traditions, rewriting them in the process.

This 'new' relationship with the audience, however, also presupposes a reconfiguration of the art of the actor. The two dominant trends that we have outlined above – one Naturalist, the other anti-illusionist – also propose new modes of acting. The directorial figures of Antoine and Lugné-Poë act as somewhat schematic reference points of the two most distinct approaches to redefining the art of the actor. Antoine's Naturalism presupposes a mode of acting that is psychological, expressive, heavily inflected by the emerging discourses of psychoanalysis and theories of the environment. The challenge posed by playwrights such as Ibsen and Strindberg required an approach to acting that focused on the inner world of the characters and its fraught relationships with environment and biology, in a sometimes heady concoction of Nietzsche, Freud and social theory. As Strindberg's 'Preface to *Miss Julie*' clearly shows, the modern character was perceived as fragmented and de-centred. It demanded a mode of acting that reflected on an intimate level the scale of this inner turmoil:

My souls (or characters) are conglomerations of past and present cultures, scraps from books and newspapers, fragments of humanity, torn shreds of once-fine clothing that has become rags, in just the way that a human soul is patched together.[14]

Naturalism was creating new demands on actors. The kind of acting it presupposed relied on the 'inner' workings of character; it was intimate, subtle, but definitely psychological and humanist, despite the levels of crisis which that very humanism was seen to inhabit, as Strindberg suggests. By contrast, it might be useful to recall in this context the types of actors that Jarry initially had in mind for the production of *Ubu Roi*. The first private productions were with puppets, and in the public production mentioned above the actors were asked to move like puppets. The actors' bodies were puppetised. And this was one of the main factors that disconcerted the audience. The approximation of a living organism to a machine always creates discomfort as it undermines most of the basic humanist assumptions: anthropocentrism, subjectivity, agency are a few of these categories. (This unease, as Jarry's contemporary Bergson was to claim in his theories on laughter, might be at the creative core of all comedy.) Under the Naturalist legacy, and no matter how critical an attitude was voiced, the basic 'humanism' of the characters was seen to remain intact. With Jarry we have a kind of acting that relies on exteriority. The movement is always from the outside. It is cruel, hard and blasphemous. Rather than drawing its definition from the great Enlightenment discourses of the subject, it identifies with the popular and carnival traditions that are seen to be resolutely anti-humanist. In turning the body of the actor into an 'object' on the stage, it undermines the fundamental distinctions between human and non-human, and outer and inner world. It is fascinating that these two trends in acting, which helped to forge the role of the modern director, run almost parallel in the theatres of Modernism. Antoine's Naturalism, heavily inflected by his encounter with Strindberg and Ibsen, will be elaborated on by Stanislavsky (through his encounter with Chekhov), and Brecht will codify the anti-humanist tradition in acting with his Epic Theatre. Still, it is important to remember that these two schools need not be read as antithetical. In some ways they even mirror each other in their attempts to chart and represent and find formal equivalents for Strindberg's 'fragments of humanity'.

However, in one particular area, that of gender, it might be equally fascinating to follow Strindberg's argument through and see how this chaotic state of the 'modern character' comes into being. His Miss Julie is such a 'modern character':

> Miss Julie is a modern character – not that the half-woman, the man-hater, has not existed in every age, but because, now that she has been discovered, she has stepped forward into the limelight and begun to make a noise. The half-woman is a type that pushes herself to the front, nowadays selling herself for power, honours, decorations and diplomas, as formerly she used to for money. [...] They engender an indeterminate sex to whom life is a torture, but fortunately they go under, either because they cannot adapt themselves to reality, or because their repressed instinct breaks out uncontrollably, or because their hopes of attaining equality with men are shattered. It is a tragic type, providing the spectacle of a desperate battle against Nature – and tragic also as a Romantic

heritage now being dissipated by Naturalism, which thinks that the only good lies in happiness – and happiness is something that only a strong and hardy species can achieve.[15]

In its proper context, the above quotation also needs to be read against what was perceived to be Ibsen's more favourable treatment of women in his plays (notably *A Doll's House* (1879), *Ghosts* (1881) and *Hedda Gabler* (1890)). Either way, as most theatre historians today concede, the 'woman question' was constitutive of Naturalism as a movement. In as much as Naturalism demanded a new type of actor, it also demanded a new type of actress. It might be interesting for us to speculate that Naturalism and its conventions are tied up with the specific representation of the female.

Ibsen's championing of the 'woman question' is matched by Strindberg's utter horror in the face of feminism as a social movement. Either way, for both playwrights, female characters become conspicuous on stage and, in many ways, set up their own demands for acting and staging. The figure of the 'new woman' is central to the formal and thematic concerns of Naturalism. Either as emblem of modernity with the hallmarks of self-reliance and self-fulfilment, or as a barren, hysterical creature deprived of her motherly function (or as a synthesis of all the above), the new woman becomes a fixture of the Naturalist stage. For James Joyce, writing in 1900, Ibsen's insight into womanhood possibly offers a broader understanding of the workings of humanity:

> Ibsen's knowledge of humanity is nowhere more obvious than in his portrayal of women. He amazes one by his painful introspection; he seems to know them better than they know themselves. Indeed, if one may say so of an eminently virile man, there is a curious admixture of the woman in his nature.[16]

And this 'admixture' was one that Joyce was to experiment with as well, notably in the last section of his *Ulysses*.

It might be interesting to try to include in this schema, which traditionally ranges from Ibsen's feminism to Strindberg's 'crisis of masculinity', the histories of the actual actresses involved in bringing these figures of the 'new woman' on to the stage. As we have mentioned earlier, the rise of the modernist director is inextricably linked with the art of the actor, as the latter was starting to be reconfigured within the theatres of Modernism. As the 'woman question' is so intrinsic to Naturalism as a movement, it is worth examining how the specific representation of the female is both informed by and comments on the broader conventions and ideologies of the movement.

'The Woman Question'

In *Women, Modernism and Performance*, Penny Farfan examines the relationship between Ibsen and contemporary performers like Ellen Terry and Elizabeth Robins, as she inserts the histories of specific actresses into the overall understanding of the history of modernist theatre. She, too, starts her analysis from Ibsen:

> Notably, though it has commonly been suggested that the door-slam at the end of *A Doll's House* signalled the advent of both modern drama and the women's movement, Nora's forgery of her father's signature is in fact the act of transgression that sets the drama in motion; and indeed, authorship and authority are linked throughout Ibsen's 'women's plays', so that acts of writing, reading, or – in Hedda's case – manuscript-burning serve to signify the female protagonists' respective degrees of critical engagement with hegemonic cultural texts that deny women status as authoritative subjects.[17]

Such claims of authorship of or on the modernist stage would have to include the history of specific female performers and their contribution to our received understanding of Naturalism. The work of Ibsen in particular had a huge impact on the newly emerging feminist movement and especially on its performative and public dimension. As Farfan states, however, the reception of Ibsen by early feminists was at least ambivalent, and she examines the work of the actress Elizabeth Robins, who initially acted in Ibsen plays and later wrote her own (*Votes for Women*, 1907). Robins, who had played the title role in *Hedda Gabler* in the first London performance in 1891, wrote in her essay 'Ibsen and the Actress' in 1928:

> If we had been thinking politically, concerning ourselves about the emancipation of women, we would not have given the Ibsen plays the particular kind of wholehearted, enchanted devotion we did give. [Ibsen's work] had nothing to do with the New Woman; it had everything to do with our particular business – with the art of acting.[18]

This essay, published by Virginia Woolf and Leonard Woolf at the Hogarth Press, touches upon one of the central issues regarding Ibsen and feminism. Robins proposes a distinction between what may be conceived as the theme and the political stance of the work, on the one hand, and its formal concerns on the other. The relationship between form and content would ignite many a heated debate among the avant-garde that was soon to follow. In underlining the link between the two, it could be said that Robins also points towards some of the shortcomings of Naturalism as a theatrical movement.

Her own play *Votes for Women* can be read as both a corrective and a supplement to Ibsen's treatment of the 'woman question'. Like many suffragette dramas it implied a more direct and demonstrative style. Farfan writes of *Votes for Women*:

> Rejecting the patient and orderly but ineffectual proceedings of the Constitutionalist suffragists in favor of a more radical and spectacular activism, Robins's play mediated constructively, through its pointedly political artlessness, between Hedda Gabler's furiously impulsive destruction of Eilert Løvborg's manuscript and the acts of vandalism that were perpetrated by increasingly desperate militants in the final phase of the suffrage campaign and that included an attack on Velázquez's masterpiece, the *Rokeby Venus*, in the National Gallery in early 1914.[19]

In fact the style employed is very similar to what the avant-garde later termed 'agit-prop' theatre. Either way, it seems that Robins's experience as an actress definitely informed her writing of the play. However, the suffragette theatre's style of performance was testing the limits of Naturalist acting. What the example of Robins indicates is possibly the beginnings of a quest of a style of theatre that approximates to the more political theatres of the avant-garde like Meyerhold's and Brecht's. Either way, this experiment in theatrical form is heavily inflected by the 'woman question'.

It is also, as mentioned earlier, inflected by the actual histories of the actresses of the period. Farfan mentions Ellen Terry, Elizabeth Robins, Edith Craig and Isadora Duncan. Sarah Bernhardt and Eleonora Duse earlier, and Zinaida Raikh and Helene Weigel later, could be added to the list. All these actresses had an impact on their art and on the art of modernist theatre in general that is comparable to the contributions made by the directors they worked with. Their approaches range from the more psychological approaches of naturalism to the abstract and stylised acting of Meyerhold's biomechanics and its progeny. And in most cases, in a performative fusion of art and life, their public personas matched the image of the new woman, as Gail Finney describes her:

> The New Woman typically values self-fulfilment and independence rather than the stereotypically feminine ideal of self-sacrifice; believes in legal and sexual equality; often remains single because of the difficulty of combining such equality with marriage; is more open about her sexuality than the 'Old Woman'; is well-educated and reads a great deal; has a job; is athletic or otherwise physically vigorous and, accordingly, prefers comfortable clothes (sometimes male attire) to traditional female garb.[20]

The other side of this coin, however, exposes tragedy and loss, as the reception of Isadora Duncan proves. And through this fusion of private and public, of their art and their lives, all these actresses, in some ways, enact the historically difficult relationship between women and the stage. We know that the classical European theatres (from the Greeks to the Elizabethans) had no female performers. This fact, coupled with the fraught legacy of the female image in representation, always as object but rarely as subject, creates some of the creative tensions and anxieties that these performers experienced. It may have also led some of them to a critical and experimental stance towards their art form. This stance usually involved some reworking of the contours and the function of the female body. Isadora Duncan for instance wrote, 'I use my body as my medium just as a writer uses his words. Do not call me a dancer.'[21]

This claim of authorship through the body rather than words runs parallel to the overall aspirations of modernist theatre to disentangle itself from the primacy of the written word. And nowhere is it located and enacted more clearly than on the body of the actress. If the modernist stage enacts a crisis of Enlightenment thought and its formal theatrical conventions, then the role of gender and the specific oppression of the female is constitutive of the structure of such thought. The female body in particular, and through the work of the female performers of the period, becomes the site that renegotiates the representational efficacy not only of the male gaze, but of the whole edifice that creates it. In a 1911 review of *Rachel: Her Stage Life and her Real Life*, Virginia Woolf insightfully comments, drawing on a performative fusion of life and the stage:

> The truth seems to be that one does not stop acting or painting or writing just because one happens to be driving in the Park; only trying to combine the two things often ends disastrously. Perhaps disaster is more common among actresses than among other artists, because the body plays so large a part upon the stage.[22]

Although acting is here seen to be on a par with textual and visual art, the fact that it involves the inscription of the female body may sometimes, as Woolf claims, lead to disaster. The female performer from Naturalism onwards enters a very interesting and challenging arena; one where she is asked through her body to be both the subject and the object of her artwork. Given the fraught relationship that classical European theatre has with the female body this may prove not simply difficult but, sometimes, catastrophic. However, it needs to be stressed that Naturalism's interest in the 'woman question' on a thematic level is matched by the broader formal experiments in representing the female body. Although the leading directors of the period rarely refer to the issue of gender in the ways we are accustomed to applying it today, most do work with leading actresses when giving shape to their theories. Rather than seeing these performers as simply and unproblematically mediating the thoughts of these directors, it might be useful and historically more accurate to assume that the actresses themselves had a considerable input in the creation of these theatrical projects. Strindberg worked with both his actress wives, Siri Wrangel and Harriet Bosse, and towards the end of his life with the seventeen-year old actress Fanny Faulikner;[23] Ibsen was served by a number of influential actresses; Gordon Craig designed for Eleonora Duse and Isadora Duncan and directed his mother, Ellen Terry; Meyerhold worked with Zinaida Raikh; Stanislavsky with Olga Kipper; Harley Granville-Barker with Lillah McCarthy; Brecht with Helene Weigel.[24]

The art of the actor, being ephemeral, is sometimes difficult to include within received theatre history. However, within modernist theatre, it starts to be systematised and recorded. As mentioned earlier, the rise of the director is also linked to his pedagogical role. Training actors is central to most projects and it invariably presupposes some concept of the body. This body, however, is always gendered and historically determined. From the Naturalism of Ibsen to the dance drama of Isadora Duncan, the new woman is making herself visible and in the process helping to forge a 'new' image of her body. And this modern female body may have been arrived at through the creative contribution of the work of actresses.

The comprehension of the 'woman question' and its representation on the stage required not only a new world-view but also a new aesthetic. If, as Engels claims, the oppression of women is constitutive of the bourgeois family, then the fascination in Naturalism is understandable. However, Engels does not provide us with an aesthetic to deliver such a materialist historical analysis. This among other reasons, is why, Naturalism (as Raymond Williams argues) tends to rely on individualism and the personal or familial in its attempt to comprehend the crisis it is charting. A more historical and critical reading of this crisis in the bourgeoisie necessitated a different aesthetic: one that is not implicated in the individualism it is trying to critique. Through notions of distance, abstraction, stylisation, shock and estrangement rather than empathy, the avant-garde attempts to forge such an aesthetic. However, it might be useful to point out that it is an aesthetic that many actresses of the period may have been experimenting with. The incongruity of their position may have forced them to step back, to strike the necessary Brechtian distance and watch the *gestus* of their representation.

It is fascinating to note that many of the prominent directors of the period started their theatrical lives as actors (Antoine, Lugné-Poë, Stanislavsky,

Meyerhold). Despite the plethora of well-known actresses during the same period, many of whom worked with the directors mentioned above, almost none – apart from Isadora Duncan (who mainly directed herself) – made the transition from performer to director. In many cases it was the attempt to address the challenges posed to the art of acting by the new drama by playwrights such as Ibsen, Strindberg and Chekhov that helped to forge the figure of the director himself. And it is a figure that has been marked by gender. To this day, the director is usually male. And when we talk of creative couplings it is usually between a male director and an actress. Within modernist theatre, this dynamic helped to create some of the most exciting experiments in the art of acting.

Naturalism and its Discontents

The reception of Naturalism has been filtered through the lens of later avant-garde and epic theatres, or through the materialist readings proposed by Raymond Williams amongst others. Either way, it is usually associated with late nineteenth-century positivism, theories of the environment and the rise of psychoanalysis where its worldview is concerned, while its aesthetic is seen as one of verisimilitude, relying on a slightly crisis-ridden humanism. Succinct as this analysis may be, it overlooks the radical potential of Naturalism: its contribution to social movements of the time and its fundamental reworking of theatrical convention. It is probably historically more accurate, although methodologically less satisfactory, to read the Naturalist movement in the theatre in conjunction with the more anti-illusionist aesthetics of the theatres of the same period. These interlock and overlap in all sorts of complicated ways, even when they are vehemently denouncing each other (perhaps particularly then) in the favoured mode of the time, the manifesto.

The lives and works of the Russian directors Konstantin Stanislavsky and Vsevolod Meyerhold could act as an apt example of the parallel/ mirroring lives of Naturalism and its antagonists. Stanislavsky, the high priest of the internal, the psychological, the view of the stage as an extension of the real, has more or less created the ways mainstream acting is understood today (in its corrupted 'method' version). Meyerhold, on the other extreme, sets the basis for what was to become Brecht's Epic Theatre, creating a language of theatricality that *comments* on the real. Robert Leach, however, has eloquently shown how these two men and their respective projects are inextricably attached. As was the case with Antoine and Lugné-Poë, it was their response to the demands created by a new type of play-text that triggered their experiments. Like their French counterparts, they too were actors. The new type of play they encountered was provided by Anton Chekhov. Robert Leach stresses this point:

> What Chekhov achieves, in fact, is a kind of dramatic equivalent to Bakhtin's notion of heteroglossia, which in literature refers to the interaction of varieties of speech types and voices. In drama, however, all the other elements of the theatre add to the medley of conflict, contradiction and doubt. The dramatic presentation then does not represent reality, but rather reworks and recreates it. In this sense it embodies the life of the human spirit. It is experience, not an interpretation of experience, which Chekhov provides. This is essentially not static, not conservative, but dynamic. It works in both the head and the heart.
>
> That is the challenge which Chekhov posed to the twentieth century theatre. It was what stimulated both Stanislavsky and Meyerhold to push forward the search for stage truth.[25]

Leach manages to undo the schematic opposition between the two men and to propose a reading of Chekhov that undermines many of the preconceived assumptions about Naturalism. The encounter with Chekhov's *The Seagull*, with Meyerhold as Konstantin Treplev, at once meshed their relationship for life and triggered the different paths they were to follow in 'search for stage truth'.

The word 'truth' is, of course, telling, as for both men their work was to introduce a new ethos into the theatre. In his opening address to the first Moscow Art Theatre company in 1898 Stanislavsky said:

> What we are undertaking is not simply a private affair but a social task. Never forget that we are striving to brighten the dark existence of the poor classes, to give them minutes of happiness and aesthetic uplift to relieve the murk, which envelops them. Our aim is to create the first intelligent, moral, open theatre, and to this end we are dedicating our lives.[26]

Although the perspective on 'the dark existence of the poor classes' is markedly different from that of Meyerhold – who instead of 'murk' finds there the potential for revolutionary change – the above quotation still indicates a desire to redefine the social function of theatre. The Moscow Art Theatre remained, more or less, faithful to its liberal roots, for instance refusing to stage Soviet plays – at least until eight years after the October Revolution. Meyerhold's project, on the other hand, was all about merging the aesthetic and the political on the stage. In contrast to Stanislavsky's political prowess (he had refused the Commissar for the Enlightenment's invitation to head the Commissariat's Theatre Department in 1918), Meyerhold was inspired by the upheavals caused by the revolution and the utopia it promised. In January 1918 he joined the Theatre Board and in August of the same year, after joining the Bolshevik party, he was made head of the Petrograd section, where he directed the 'first Soviet play', Mayakovsky's *Mystery Bouffe*. The first years of the October Revolution, before the Stalinist purges and the Great Terror of the late 1930s, provided the context for various utopian explorations of his into the possibility of a revolutionary theatre.

Meyerhold's theatre was to experiment openly with the possibility of radical theatrical forms, embodying the ideology of the Revolution. The experimental legacy that Meyerhold inherited from Russian Symbolism and Formalism was infused with a new invigorating energy from the October Revolution. Unlike Stanislavsky, whose concept of the individual was stubbornly personal and introverted, relying on psychology and a positivist view of the environment, Meyerhold was attempting to establish a concept of the individual as part of a historical, dialectical process. The world around him was in revolutionary turmoil and his theatre was to partake in that, not only thematically but also in terms of its modes of production. It was to comment on life, maintain a critical distance and amaze its audience, rather than to present itself as a direct extension of that life. In a characteristically avant-garde manner, Meyerhold theorises this engagement:

> The theatre is faced with a new task. The theatre must work on the spectator in order to awaken and strengthen in him a militancy strong enough to help him conquer the oblomovism, manilovism, hypocrisy, erotomania and pessimism within himself. How can we acquaint the manual labourers of socialism with the full magnitude of the revolution? ... How, indeed, if not through the theatre?[27]

This bridging of manual, aesthetic and intellectual labour was one of the goals of the historical avant-garde and Meyerhold's theatrical experiments make a vital contribution to it. No matter how naive or romantic his Marxism may have been, there is a clear attempt to see the act of making theatre as a democratic project, informed by the oral and popular traditions in performance and by modern technologies. But as was the case for Stanislavsky, this new function of the theatre was to be defined through the art of the actor:

> And once again the actor stands out as the main transmitter of the invigorating shock. But what must we do to make this shock effective, to help the actor transmit

it to the audience? Above all, we must strengthen those elements of the production which strike directly at the spectator's emotions.[28]

The shock, the amazement, the wonder, the distance and the final estrangement are to be achieved through the spectator's emotions. This needs to be highlighted as this tradition in acting is sometimes read, particularly in the reception of Brecht, as associated with emotional coldness and 'intellectual' activity alone. However, as Meyerhold succinctly puts it, 'the invigorating' shock addresses the audience in both a psychological and physical manner, both intellectually and emotionally; indeed, it is based on the premise that these entities are inseparable and not in binary opposition. His notion of the *dialectical actor*, who both inhabits and comments on the role she or he is playing, can be read as an extension of the same principle: one that constantly negotiates the relationships between emotion and intellect, inner and outer world, reality and theatrical representation. The actor becomes a lens through which the relationship of the individual to the historical process is examined, tested and contested. Brecht's notion of *gestus* finds a precedent in such theories of acting. Meyerhold writes of the 'actor-tribune':

> Nowadays, when the theatre is once more being employed as a platform for agitation, an acting system in which special stress is laid on preacting is indispensable to the actor-tribune. The actor-tribune needs to convey to the spectator his attitude to the lines he is speaking and the situations he is enacting; he wants to force the spectator to respond in a particular way to the action that is unfolding before him … The actor tribune acts not the situation itself, but what is concealed behind it … When the actor-tribune lifts the mask of the character to reveal his true nature he does not merely speak the lines furnished by the dramatist, he uncovers the roots from which the lines have sprung.[29]

It is important to underline the fact that this view of the actor-tribune does not dissolve into sheer propaganda. It draws its energies from the irreverent popular tradition, with a dose of Taylorism and a general fascination with technology, but in its new *biomechanical* guise maintains a critical distance from both. Whereas Stanislavsky's system was working in the opposite direction – from the inside towards the outside – attempting to create a stage that was a seamless continuation of reality, Meyerhold's approach was definitely external, one of constant framing, distance and critique.

This does not, however, imply that psychology played no part in his project. The last production that Meyerhold was to stage was Dumas fils' *The Lady of the Camellias* with Zinaida Raikh as Marguerite in 1934. This, according to most commentaries, was possibly his greatest achievement on the stage and presented the culmination of his work on acting. Once again highlighting the 'woman question' as central as much to Naturalism as to the avant-garde, this iconic text was given the full Meyerhold Treatment. Both Sarah Bernhardt and Eleonora Duse had played Marguerite, as had several *divas* in Verdi's operatic version, and their performances had had a somewhat mythological quality about them. In an iconic fusion of character, role and actress the figure of Marguerite had come to stand for the ambivalent position of women within the bourgeoisie, and so was able to comment on the equally ambivalent position of women on the stage.

Meyerhold was fascinated by the character in his own way. The use of the figure of the woman as a lens (or a *gestus*) through which to study the workings of capitalism was not unfamiliar to his epic tradition. For him, the encounter with the figure of Marguerite, her performance history and the specific contribution of the actress Zinaida Raikh led to a reconsideration of some of his more staunch formulations on the physicality of acting. This was a performance that made room for psychology as well, albeit a

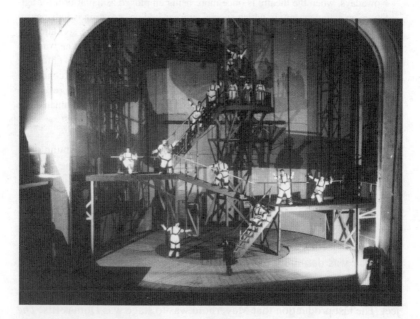

5   *The Bathhouse*, by Mayakovsky, directed by Meyerhold, 1930

6 *The Bedbug*, by Mayakovsky, designed by Aleksandr Rodchenko, directed by Meyerhold, 1930

psychology that is rooted in physicality and historicity. Robert Leach comments:

> Meyerhold created a theatre in which the actors were no longer simply the most dynamic elements in an intellectually-conceived polyphony. When he accepted that Chekhov's characters, Marguerite in *The Lady of the Camellias*, and others, were not only inherently theatrical, but also had – or seemed to have – an individual 'inner life', that they were psychologically 'true', he added a new dimension […]

> Stanislavskian techniques became not only permissible but mandatory, for the psychological dimension which gave Meyerhold's images of life a new depth and resonance … In this way, the psychological detail grew out of the theatricality, not the other way round. Movement created psychology in the final Meyerholdian psychological acting method.[30]

It is fascinating to note that such a formal 'reconciliation' was achieved through the specific representation of an iconic female theatrical role. Although Meyerhold had previously tried to stage Tretyakov's *I want a Baby*,[31] a radical piece about the politics of reproduction, his attempts were blocked. With *Camellias* he combines a similar approach to sexual politics while also addressing formal questions of representation and actor-training. Leach continues:

> Perhaps Zinaida Raikh's feisty, beautiful, ironic, unconventional and sexy per-
> formances, which jolted Soviet complacency sharply, were among Meyerhold's
> greatest achievements as a director-cum-actor trainer. Certainly it was Zinaida
> Raikh's work in these productions which lifted them to unexpected heights and
> which was resentfully rejected – as was her feminism – by many Soviet critics.[32]

Raikh emerges as having had an important part in the formation of the aesthetics and the training method that aspired to combine the 'psychologism'
of Stanislavsky with the 'formalism' of Meyerhold.

Although close to Meyerhold in many ways, Craig could not be further
in terms of sexual politics, or indeed in politics of any sort. It was with
Craig though that another 'hybrid' experiment had already taken place
that both pushed the limits of Stanislavsky's Naturalism but also, and crucially, tested the possibility of its co-existence with other more anti-
illusionist and more abstract schools pf performance. As early as 1908
Craig starts discussing the staging of *Hamlet* with the Moscow Art
Theatre. The role of Isadora Duncan is crucial in this context. During her
first tour of Russia her enthusiasm for Craig managed to convince
Stanislavsky to extend an invitation to the charismatic Englishman. Craig
accepted and started a series of visits to Moscow between 1908 and 1912,
by which time his production of *Hamlet* had been staged at the Moscow
Art Theatre. This is a notorious production that has gone down in theatre
history primarily as a 'failure', with Craig's famous screens collapsing on
the opening night.[33] Sometimes, however, such 'failures' prove more
interesting in their original aspirations and the experimental processes
involved than they do in the final result. And this was a bold experiment,
bringing together two traditions (although at this early stage they could
hardly be termed that) that could not be further apart. How was Craig
going to work with Stanislavsky when he affected to despise real actors?
Who was going to direct? Were design and directing to be kept separate?
Surely both men could foresee the potential for disaster. Or possibly that
was part of the attraction of such a collaboration, since it is important to
stress that both these approaches, almost at the start of their respective
projects, encountered each other not as opposites but as parallel and in
places overlapping endeavours.

Craig's ideas were not new to the Russian theatre when he first went
there in 1908. However, it was not Stanislavsky but the Russian

7 Zinaida Reikh as Vera in *The Second Commander* by I. L. Selvinsky, directed by V. E. Meyerhold, 24 July 1929, Kharkov

Futurists and Symbolists that had already been influenced by Craig. *Theatr: A Book about the New Theatre* was published in St Petersburg the same year that Craig arrived in Moscow. In it designer Aleksandr Benois, poets Bryusov and Bely and theorists like Lunacharsky and Meyerhold himself outlined a vision for a theatre of the future that seemed very Craigian indeed. Highly stylised and abstract, relying on puppets rather than living actors, the vision presented could have been of Craig's own devising. And in a sense it was since the Englishman's influence was profound in this circle. Craig's 'First Dialogue on the Art of the Theatre' had been pirated and published in Russia in 1906. Meyerhold wrote of Craig in 1909:

> It is remarkable that in the very first year of this new century E. G. Craig flung a challenge to the naturalistic theatre ... therefore, this young Englishman is the first to set up initial guideposts on the new road of the Theatre.[34]

It was, however, with the 'high priest' of Naturalism himself that Craig had come to work and not with Meyerhold.

Unlike Meyerhold, Stanislavsky was not well up in Craig's work and knew of it only through reputation (Duncan's accounts of it not least). It is also possible that Stanislavky was so taken with Duncan's performance as to identify it mistakenly with Craig's overall approach. Either way he was having problems with his 'system' and, in an attempt to expand the aesthetic horizons of his company, he invited Craig to Moscow. The encounter between these two seemingly opposed approaches to the 'new theatre' has been extensively documented by Craig in his journal *The Mask*. Despite their enormous differences, *Hamlet* was finally staged and Craig maintained his respect for Stanislavsky and the Russian tradition in theatre throughout his life. He writes in his review of Stanislavsky's *My Life in Art* in 1924:

> It has been proved by you, more than by anyone else at any time, that the artist may only (can only) work in a material, which is 'dead' material (I search for better word in vain) if he will create a work of art ... Your book must live because of the sincerity, which breathes out of every page of it. You have raised the entire profession of Theatrical workers to a position it cannot recede from. You have at last made it impossible to retreat. We salute you with affection and with reverence.[35]

In typically Craigian fashion Stanislavsky's insistence on the art of acting as an extension of the laws of nature, as an organic entity, is rewritten as 'dead material'. This could be read as a backhanded compliment, another opportunity to emphasise Craig's inorganic actors (marionettes or quasi-marionettes). In another sense, however, Craig is also tapping into Stanislavsky's concerns with the body of the actor, its physicality and its overall 'material' qualities, both internal/psychological and external/physical. Just as Stanislavsky's long-term working relationship with Meyerhold threw up problems in both their approaches, from which both men benefited creatively (as Robert Leach has shown), so his encounter with Craig in the production of the Moscow *Hamlet* probably served its purpose of addressing at least some of his concerns about psychological approaches to acting and the aesthetic of Naturalism more generally. The famous disaster that was the Moscow *Hamlet*, in this sense, is seen as a modernist experiment in performance that bridges two seemingly opposing aesthetics. Both the strict, anti-humanist abstraction of Craig and the slightly reductive aspects of Stanislavsky's psychological expressivism are reworked in the process.

The period's experiments themselves need not be read in opposition, for, despite the manifesto quality of much of the writing by the modernist directors, their actual projects display attachments that might seem incongruous. Brecht, in whom much of this experiment culminates and despite his passionate attacks on Naturalism and on Wagner, owes a debt to both traditions. His quest for a 'new realism' could be read as inflecting Naturalism's commitment to the 'real' *and* rewriting Wagner's totalising renditions of

Photograph of a model stage setting for a scene in Hamlet. 1912

8 Edward Gordon Craig, *Photograph of a model stage setting for a scene in Hamlet*, 1912

epic. Both the Naturalist and the anti-illusionist tradition form part of the 'new movement' in the theatre. Sometimes for the sake of methodological clarity, and in conjunction with the manifesto fervour of their theoretical works, these schools are defined against each other. They all converge, however, in the figure of the modernist director.

4

'... as if the words themselves could sing and shine': Poetic Drama and Theatricality

> Ibsen has sincerity and logic beyond any writer of our time, and we are all seeking to learn them at his hands; but is he not a good deal less than the greatest of all times, because he lacks beautiful and vivid language? 'Well, well, give me time and you shall hear all about it. If only I had Peter here now' is very like life, is entirely in its place where it comes, and ... one is moved ... and yet not moved as if the words themselves could sing and shine.
>
> (W. B. Yeats, *Plays and Controversies*, 1923)

Yeats's response to Ibsen's *A Doll's House*, while polite and measured, manages to delineate the main concerns of the primarily Anglophone phenomenon of poetic drama. The term, usually coined in opposition to the more daring theatricality of the avant-garde, has come to describe the dramatic works of writers we otherwise associate with literary experimentation. The dramatic works of W. B. Yeats and T. S. Eliot form the main corpus of this 'trend', accompanied by the dramatic works of W. H. Auden and Christopher Isherwood. This categorisation tends to posit European Symbolism (as seen in the works of Maurice Maeterlinck and Stéphane Mallarmé) as its predecessors and sees as its successors the theatres of Harold Pinter and Samuel Beckett. It is a tradition that focuses on the tension between the written word and the stage, highlighting, as Yeats's quotation shows, the power of the written word.

However, as the quotation also indicates, it is a legacy that exhibits a fraught and contradictory relationship with the workings of the stage. Even as he is exerting the power of the words to 'sing and shine', Yeats himself resorts to a type of theatricality in assuming the guise of an 'Ibsen character'. This act, more one of ventriloquism than acting, underlines the passionate attachment that many of these writers feel towards the stage; an attachment, however, that is at once informed and undermined by the workings of anti-theatricality. And this love-hate relationship with the stage that many of these writers-cum-dramatists exhibit helps to create its own language of performance. More often than not, this language is one of un-performability, as many of these plays present difficulties in their shift from the page to the stage. Indeed, these 'difficulties' appear almost deliberate, endemic to poetic drama itself.

The sometimes fraught relationship between the poetic word and the stage is also a prime concern of many Continental experiments of the period, prompting Jean Cocteau to differentiate between 'poetry in the theatre' and 'poetry of the theatre' in his famous preface to his own poetic drama, *Les mariés de la Tour Eiffel* (1922). Indeed, as this analysis hopes to highlight, this poetic imperative of modernist drama allows us to read the Anglophone experiments in conjunction with those of the historical avant-garde, and not in opposition to them. The difficulty of transmitting poetry onto the stage creates its own language of theatricality, one that is usually accompanied by its own body of theory in the form of essays, debates and manifestos. Rather than feed into a Platonic anti-theatrical tradition, one that opposes the workings of 'poetry/philosophy' to those of the stage, these experiments gesture towards a new, modernist relationship between the 'word' – with all is philosophical efficacy – the body of the actor, and the theatrical event in general. In doing so, and under the rubric of the mani-festo, some of its proponents – mainly the literary, Anglophone 'high mod-ernist' poets – make vivid proclamations against the stage. These, however, usually result from a passionate attachment to theatrical form. Whether with the Japanese dancer Ito or with Craig, or with the actors at the Abbey Theatre, Yeats, for example, was involved in some form or another with the practicalities of making theatre throughout his life.

Rather than read the Anglophone tradition in poetic drama as opposed to the theatrical experimentation on the Continent, this study underlines the parallels and intersections between the two. The work of Eliot and Yeats is read in conjunction with the work of Gertrude Stein, Auden and Isherwood and Brecht, opening up the whole category of 'poetry' in the theatre. In turn, the emphasis on the poetic word creates its own demands on theories of acting. Once again, the actor is a key figure in all these discussions. The possibilities offered by the newly emerging movement of what was to be known as 'modern dance' are enthusiastically explored by many of the proponents of poetic drama. Diaghilev's Ballets Russes, with its twenty-year-long run on the Parisian stage (1909–29), and its phenomenal international success, was very influential not only on theories of dance, but on acting too. Cocteau was a regular at the Ballets Russes and his own work is marked by this encounter. Eliot, too, is not unaffected by the possibilities presented for poetic drama by modern dance. Although the personal relationship between Craig and Isadora Duncan has been documented and explored, there is very little on the potential influence of her experiments in dance drama on Craig's theories of acting. This creative interaction between dance and theatrical experiment (the two in many ways intertwined) is approached as yet another way of addressing the use of poetry on the stage.

This use of poetry is further complicated in this instance by the fact that the *poetic* is usually underpinned by an equally strong *philosophical* imperative, where the poetic comes to stand in for the philosophical. Whether it is Eliot's Christianity, Yeats's mysticism, Stein's phenomenology or Brecht's Marxism, most poetic dramas are philosophically framed. And in each case this philosophy does not appear simply as a theme, enacted through character and action, but comes to inform the conventions, the modes of dramatic presentation itself. This quest for a *philosophical* theatre ignites much of the contradiction, tension and difficulty when it comes to actual performance. This modernist enactment of the difficult relationship between theatre and philosophy creates its own forms of theatricality. For Puchner, however, it is a continuation of the anti-theatrical tradition. He writes:

> Modernist drama and theatre is a Platonic theatre, by which I mean not a theatre of abstract ideas but a theatre infused with types of anti-theatricality first developed in Plato's closet dramas.[1]

It is a Platonic theatre in *both* the above senses and in many ways the 'new theatricality' (rather than anti-theatricality) results from such a desire to reconcile philosophy and theatre. As the very genesis of theatre relies on such a Platonic distinction, the desire to philosophise theatre necessarily sets in motion all the basic tenets of anti-theatricalism. Poetic drama rehearses all the debates about the fraught relationships between philosophy and the stage. Indeed, usually, these debates are present both formally and thematically. The tensions between the written word and the body of the actor, between the acts of reading and seeing, between individual and collective response are all experimented with in an attempt to present a 'theatre of abstract ideas', a philosophical theatre. Eliot's attempt at creating a modernist liturgical drama in *Murder in the Cathedral* (1934),

Yeats's quest for a ritualistic theatre that blends the Noh forms with an oral Irish tradition, Brecht's search for an aesthetic equivalent of dialectic materialism all go against a basic premise of Aristotelian theatre (and Platonic anti-theatricalism): the separability of theatre (as performance) and philosophy. In this sense the most poetic of modernist drama also transpires as the most philosophical. To separate the two, as some studies particularly of Brecht tend to do, would be to misread one of their fundamental drives. In turn, and inevitably, this legacy engages with the long anti-theatrical tradition initiated by Plato.

It is fascinating to note in relation to this philosophical imperative that poetic drama very deliberately rewrites another moment of separation between theatre and philosophy. Indeed, the violent banishment of theatre from the public sphere by Christianity in the fourth century CE is an event that much modernist theatre directly or indirectly visits. If we take as our reference points Eliot's fascination with mediaeval liturgical drama at one end, and Gertrude Stein's radical reworking of Christian myth in plays like *Dr Faustus Lights the Lights* (1938) and *Four Saints in Three Acts* (1927) at the other, what transpires is an obsession with Christian myth, iconography and ritual. Whether in Brecht's appropriation of Christian parable (*The Caucasian Chalk Circle*, 1944) or in Yeats's late play *Purgatory* (1939), the presence of Christianity appears not only as a critique or means to the redemption of modernity but as a Platonic *topos*: as the stage where the final separation between theatre and philosophy took place. Other than in the work of Eliot, where there is a search for a genuine Christian drama, most modernist drama engages with Christianity as if it were a new form of Platonism, at least in its attitude towards the theatre. As such it needs to be retheatricalised. In another sense, what these rereadings of Christian 'drama' show – as is the case in the works of Plato – is the absolute fascination that Christian philosophy and ritual display towards the very theatricality that it banished. Like many of the modernist dramatists themselves, Christianity exhibits a similar fraught relationship with things theatrical.

One of the main sites on which this difficult relationship is enacted is the actor's body. As is the case with Christianity, poetic drama stumbles across the *presence* of the actor's body in its attempt to mediate the power of the word, in this case the *poetic logos*. With expressive psychologism at one extreme and stylised abstraction at the other, the body of the actor becomes the lens through which modernist theatre experiments with the limits of mimetic representation. Puchner sees the actor as the 'scapegoat of modernist theatre'[2] and sees poetic drama's reactions towards it as primarily hostile, true to the Platonic legacy of *somatophobia*. Inflecting that position, this analysis stresses the varied and contradictory reactions to the actor. Rather than expressing an unmodified, anti-theatrical hostility towards the actor, the playwrights of poetic drama engage with these debates not univocally but with a multiplicity of positions. In fact, these attitudes may also help us to differentiate between the various projects and not to read 'poetic drama' as a specific Anglophone tradition that is framed by a supposed distrust of theatre, coupled with a similar fear of its democratising potential. At the same time, 'poetic drama' itself need not be read in opposition to the European avant-garde but as parallel to it, overlapping in places and dealing with similar theoretical entanglements.

In their quest to make the words 'sing and shine', Eliot and Yeats see the body of the actor as primarily a vehicle, there to mediate the power of their verse. On the other extreme of this spectrum Meyerhold, working with the poetic dramas of Mayakovsky, formulates his biomechanics in an attempt to create material presence for the actor on the stage beyond mimetic representation. Similarly, Gertrude Stein's versions of 'dramatic character' are heavily inflected by cubist notions of space and linguistic experimentation. These are not all simply uniform, stock anti-theatrical reactions to the representational efficacy of the human form. For example, here is how Martin Browne, Eliot's faithful director, assesses Eliot's attitude towards the actor's art:

> Lack of contact with the theatre has imposed an ignorance more fundamental: he has no experience of the actor's art except from 'the front', and no means of discovering what are the true reasons for the success or failure of a line or a situation … So when he labours to create his own play, he has to judge his work, not by the actor's effort to bring it to life in rehearsal, but by his own ear as he hears it in his head, and his own eye scanning the page.[3]

In this sense, it would then be the actor's job to try to approximate the sound of poetry as the playwright 'hears it in his head'. Interestingly enough, the action that the actors are invited to simulate is that of reading. The eye, usually the locus of the stage, is confined to 'scanning the page'. In the above quotation, Browne touches upon another vital tension within poetic drama: that between the act of seeing a play and the act of reading. Much of modernist drama aims to reintroduce the act of reading onto the stage. Brecht covers the stage with text, textuality itself becomes thematically present in much of his work. In the Dadaist and Futurist theatres words become characters on the stage. Gertrude Stein's plays also rely on this tension between seeing and reading. She writes in 'Plays':

> Is the thing seen or the thing heard the thing that makes most impression upon you at the theatre. How much has the hearing to do with it and how little. Does the thing heard replace the thing seen. Does it help or does it interfere with it.[4]

And talking of her theatrical education she says:

> So then for me there was the reading of plays which was one thing and then there was the seeing of plays and of operas a great many of them which was another thing.[5]

As this analysis hopes to show, taking dramatists at opposed ends of the poetic drama spectrum, the ways this issue is approached are radically different in the works of Eliot and Stein. Whereas Eliot's plays reconcile the differences between seeing and hearing within the figure of the playwright, as Browne's quotation insists, Gertrude Stein's experiments in plays and operas do something altogether different. The actions of seeing and hearing, the eye and the ear are 'torn apart' and put together again in cubist manner, this time on the surface of the stage. The workings of the stage are reconciled with the workings of the text in a new form, 'the landscape play'. She writes of *Four Saints in Three Acts*:

> In Four Saints I made the saints the landscape. All the saints that I made and I made a number of them because after all a great many pieces of things are in a landscape all these saints together made my landscape. These attendant saints were the landscape and it the play really is a landscape.[6]

This blending of geography and textuality proposed by Stein owes much to cubist notions of space and, like Eliot's experience of theatre, it does tend to view actors from 'the front', flattening psychology and relying more on the idea of the 'still life' than on the inner workings of character. However, unlike Eliot, who returns his albeit slight stylisation to the 'head' of the author for ultimate resolution, the plays of Stein never actually resolve this difficulty but make it a constitutive part of the *landscape*. In this sense, the theatre of Eliot partakes in the discourses of anti-theatricality, elevating the ear over the eye, while Stein's theatre could be read as trying to retheatricalise the stage, partly engaging in the same anti-theatricality, and in a cubist vein, often substituting the eye for the ear. *Four Saints* was written as an operatic collaboration with Virgil Thomson. The presence of the music, and its contribution to the making of the piece, no doubt added to this heightened position accorded to the ear.

Of course, human actors are not the only obstacles for poetic drama. In some cases the stage design and the still conflated roles of the director/designer come under attack as well. As much of the poetic drama is concerned with re-establishing the role of the playwright, the emerging figure of the modernist director and all he represents are also seen as targets in the struggle to clear the stage for the presence of the 'word'. This is particularly interesting in the case of Yeats. Although his early dramatic works are greatly influenced by Craig, whose screens he used in the 1910 production of *The Hour Glass* (1904), still he feels the need to attack the autonomy of the physical presence of the stage. On the occasion of the opening of the Abbey Theatre in December 1904, he writes in *Samhain*:

> I have been the advocate of the poetry as against the actor, but I am the advocate of the actor as against the scenery ... the actor and the words put into his mouth are always the one thing that matters, and the scene should never be complete of itself, should never mean anything to the imagination until the actor is in front of it.[7]

So for Yeats there is a clear hierarchy of signification on the stage, with the scenery at the bottom and the words at the top, the actor hovering somewhere in between, not quite sure what position to occupy. This ambivalence about the actor is resolved later in his playwrighting life, as he gets more involved with the Abbey Theatre, becoming notoriously hostile. What Yeats called his 'big scheme of poetic drama' was a specific project meant to promote the dominance of the word on stage. Despite all his interest in staging conventions through his encounters with Craig or the Noh theatre, his main drive was to rescue the stage for the word and the poet-cum-playwright. In fact, Yeats very systematically applies formal stage conventions, and quite elaborate ones at that, to the service of the poetry on stage.[8] For him poetic drama only partially takes part in the scenic experiments identified with the European avant-garde and in a sense he also proposes it as a corrective to the theatrical excesses of the Continent.

In 1913, while Yeats was staying with Ezra Pound in Sussex and was familiarising himself with the Noh, he considered joining Craig's School for the Art of the Theatre in Florence. Craig discouraged him from doing so ('You could learn nothing there. What you've learnt you've learnt already').[9] Still, Yeats was intent on promoting his ideas on poetic drama and was planning a volume of theatre criticism with drawings by Craig and Robert Gregory. He wrote to his publisher:

Coming at this moment when people have in their memories the Reinhardt productions, the scenery and costumes of the Russian ballet, the Barker productions of Shakespeare – all examples of the new decorative method – it would probably get considerable attention. It would contain the only serious criticism of the new craft of the Theatre. It is the exact moment for it.[10]

It is also the moment that Yeats starts to put his own ideas into practice, having encountered Ito and the Noh (as we'll see in the next chapter). However, the insistence on the poetic dimension of the stage rather than the theatrical adds a manifesto quality to much of his writing. This is also mirrored in Eliot's writings on the theatre, which seek to continue the long literary tradition in Anglophone poetic drama. Many of his essays are concerned with Elizabethan and Renaissance drama. His writing also refers to Yeats's work, the late essay *Poetry and Drama* (1950) proposing Yeats's *Purgatory* as the play that solved the problem of the use of verse.[11] Although the writing on poetic drama presents itself as a 'serious criticism of the new craft of the theatre', it does so in tones that are more akin to the philological essay than to the polemical manifesto. Still, quite consciously Yeats presents his excursions into poetic drama as a theoretical and practical alternative to the new 'craft'. His clumsy turn of phrase ('the words put into his mouth') only highlights the condescension he feels towards anything other than the poetic word on stage.

The poetic word on the stage, however, is not a simple matter; immediately the problem of whether to use verse or prose is posed. The body of the actor and the impact of the written word transpire as the main concerns of poetic drama. The debates about the uses of verse and prose are passionate and equally engaging. More often than not they spill out into debates about reception. The impact of verse is sometimes seen as an estranging device, one that some writers find attractive, others problematic. The use of verse, or heightened poetic language, is used both to differentiate poetic drama from naturalism *and*, in some cases, to usher in a new type of realism, as is the case with Brecht's Epic Theatre. What many of these debates centre on is the seeming incompatibility between verse, poetry and any type of realism. Furthermore, there is a clear attempt to prove that poetry is able to have at least as much impact on an audience as general 'stage crafts'. Eliot concedes that in his earliest full-length play, *Murder in the Cathedral*, he was in a privileged position, as the play was commissioned and performed at Canterbury Cathedral on 15 June 1935 for an eager and willing audience of practising High-Anglican Christians. He writes:

When I wrote Murder in the Cathedral I had the advantage for a beginner of an occasion which called for a subject generally admitted to be suitable for verse.

Verse plays, it has been generally held, should either take their subject matter from some mythology, or else should be about some remote historical period ... Furthermore, my play was to be produced for a rather special kind of audience – an audience of those serious people who go to 'festivals' and expect to have to put up with poetry ... And finally it was a religious play, and people who go deliberately to a religious play at a religious festival expect to be patiently bored and to satisfy themselves with the feeling that they have done something meritorious.[12]

In many ways this was the perfect audience for Eliot's play. However, as he concedes himself, it was almost too perfect, as the use of verse in this particular play did not throw up any solutions applicable to other types of plays, as Eliot himself discovered when he agonised over the use of verse in the later 'society' dramas, *The Family Reunion* (1939) and *The Cocktail Party* (1949). Instead of 'preaching to the converted', in these plays he had to make another case for the use of verse and this is the one, more or less, followed by Yeats as well: that the verse should permeate every aspect of language on stage. It should be incorporated to such a degree as to appear unforced and totally appropriate to the scenic situation. He writes:

I believe that prose should be used very sparingly indeed; that we should aim at a form of verse in which everything can be said that has to be said; and that when we find some situation which is intractable in verse, it is merely that our form of verse is inelastic ... For we have to accustom our audiences to verse to the point at which they will cease to be conscious of it.[13]

In other words the problems posed are not those that pertain to the shift from the text to the stage but primarily those that relate to the transmission of the poetry, that is, recitation not performance. The poetry itself needs to be 'elastic' enough to contain all human emotions, as Eliot claims. In this sense, he believes that if the audience response is not the desired one, then it is the fault of the poetry, or its transmission through the words 'put into the actors' mouths', as Yeats elaborates. Either way, the problem is seen as a textual one, not one of staging. He goes on to chart out the development of Yeats's work in the theatre as a fine example of the evolutionary process he has schematically outlined. Initially he claims Yeats wrote plays in verse 'about subjects conventionally accepted as suitable for verse', that is, myth or history. His *Plays for Dancers* are seen as 'very beautiful, but they do not solve any problem for the dramatist in verse: they are poetic prose plays with important interludes in verse'. His last play, *Purgatory*, is presented as the best solution to his posed problem.

More specifically, what Eliot finds unacceptable is the mingling of prose and verse because, as he claims, 'each transition makes the auditor aware, with a jolt, of the medium' (note the use of the tem 'auditor' and not 'spectator'). But it is precisely this jolt that the plays of Brecht and Stein, W. H. Auden and Isherwood aim to create. (And in this specific instance Eliot is reading against something he had been much influenced by: W. H. Auden and Christopher Isherwood's *The Dog Beneath the Skin*, which combines jaunty prose and superb high-style choruses.) It is the jolt that makes the audience look again, through the lens of distance; although, as Eliot's quotation makes clear, the audience doesn't necessarily 'look' but mainly 'hears'. And again we find ourselves in the fraught territory of the visual versus the auditory response. As we have noted, some playwrights will go with one and some with the other, or as Yeats does, apply different approaches for different plays. Interestingly enough, the playwrights whose concerns are more aligned with the European avant-garde tend to mix modes up within the same play. For Brecht the poetry and the prose exist within the same play but are usually kept separate, usually the prose conveying action and relationships between roles, while the verse provides a comment, with the necessary jolting effect on the audience. In some cases the verse is part of a song, accompanied by music. The use of verse in the plays of Gertrude Stein is even more experimental. Here, the verse itself seems to be part of the overall theme. The physicality of the verse becomes part of the *landscape*, in a gesture that again combines, mixes and substitutes seeing and hearing. Here is an example of the use of verse from *Dr Faustus Lights the Lights* (1938):

> Faustus
> Yes they shine
> They shine all the time.
> I know they shine
> I see them shine
> And I am here
> I have no fear
> But what shall I do
> …
> It is all to me
> Ah I do not like that word me,
>
> Why not even if it does rhyme with she. I know all the words that rhyme with bright with light with might with alright, I know them so that I cannot tell I can spell but I cannot tell how much I need not have that, not light not sight, not light

not night not alright, not night not sight not bright, no no not night not sight not bright no no not bright.[14]

Indeed, Yeats could not have asked for a better example of words that 'shine'. This use of verse, brash and bold as it is, is not simply interested in the divisions between verse and prose and their reception by the audience. In a play about light, sin, redemption and the Enlightenment, this use of verse, blending the themes with the formal experimentation, explodes the category of 'verse' altogether, having first exhausted all its possible uses. Through the repetition and the multiple negation towards the end, the whole category of sight in the theatre is analysed and de-composed. The audience in this instance are not only auditors; they are also 'seers'. And it is this faculty of sight – one so central to the project of the Enlightenment that Faustus embodies – that is read into the verse itself, making it materialise on the stage, not only for the benefit of the audience's ears but also, and crucially, for their eyes. This is verse going against the auditory imagination. Just as the whole play itself presents a radical reading of the most classical of genres – tragedy – the verse employed goes against the most classical of formats: the identification of verse with the voice and, in turn, with auditory reception.

Poetic drama has been primarily identified with the concerns, aspirations, experiments and politics of the predominantly Anglophone tradition of so-called 'high Modernism'; and indeed it is often used as the benchmark that separates the radical experimentations on the Continent from the more conservative anti-theatrical tradition of canonical literary Modernism. However, *most* of the experiments taking place on the stage within Modernism had to encounter the problem of 'poetry on the stage', regardless of political, religious or aesthetic affiliation. The category of the poetic should not be solely applied to playwrights who are also poets. Also, it is not the sole preserve of the more conservative traditions in politics. Usually the preponderance of the poetic word on stage has been read in conjunction with an anti-theatrical tradition, on the one hand, and an anti-democratic one, on the other. However, just as poetry is not the sole preserve of the conservative modernist legacy, the workings of the stage cannot inherently imply a more democratic approach either. The European avant-garde clearly shows that whether in the dramas of the Italian Futurists or the Russian Constructivists (or in the fascist spectacles), the privileging of the stage does not automatically imply a more democratic approach.

The working of poetry on the stage is, however, a fundamental concern of most modernist drama. The anxieties about the conceptual and communicative efficacy of poetry in the theatre inflect most modernist theatre from Yeats to Brecht. This is a trajectory that ideally would also cover many projects in between, like the plays of Mayakovsky, the Italian Futurists and the Dadaists. The highlighting of poetry immediately throws all the stage properties into crisis: the actor, the design, the relationships with the audience and the playwright. These are categories that are quite consciously experimented with. Ironically, in most cases the solutions to the problem of the word on the stage, far from being anti-theatrical, usher in a new type of theatricality. Interestingly enough, and against the reading that sees poetic drama as inherently unstageable, poetic drama emerges as very theatrical, indeed meta-theatrical. Coupled with the theoretical propensity of most of its practitioners, it appears as the most philosophical as well. The following section will be concerned with looking at specific cases – Yeats, Eliot and Gertrude Stein; Brecht, Auden and Isherwood – of poetic drama that try to reconcile this philosophical imperative, defined by their broader concerns and outlooks with the theatrical one dictated by the requirements of the stage. The embodiment of the poetic word on the stage, in turn, finds dynamic models in much of the dance experimentation of the period.

W. B. Yeats: Poety, Philosophy and Nationality

> I had three interests: interest in a form of literature, in a form of philosophy, and belief in nationality. None of these seemed to have anything to do with the other.[15]

We could say, contrary to Yeats's own claim, that all three did come together for him on the stage. The various phases of Yeats's development as a playwright may signify a preponderance of one category over the other, but most of his work in the theatre is driven by the desire to forge an aesthetic that would combine all his interests. The early plays like *The Countess Cathleen* (1882), *Cathleen Ni Houlihan* (1902) and *Deirdre* (1907) exhibit a strong engagement with Irish popular tradition and its oral performative aspects, placing Yeats within the legacy of the Celtic Twilight and its romantic undertones. At this early stage Yeats, still writing in blank verse, has two significant encounters: one with Lady Gregory, a folklorist herself and a stern supporter of Irish nationalism; the other with the Abbey Theatre in Dublin. Unlike most of his Anglophone contemporaries but like his Continental peers, throughout his involvement with the stage, Yeats worked with a changing but challenging group of actors at the Abbey Theatre, all also committed in some measure to the cause of Irish nationalism.

These encounters do not always prove to be harmonious, as the premiere of *The Countess Cathleen* showed. The play was premiered at the opening of the Irish Literary Theatre (May 1899) and was greeted with a mixed reception. The Countess Cathleen's offer of self-sacrifice in order to stop the peasants selling their souls to two demons for food during a famine was met with religious outrage. The play was even attacked as anti-patriotic on the grounds that Irish peasants would never sell their souls in the first place. What Yeats saw as an oral tradition – one he could formally experiment with – was considered by the religious segments of the audience and critics as sacrilegious. Yeats himself conceded: 'In using what I considered traditional symbols I forgot that in Ireland they are not symbols but realities.'[16] And this is an attitude towards the 'popular' and oral traditions that marks much of the avant-garde as well, as usually the encounter with orality, be it in Yeats or Meyerhold, involves an element of elevation and heightening. Seen either as inherently metaphysical or revolutionary, the oral and popular traditions, for all the attention they receive, sit uncomfortably within the broader philosophical and political claims of the respective projects. In many ways, the attitude displayed towards the 'popular' is parallel to that towards the 'Oriental theatres', and it is equally fraught and contradictory.

The production of this early play also sets the agenda for Yeats's experiments in stagecraft. The play used static tableau-formations, non-realistic sets, chanted dialogue and creative lighting to portray the set but also the mood. Yeats later called the play 'a tapestry'. It also introduces, through the character of Aleel, the familiar narrator/bard/commentator/musician figure, who appears in most subsequent plays. In these plays these figures are there primarily for the benefit of the poetry. They also help to mediate the general philosophical position of the pieces in a classic epic manner. However, although they perform all these meta-theatrical functions, they also point to a more general difficulty that the early drama poses. These early plays also exhibit an awkwardness regarding the art of the acting, as this has been subsumed under the notion of recitation. One reviewer writes:

> Chanting is hard to follow until the ear grows accustomed to listening to measured rhythm. Many of the artists failed to allow those in front to clearly understand what they spoke. This should not be, of course, as the first essential of effective stage work is the clearness of articulation in the speech of the actors.[17]

Indeed it is that 'clearness of articulation' that Yeats was striving for. It is a clearness that, while exhibiting its faithfulness towards the playwright's poetry, nevertheless neglects the main vehicle of performance, the actor's body. The physical presence of actors on stage, even in these early plays, is treated with ambivalence. Later, not being able to resolve this difficulty, Yeats proposed more extreme measures when he asked for the actors to rehearse in barrels so their bodies would not interfere with the articulation of the poet's words. The physicality of the voice is ignored altogether or, in a Platonic twist, it is subsumed under the all-powerful sound of the word. Sound itself, divorced from any materiality, is seen as simply transmitting the unmediated words of the playwright. Yeats writes:

> The barrels, I thought, might be on castors, so that I could shove them about with a pole when the action required it.[18]

This is the same Yeats, however, who is fascinated with dance and later in his life writes *Plays for Dancers*. The aphoristic and paradoxical nature of the above quotation echoes Craig's pronouncements on actors according to which the greatest obstacle to non-realistic portrayal on stage was the body of the actor. As long as the word was seen as the most significant element on the stage, the actor's body would be viewed solely in terms of how well it could transmit that word. The image presented above is that of a marionette and marionette-master. We begin to understand Yeats's attraction to the work of Craig in all its contradictory splendour.

Yeats's more theatrical period is defined by his encounters with both the work of Edward Gordon Craig and the Japanese Noh. Indeed, the negative reception of *The Countess Cathleen* urged Yeats to get further involved with 'stagecraft'. Interestingly enough this quest leads to Craig, the most anti-theatrical of all his contemporaries, especially when it came to the art of the actor. He had hoped to raise enough money to fund a Craigian staging of *The Countess*, as he believed that Craig could help materialise his ambitions. Instead Yeats applied many of Craig's ideas in 1911 in the Abbey Theatre's production/revival of his play *The Hour Glass*. Yeats saw in Craig's experiments ways of conceptualising scenic space and presenting a non-illusionist view of the stage. Craig's famous screens were set up on the stage of the Abbey Theatre for the first time in November 1910. The result was heralded in *The Irish Times* as 'a great improvement on the old staging of *The Hour Glass*', and Yeats found in Craig's screens what he believed at the time to be the scenic counterpart of his poetic language. However, this theatre was to remain the domain of a single genius, as the poetic drama requires. Yeats had already expressed concerns about the design 'taking over' from the main thrust of the words. This production of *The Hour Glass* was as much a success for Craig as designer as it was for Yeats as playwright. The reviewer in *The Irish Times* appropriately congratulates Craig:

> The success of these aims is the result of the genius of an individual producer, who combines with artistic and thoughtful ideas on the principles of staging, an

unusual ability to deal with the mechanical problems involved in giving effect to those principles.[19]

This is not merely Yeats and Craig squabbling over whose name will appear first in the programme notes, but more a matter of epistemology (although Craig could never really work collaboratively with anyone). The end result, the performance, was still to be regarded as the product of a single aesthetic will. Yeats saw stage design, no matter how important and radical, as an apprentice to the poetic word. Craig was helping to forge a model of the artist that would evolve into the all-powerful director. The tensions were inevitable.

The encounter with the Japanese Noh presented no such problems of authorship and was, indeed, a breakthrough in the quest for a 'model'. Here was a form of theatre that was non-illusionist, non-representational, stylised, used gesture and music while relying on a philosophical interpretation of the world. In as much as it can be read as Zen philosophy in motion, or embodied Zen, Noh theatre offered ways of presenting Yeats's

7. Mask of the Fool in *The Hour Glass* by W. B. Yeats, designed and engraved by Edward Gordon Craig, Vol. 3, Nos. 10–12, p. 147a, 1911.

9 Edward Gordon Craig, Mask of the Fool in *The Hour Glass* by W. B. Yeats metaphysical concerns on stage. The Noh was also aristocratic, catering for Yeats's fear of large choruses and the potential mass appeal of theatre. As a result of his encounter with Ito and the Fenollosa manuscript, Yeats wrote *Four Plays for Dancers: At the Hawk's Well* (1917); *The Only Jealousy of Emer* (1919); *The Dreaming of the Bones* (1919) and *Calvary* (1920). The first two of these are Cuchulain plays where the protagonist is fighting natural and supernatural powers. *The Dreaming of the Bones* was Yeats's response to the Easter Rising of 1916 and *Calvary* his version of the New Testament story. Later in 1926 he also wrote *The Cat and the Moon*, his version of a 'kyogen', a kind of satyr play of the sort that traditionally interspersed cycles of Noh. Although these plays were later to reach larger audiences, initially Yeats claimed to be writing for his friends and 'rejoiced in my freedom from the stupidity of an ordinary audience'.

The Noh suited Yeats's formal experimentation but also his general attitude towards audiences. However, his reworking of the style introduced his own conventions, for example his use of a folding curtain to open the plays. He writes:

> Two of these plays must be opened by the unfolding and folding of the cloth, a substitute for the rising of the curtain and all must be closed by it.[20]

This cloth or veil, which Yeats proposes, has been interpreted by Puchner as a meta-theatrical gesture that 'epitomizes the struggle between diegesis and mimesis by giving their confrontation a tangible and theatrical form'.[21] While this is certainly true, I would claim that it is also a reworking of Craig's screens. Yeats had already used these on the production of *The Hour Glass* and was already sceptical of the overwhelming impact of stage design, particularly as expressed in the figure of Craig. His use of curtains, cloths and veils could also be read as a scaled-down version of Craig's screens, there to conceptualise space on the stage, in an architectural non-mimetic fashion, and to mediate between the stage and the audience. This folding and unfolding of a piece of cloth conflates the functions of the traditional curtain and the mimetic use of scenic space.

Yeats continued to write plays until the late 1930s, but the Noh became an integral part of his approach to playwrighting and performance. He produced two more dance plays, *The King of the Great Clock Tower* (1935) in prose, then rewrote it in verse as *A Full Moon in March*. Both are based on Irish legend and both centre around ecstatic dances before severed heads. These plays can also be read in conjunction with one of the greatest poetic dramas, Oscar Wilde's *Salomé* (1892 French edition, 1894 English edition), whose ghost can be seen through its text and its staging. Indeed these plays, with their sexual and ecstatic energy of dance, should be read in dialogue with *Salomé*, one of the most haunting and beautiful early poetic dramas.

It is one of Yeats's last plays *Purgatory* (1939) that Eliot exalts as the most successful poetic drama, having solved the issue of verse. This is written in four-stress verse and has no songs and no masks. The set comprises a ruined doorway and bare trees: 'wicked, crooked, hawthorn tree'. It is minimal and haunting. The narrative revolves around guilt, repetition, parricide, and the possibility or not of redemption. An old man and his son visit the ruins of the great house where the father was born. This house of the father is also the site where he hopes to redeem the rape of his mother, a rape, however, that resulted in his birth. The primal oedipal story is enacted as the son – the old man in the story – narrates how he grew up to kill his father. In the fight that occurs between the onstage father and his son, the father (and not the son this time) kills his son, thinking he is ending the cycle of repetition, only to discover that he is 'but twice a murderer and all for nothing'. These final words he addresses to God. This play, with its *Oresteia*-type theme, combines Noh influences with the classical European tradition in tragedy. Also, apart from the appeal to God at the end, the play prefigures both in its set (the tree, the empty ruined house) and in its themes (the possibility or not of redemption, the cycle of repetition of sin and suffering) the work of Samuel Beckett, which can be seen as expanding on the legacies of such poetic dramas as *Purgatory* and *The Cat and the Moon*.

Yeats's 'big scheme of poetic drama' formed an integral part of his aesthetic and political project. Probably more so than the poetry, the drama's appeal to a sense of communitas helped him to integrate his nationalist aspirations. This appeal, however, is not in and of itself a democratising force and in the Noh Yeats found a form of theatre that was stylised, ritualistic and aristocratic. Moreover, his attitude towards actors also portrays an anti-theatricality that at once wants to embrace the process of performance, while still fearing its collective and potentially democratising power. It is no coincidence that many of his plays were written as chamber pieces and, like Strindberg's, were meant to be performed amidst groups of friends. At the same time, however, his involvement with the Abbey Theatre is an attempt to stretch the aesthetic and political efficacy of these pieces to include a wider audience. All these issues are reworked thematically and formally through Yeats's particular brand of mysticism and metaphysics, creating a heady cocktail, one where the use of poetry on the stage makes the words 'sing and shine' at times, but also inhabits an anti-theatrical trajectory with all its ambivalence and contradiction towards the collective and physical dimension of performance.

T. S. Eliot: 'He do the police in different voices'

The dramas of T. S. Eliot are equally concerned with bridging the gap between the elevated aestheticism brought by the use of poetry on the stage and its broader appeal. After *Murder in the Cathedral*, which as Eliot himself concedes was presented before an ideal audience, he is quite consciously aware of creating an aesthetic that would 'solve' the problem of the use of verse on stage while also appealing to a more general audience. Eliot is acutely aware that writing for the stage is fundamentally different than writing for the page. Again the problem for Eliot centres around the issues of the voice/verse and their relationship to authorship. He writes:

> The first thing of any importance that I discovered was that a writer who has worked for years, and achieved some success, in writing other kinds of verse, has to approach the writing of a verse play in a different frame of mind ... In writing other verse, I think that one is writing, so to speak, in terms of one's own voice: the way it sounds when you read it to yourself is the test. For it is yourself speaking. The question of communication, of what the reader will get from it, is not paramount: if your poem is right to you, you can only hope that the readers will eventually come to accept it ... But in the theatre, the problem of communication presents itself immediately. You are deliberately writing verse for other voices, not for your own, and you do not know whose voices they will be.[22]

The problem of communication, indeed of creation itself, is again focused on the poet's voice. And Eliot interestingly differentiates between the textual function of the voice and the physical one on the stage. He believes that in both cases what needs to be heard through the text or through the body of the actor is the voice of the poet, his own voice. Somehow textual mediation is seen as more innocent while transmission through another's voice appears more problematic. What Eliot really wants the audience to hear *through* the voice of the actor is the voice of the poet. Acting is thus viewed as an act of ventriloquism rather than artistic creation. This use of ventriloquism is, I believe, present in Eliot's poetry as well, particularly when he tries to speak through characters of different, usually lower, classes. This is apparent in the pub and rape scenes of *The Waste Land*, where the device of the dramatic persona is used. Like in the dramas, the mediation of the voice creates all sorts of tensions between the categories of role/character/ caricature. Most of these voices, transmitted through the body of the actor, while ignoring it, are there to transmit the sound of Eliot himself.

After the success of *Murder in the Cathedral* and despite invitations to do so, Eliot refused to write any more religious dramas. He was now interested in writing about 'a theme of contemporary life, with characters of our own time living in our own world'. Unlike Yeats, who in his most experimental period longed for a studio-type intimate audience, Eliot was reaching out to the audiences of the West End London stage. And it is this attempt to write for this 'unknown audience' who 'cannot be expected to show any indulgence towards the poet'[23] that forces him to rethink the function of verse on the stage in terms of its impact on the audience. Unlike the High Anglicans at Canterbury Cathedral, with the plays that followed, principally *The Family Reunion* and *The Cocktail Party*, Eliot would not necessarily be preaching to the converted. Through these plays he tries to bring the poetry of liturgical drama into the drawing rooms of high society. He says of audiences:

> Audiences are prepared to accept poetry recited by a chorus, for that is a kind of poetry, which it does them credit to enjoy. And audiences (those who go to a verse play because it is in verse) expect poetry to be in rhythms which have lost touch with colloquial speech. What we have to do is to bring poetry into the world in which the audience lives and to which it returns when it leaves the theatre ... What I should hope might be achieved, by a generation of dramatists having the benefit of our experience, is that the audience should find, at the moment of awareness that it is hearing poetry, that it is saying to itself: 'I could talk in poetry too!' Then we should not be transported into an artificial world; on the contrary, our own sordid, dreary daily life would be suddenly illuminated and transfigured.[24]

The function of the poetry here is one of redemption and elevation. The idea that the audience might already speak 'in poetry' before being initiated by Eliot's dramas seems inconceivable in this context. Unlike Eliot's life, as he sees it, their own lives might not be sordid and dreary. And it is this view of the audience's voice that leads Eliot to an act of ventriloquism. The idea that the audience might then take up this act of ventriloquism, caricaturing themselves, as it were, seems ludicrous. However, this seems to be the desired response in Eliot's scheme of poetic drama. The poetry needs to be so organically integrated that it becomes 'the natural utterance, because it is the only language in which the emotions can be expressed at all'.[25] However, such an organic unity can never be achieved as long as the actor's body and voice remain mechanical channels through which the voice of the poet is transmitted. Rather than 'natural', the end result appears forced, artificial and condescending towards those it is portraying and addressing.

This tension between Eliot's desire to create an organic form of stage verse, while deliberately ignoring the presence of the actor or even the stage itself, could account for some of the challenges that these society dramas pose when it comes to staging *The Family Reunion* (1939) and *The Cocktail Party* (1949). Despite their deceptively domestic and Naturalistic titles, both plays rework classical themes, experiment with ritual and continue Eliot's quest for the 'organic' use of verse on stage. *The Family Reunion* is Eliot's reworking of Aeschylus's *Oresteia*. His 'Sweeney' poems and the dramatic fragment 'Sweeney Agonistes' act as precursors for the character Harry, the Orestes figure who returns home thinking he has killed his wife. These plays also touch upon the fraught position that the female occupies in Eliot's works. The Gorgonesque witch of 'Sweeney Erect' transforms to Agatha and Mary (as maiden Kores) of *The Family Reunion*, as modern Eumenides. This play is usually read in the context of Eliot's Christian vision and his attempt at creating a 'Christian tragedy'. However, the play might owe more to its classical legacy than to its Christian one. Martha C. Carpentier writes in her study *Ritual, Myth and the Modernist Text*:

> Most analyses of the Sweeney poems and their culmination in The Family Reunion have focused on Eliot's ultimately Christian vision, while the powerful female archetypes in those works and their Hellenic parallels have been largely misunderstood or dismissed.[26]

Eliot's fascination with female archetypes is read here in the context of the work of the so-called Cambridge Ritualists. Their impact on modernist drama has remained largely undervalued, but Carpentier claims that Eliot in particular was more influenced by the renegade in that group, the Cambridge classicist Jane Ellen Harrison. Where Harrison reread the birth of religion in terms of drama and ritual, where the feminine principle is central, Eliot's poetry seems to express fear and loathing of the same feminine principle. Hugh Kenner mentions Eliot's propensity for killing women in his work: 'Throughout *The Waste Land*, in *Sweeney Agonistes*, and in *The Family Reunion*, Prufrock disguised as Sweeney and as Harry, drowned this woman over and over.'[27] This neo-classical fascination with the 'monstrous female' surely derives from contemporary anthropological and classical studies, but is clearly reworked by Eliot's particular misogynist sensibility and his modernist aesthetics. The centrality of the female in his work, despite its negative function, still partly results from his encounter with the work of Jane Harrison. Carpentier continues:

> Her emphasis was not on the phallic energy of Dionysus, nor on the material renewal of fertility ritual, but always on the mysticism and communal worship of the matriarchal daimones, among which he is preeminent. This predilection is unique to her among the Cambridge Anthropologists, and because Eliot was also

influenced by French sociology, his dramatic theory is closer in spirit to Harrison than to Cornford or Murray. He shared her desire to evoke a collective spiritual experience through resurrecting the ancient ritual 'mould' in Greek drama, not only in theory but on the modern stage.[28]

And *The Family Reunion* was such an attempt at resurrecting the ritual 'mould', equipped with Orestes-type male protagonist, Harry, and menacing Furies-cum-Eumenides, centred round the possible murder of a female (characteristically by drowning).

Another aspect of Harrison's work that relates to Eliot's project for poetic drama is her emphasis on rhythm as the structuring force of ritual. Ritual itself is seen as an abstraction from life, halfway between art and life. Always close to a strongly felt emotion, ritual is read as both expressive and formal, as both experiential and aesthetic, encompassing the kind of organic quality that Eliot sought in his dramas. Rhythm transpires as the heart and soul of ritual, as its *psyche*. It is both material and psychological; it is external and internal, and, of course, the vehicle for rhythm for Eliot is verse. Carpentier writes:

> That Eliot should want to strip drama down to its most elemental, emotional basis – rhythm – argues for Harrison's influence. Like Harrison, he saw the restoration of rhythm to drama as a return of the 'living spirit', and in the communal cathar-sis of rhythm they both saw a human expression of divinity.[29]

However, the type of divinity the respective parties have in mind might be of significance here. The 'living spirit' Harrison evokes in her study of ancient ritual[30] is an embodied one, and one that has a strong identi-fication with the female. Eliot's reworking of this sense of rhythm relo-cates it clearly within Christian philosophy, exhibiting an equal difficulty with the body and, in particular, with the female body. Rhythm itself is relocated from the body to the voice; the voice itself, as we saw, is sim-ply there to mediate the original voice of the author, or the *logos* of God, as the case may be. In this way, via the excursions through anthropology and religion, poetry is further heightened on the stage. Through the use of ritual and rhythm it becomes the channel though which not only the voice of the author is ventriloquised, but, in its truest moment, so is the voice of God.

This classical inheritance that Eliot engages with is combined with his equally charged Christian legacy in an attempt to negotiate the function of poetry on stage. However, it is not a harmonious combination, as it constantly comes up against the presence of the body on that same stage. The embodied ritualistic tradition, filtered as it was through the work of

Jane Harrison (with its particular attachments), sits uncomfortably, in an almost oxymoronic manner, with the *asomatos* legacy of Christianity. Eliot, however, continues his impossible quest for such an aesthetic and again uses a Greek model for his next play, *The Cocktail Party*. Towards the end of his apologia for poetic drama, *Poetry and Drama*, he writes:

> You will understand, after my making these criticisms of The Family Reunion, some of the errors that I endeavoured to avoid in designing The Cocktail Party. To begin with, no chorus, no ghosts. I was still inclined to go to a Greek drama-tist for my theme, but I was determined to do so merely as a point of departure, and to conceal the origins so well that nobody would identify them until I pointed them out myself. In this at least I have been successful; for no one of my acquain-tance (and no dramatic critics) recognized the source of my story in the Alcestis of Euripides.[31]

The Euripidean play remained well hidden partly because it was so trans-formed as to look more like 'Noel Coward's *Private Lives*', as Glenda Leeming puts it. *The Alcestis*, a problem-play, an *hilarotragoedia*, about self-sacrifice and resurrection within the context of marital rights and obligations in conjunction with male-to-male *philia* and male heroism, is turned into a society drama about infidelity, male identity and the possi-bility of spiritual transcendence. Two society couples – Edward and Lavinia, and Peter and Celia – are entangled in affairs. Lavinia, who has mysteriously disappeared at the opening, is, unbeknown to her husband, having an affair with Peter. Edward is having an affair with Celia but refuses to continue seeing her when his wife leaves. This leaves Celia des-olate but makes her attractive again to Peter. This neat, over-schematic exchange is plunged into crisis by the news that Celia – whose despair has led her to join an 'austere order' in a tropical country – has been crucified beside an ant hill. This female death, like the 'murder' Harry commits in *The Family Reunion*, forces everyone else to reassess their life and yet again explores the possibility of transcendence. In place of a chorus this play has a psychiatrist, Sir Henry Harcourt-Reilly, functioning as the slightly comic mediator and the voice of authority in this secular drama. The characters indulge in quasi-existential anxieties ('What is hell? Hell is oneself / Hell is alone, the other figures in it / Merely projections.'),[32] always 'Contre Sartre', as Eliot whispered to Martin Browne when these lines were spoken on the opening night. However, the problem of secular-ising tragedy through this domestic appropriation remains, especially since the new encounter between the ancients and the moderns that Eliot was undertaking still refused to engage with the presence of the actor's body and the overall physiognomy of the stage.

All the above factors did not stop the play from becoming a West-End success and transferring to New York. In this respect Eliot had achieved his goal of constructing a poetic drama that would be acceptable to a general audience. This is how one contemporary satirist, 'Sagittarius' in *The New Statesman*, presented the whole affair:

> *Nightingale among the Sweenies*
> This is the vulgarest success, blasting
> A hitherto immaculate reputation,
> The voice
> *Par excellence* of the waste land and the wilderness.
> Can the exalted oracle rejoice
> Who, casting
> Pearls before swine, wins swinish approbation?
> *Tereu*, twit, twit, this metaphysical mime
> That should have been
> The most distinguished failure of all time
> Proves quite the opposite.
> Between the conception and the reception, between
> The curtain calls the Shadow falls –
> The deep damnation of a Broadway hit,
> Groomed for some critic *coterie's* diploma,
> Dear God, like *Oklahoma!*
> (O what a terrible morning)
> Seeing (let's face it) not alone the arty
> But the dim rabble crash *The Cocktail Party*.
> Has the hautboy of attenuated tone
> Become the uncultured herd's unconscious saxophone?[33]

Despite the satirist's biased opinion, Eliot's attempt to heighten the dreary and lowly life of his audience, primarily by making them realise they 'too can speak poetry', does contain an endemic element of condescension. Equally endemic and irreconcilable remains his fusion of the poetic and the mundane, the everyday and the transcendent. This anxiety permeates his late study *Poetry and Drama*, which he wrote after the success of *The Cocktail Party*. After claiming that it seems 'extremely unlikely' for a man writing prose plays to offer any solutions to the problems of poetic drama (Ibsen and Chekhov are said to be 'hampered in expression by writing in prose'), he remains faithful to his conviction that the poet is the rightful heir of the 'poetic' on the stage. The possibility of a different genealogy eludes him. In true Platonic manner he presents his model of a poetic drama as 'an unattainable ideal'. Towards the end of his essay he writes:

> Nevertheless, I have before my eyes a kind of mirage of perfection of verse drama, which would be a design of human action and of words, such as to present at once the two aspects of dramatic and of musical order.[34]

Writing this in 1950 Eliot appears nostalgic for the radical aestheticists of the late nineteenth century like Walter Pater. Ignoring the years of stage experimentation that intervened, he in many ways takes the argument *back* to a premodernist agenda. The elevation of music as the ultimate abstract ideal is one that all other artworks try to achieve in vain. This Platonic impossibility is further intensified by positing the poetic word against the physicality of the stage and the actor's body. Eliot continued his experiments in poetic drama in plays that followed, *The Confidential Clerk* (1952) – a reworking of the *Ion* by Euripides – and *The Elder Statesman* (1954) – his version of *Oedipus at Colonus*, but never repeated the success of *The Cocktail Party*. His quest for a Christian tragedy, where the physicality of the drama needs by definition to be elevated into the spirituality of the poetic verse, has created a mixed body of work; it has also helped shape the theoretical framework within which much poetic drama was written and continues to this day to be critically assessed.

Gertrude Stein: The Landscape Play

The problems of verse drama and their impact on the redefinition of the stage are also addressed in the formidable number of works for the theatre written by Gertrude Stein. Between 1913 and 1946 Stein wrote almost eighty plays. All her plays, from the early *It Happened, a Play* (1913) to the last *Yes Is for a Very Young Man* (1946), consistently defy referentiality and address the issues discussed here in a radically different manner. Stein's dramatic works have been read in conjunction with the historical avant-garde in Europe, where she spent most of her creative life. Her works display clear parallels with the concerns of modernist painters like Picasso, Cézanne, Matisse and Braque. To these influences Stein adds her particular brand of feminist philosophy and North American optimism; the result is a diverse and provocative body of theatrical works that inflect the debates about poetic drama in challenging ways.

First, her general disposition towards modernity was not filled with the gloom and doom displayed by Eliot and many of his contemporaries. Stein, like many feminist writers, embraced modernity and saw it as a possible site of change. Bonnie Marranca writes in her introduction to Stein's plays that, 'unlike many of her contemporaries, she was more interested in the world as paradise than as wasteland, the miraculous not the tragic'.[35] Her interest in Christianity, for example, displays a fascination with the ritualistic, the aesthetic and the pleasurable aspects of Christian faith. There is no anxiety about lost sacred practices, but a revelling in the iconographic and overall aesthetic imagery of Christianity (*Four Saints in Three Acts*). Her fascination with technology, while critical, contains none of the deeply technophobic attitudes of her contemporaries (*Doctor Faustus Lights the Lights*). For Stein, modernity transpires as a site of potential emancipation not as the debris of a lost humanity that was once organically whole.

In her dramatic works this critical optimism adds energy and humour. It is also linked with her broader epistemology as she brings to the problems of poetic drama a phenomenological twist. Her plays address general problems of perception and representation and the particular ways that theatre inflects these. In this, she in many ways transposes the lessons she learnt from painting onto her philosophical concerns about perception (she studied psychology with William James and medicine at Johns Hopkins University from 1897 to 1901). Her experiments in dramatic writing are part of this attempt to write beyond stories, to explore the materiality of creation and of perception. She writes in her essay 'Plays':

> Everybody hears stories and knows stories. How can they not because that is what anybody does and everybody tells. But in my portraits I had tried to tell what each one is without telling stories and now in my early plays I tried to tell what happened without telling stories so that the essence of what happened would be like the essence of the portraits, what made what happened be what it was. And then I had for the moment gone as far as I could then go in plays and I went back to poetry and portraits and description.[36]

For Stein, the stage presented the possibility of fusing poetry and portraits and description, examining the ways we hear, see or read in the theatre. The notion of the landscape play was to provide the basis for the fusion of all these ideas. The materiality of the poetry, the actor and the stage would all fuse into the idea of a landscape. This was not meant metaphorically, but used ideas similar to those expanded on later by the concrete poets. The very 'thereness', the presence of the theatre was to be presented both thematically and formally. In turn this presence was posited against the presence of the real for the audience. In the process the whole 'aesthetic' (i.e. sensory) encounter would also be broken down and, in cubist fashion, the acts of hearing, reading and seeing would be intermingled, fragmented and composed anew. The resulting composition would usually bear the marks of the organising principles of the portrait, the still life and the landscape. This view of the stage also radically reconceptualises performance. Bonnie Marranca writes:

> This spatial conception of dramaturgy elaborates the new, modern sense of a dramatic field as performance space with its multiple and simultaneous centers of focus and activity, replacing the conventional nineteenth-century, time-bound and fixed setting of the drama. The effect is a kind of conceptual mapping in which the activity of thought itself creates an experience.[37]

This could be read as philosophical theatre *par excellence*. The grand stories of the past (like Christianity in *Four Saints*) or the present (like technology in *Doctor Faustus*) appear emblematically perhaps as part of the landscape. They provide the visual and auditory set but can no longer equip the stage with that grand framework, philosophical efficacy. Rather, this is taken over by the now literal frame of the landscape. This is how Stein describes the saints in her version of a miracle play, her operatic collaboration with Virgil Thomson, *Four Saints in Three Acts*, which was staged to critical acclaim on Broadway in 1934:

> In Four Saints I made the saint the landscape. All the saints that I made and I made a number of them because after all a great many pieces of things are in a landscape all these saints together made my landscape. These attendant saints were the landscape and it the play really was a landscape.[38]

This is stagecraft beyond pictorial arrangement, beyond scenery; this immersion of everything into the landscape creates a stage that is not the representation of somewhere else. It is not merely abstract or expressionist; it creates a presence in and of itself. This physical presence, the landscape, is not an analogy but a material being-in-the-theatre. This creates a vision for the autonomy of the stage that is far more radical than any proposed by Craig or any Anglophone poetic drama.[39] Stein's plays set out to reconstitute the very essence of the theatre itself. This is not an exercise in reconciling the ancients with the moderns, in trying to write a Christian or a modernist *version* of a genre in need of resuscitation. This view of the stage rewrites the mould. Interestingly, this feat is undertaken through the use of the poetic word. In turn the stage possibly offers Stein an arena that allows her to quite literally materialise her poetry, to give it substance and embodiment, to make it spatial.

Doctor Faustus Lights the Lights is a fine example of how Stein uses genre, classical dramatic structure, character and plot. The story starts after Faustus has sold his soul and without one he is unable to go to hell.

The power of the divine is replaced by technology and the familiar story is given a feminist twist with the introduction of the female character Marguerite Ida – Helena Annabel (with at least a dual identity as her name suggests). It is the familiar tragic story of the original; the absolute of the soul impeded by progress and technology. However, in this version the debate about the soul is gendered. Faust has lost his soul and cannot go to hell while Marguerite Ida – Helena Annabel survives hell, even though she has been bitten by a viper. Doctor Faustus is the only one who can cure her:

> Woman at the window
> A viper has bitten her and if Doctor Faustus does not cure her it will be all
> Through her.
>
> Chorus in the distance
> Who is she
> She has not gone to hell
> Very well
> Very well
> She has not gone to hell
> Who is she
> Marguerite Ida and Helena Annabel
> And what has happened to her
> A viper has bitten her
> And if Doctor Faustus does not cure her
> It will all go through her
> And he what does he say
> He says he cannot see her
> Why cannot he see her
> Because he cannot look at her
> He cannot look at Marguerite Ida and Helena Annabel
> But he cannot cure her without seeing her
> They say yes yes[40]

This deceptively minimal use of words manages to contain all the necessary references: the viper from Christianity, the classical tragic connection between sight and understanding, indeed between the eye and knowledge, and the structural link between the emblematic use of the eye and the power to cure, bringing the whole play to its *katharsis*. All these are inflected by gender and framed by the notion of the landscape play.

The fragmentation of character in this play coupled with the spiritual uncertainty and the overwhelming presence of technology has been often read in a quasi-existential vein as foreshadowing the later so-called 'absurdist' drama inspired by French existentialism. Although this reading could be sustained on some level of interpretation, it misses the radical potential of these plays, both thematic and formal. And it tends to read them as stories; usually in terms of the very stories that the plays are trying to explode. Doctor Faustus in the end manages to go to hell (by killing something, as he is instructed), but not before realising that the gift of light (and everything it stands for) has been acquired by a woman:

> Here we know because Doctor Faustus tells us so, that only he can turn night into day but now they say, they say (her voice rises to a screech) they say a woman can turn night into day, they say a woman and a viper bit her and did not hurt her and he showed her how she can turn night into day, Doctor Faustus say you are the only one who can turn night into day, oh Doctor Faustus yes do say that you are the only one who can turn night into day.[41]

After the interjection of the chorus Faustus responds:

> Well then I can go to hell, if she can turn night into day then I can go to hell, come on then come on we will go and see her and I will show her that I can go to hell, if she can turn night into day as they say then I am not the only one very well I am not the only one so Marguerite Ida and Helena Annabel listen well you cannot but I can go to hell. Come on every one never again will I be alone come on every one.[42]

This female 'character', unlike the other 'Helen' she alludes to, does not 'launch a thousand ships'. She is not a pretext, a romantic excuse in this tragedy between man, God and the devil, but in all her fragmentation – and because of it – becomes a central character of the story, rewriting its politics in the process. Not so much a female counterpart to Faust as an altogether different way of 'inhabiting' the same issue, Marguerite Ida and Helena Annabel create a new landscape for the tragedy of Faust. It is one where gender prefigures and helps to rewrite the story and, significantly, also recreate the stage for the telling.

The Marguerite of this composite name could be a reference to one of the most alluring fictional female presences on the stage at the turn of the nineteenth century: Marguerite Gautier. This was the part from *La Dame aux camélias* that Sarah Bernhardt and Eleonora Duse had made famous with their languorous performances; it was also the last part to be approached by Zinaida Raikh. It is this dying romantic heroine who epitomises the difficult relationship between women and the stage. Vulnerable, but ultimately desirable, always on the verge of death, Marguerite Gautier seems to be infected by capital itself, as Meyerhold implied. She at once represents a decaying Europe and its eroticisation through the female body. These two fictional characters, Helen of Troy and Marguerite Gautier, frame the story. It is the story of Enlightened Europe, starting with the expansion of the Greeks towards the east (read through the eroticisation of the body of a woman, complete with abduction, rape, war and recovery) and ending with the crisis that Modernism brought to that same project. The body of Marguerite Gautier may be said to be infected by the same virus. As Meyerhold claimed, she comes to represent all the evils of capitalism; she is the woman-commodity. Bringing these two images together – one from the classical epic tradition, the other from the mythology of female performance – creates an explosive combination. It is one, however, that can no longer be contained within the representational economies of either system. Instead, Stein presents us with a composite yet fragmentary character, one that nods towards the traditions of both epic and tragedy but, significantly, inhabits neither.

The only space that a character like Marguerite Ida – Helena Annabel can inhabit is the landscape play. Indeed, she forms part of that landscape as all the characters in this play need to be read as forming the landscape. They do not simply animate it but blend into it. In Platonic terms, this approach to representation is not concerned with the drawings on the wall of the cave, as it were, but with the substance and texture of the cave itself. It is concerned with the prerequisite for representation, its basis. This is particularly apposite since in the discourses of Western metaphysics, including psychoanalysis, this basis/cave is identified with the female body.

The above phenomenological approach to the construction of dramatic character poses a number of difficulties for the performer. This is definitely a poetic use of language but one that moves radically away from notions of recitation or pure mediation of the author's voice. The conventions of persona, mask, ventriloquism, psychological character are all disposed of, together with the modes of reception they presuppose. Instead the actor is asked to confront the very materiality of the words. Interestingly, unlike other avant-garde theatremakers like Meyerhold and Brecht, also concerned with the art of the actor, Stein writes very little about acting as such. Everything she asks the actor to engage with is in the text of the plays. The stage directions, for example, are meant to be read as part of the play-text. It is not clear whether they are meant to be diegetic or mimetic, as the following sequence from *Doctor Faustus* shows:

They stand repeating have I and yes it does happen and then Marguerite Ida and Helena Annabel says let me show you and the woman says oh yes but I have never seen anyone who has been bitten but let me see no I cannot tell she says but go away and do something, what shall I do said Marguerite Ida and Helena Annabel do something to kill the poison, but what said Marguerite Ida and Helena Annabel, a doctor can do it said the woman but what doctor said Marguerite Ida and Helena Annabel, Doctor Faustus can do it said the woman, do you know him said Marguerite Ida and Helena Annabel no of course I do not know him nobody does there is a dog, he says thank you said the woman and go and see him go go go said the woman and Marguerite Ida and Helena Annabel went.

As she went she began to sing.[43]

The song that follows is clearly sung by Marguerite Ida – Helena Annabel but it is not clear who is speaking in the above section. What should have been a quick and direct question-and-answer sequence with comedic undertones, eliciting information and promoting the narrative, turns into an exercise in acting that challenges dramatic character and its conventions. This particular sequence, I believe, with its references to doctors, vipers, poison and cure, is a direct take on popular European folk plays (like mumming plays). Most of these folk plays are associated with ideas of fertility, death and resurrection and some are associated with the cycles of harvest etc. Hence the appearance of the country woman with the sickle to help her find the cure.

These philological references exhibit Stein's familiarity with the history of theatrical convention. The mode referred to above belongs to the oral tradition and carries its own performance conventions. The conventions of type and caricature are taken further and further flattened, as it were, to fit into Stein's notion of the landscape play. Still, the problems confronted by the actor in her plays remain. Puchner reads these as part of Stein's anti-theatrical legacy:

> Stein's reform of the dramatic text seeks to avoid the 'thereness' of actors and characters from the beginning, to make the act of viewing theatre more like the act of reading. For this purpose, Stein disassembles the entire apparatus of theatrical representation, but most importantly the figure of the actor ... In so far as the dramatic text encourages theatrical representation and impersonation, it must be radically changed. And so Stein devises a dramatic form that would make regular impersonation impossible, an anti-theatrical drama.[44]

It is true that Stein works textually; everything that she wants the actors to engage with is in each play-text and not in theoretical works. It is also true, as Puchner claims, that she wants to introduce the act of reading to the theatre. This, however, need not be part of an anti-theatrical drive. She equally wants to introduce theatricality to the act of reading. As the previous quotation with the country woman with the sickle clearly shows, Stein is very familiar with the history of theatrical conventions, their gender politics and their representational efficacy. All these she rewrites critically not so much sublimating the workings of the stage to the act of reading, as turning the act of reading itself into a material, performative event. It is this blending of senses, materials, text and characters that her inclusion of 'stage directions' gestures towards. And it is not an anti-theatrical gesture; it is one that critically engages with the Platonic legacy but, equally importantly, rewrites it.

The aura of the words on the stage, the 'shine' that Yeats was after is here stripped down and the words appear as solid objects on the stage, as solid as the body of the actor asked to confront them. Indeed, the actor is directly invited to confront this material performativity of the words on stage. She is not simply asked to recite or read them. She is asked to perform them, and in doing so she is confronted with the materiality of her own voice, and her own body. The medium of the actor's body and the medium of the verse both acquire an objectivity, reminiscent of the objective poetry that was to follow. They are blended, broken down and composed anew within the landscape of the play. Unlike many of the approaches to the actor's body that separate its physicality from its textuality, Stein's insistence on the function of the word on the stage also underlines the constitutive relationships between bodies and texts. Indeed, through her insistence on the interchangeability of seeing, reading and hearing she proposes a textual reading of the body but also a three-dimensional, performative reading of the text. This use of poetic drama undoes all the usual charges of anti-theatricality associated with this tradition. The words shine, but in very different ways to those proposed by Yeats.

'Solely because of the increasing disorder': Poetic Drama and Epic Theatre

> Solely because of the increasing disorder
> In our cities of class struggle
> Some of us have now decided
> To speak no more of cities by the sea, snow on roofs, women
> That smell of ripe apples in cellars, the senses of the flesh, all
> That makes a man round and human[45]

As Brecht's poem from 1934 states, the poetic imperative of the day is charged with a political urgency. Indeed both become so intertwined that the radical dimension of the one demands a formal, aesthetic equivalent. It is not poetry as a whole that poses the problem but the *type* of poetry that Brecht ironically refers to above. Nevertheless, in the process he produces a poem about the engagement of art that is witty, evocative, economical and rhetorically sophisticated. Like his 'Bad Time for Poetry' (1939) it makes a plea for commitment while seriously engaging in the types of formal experimentation that are associated with the autonomy of the high-modernist tradition.

For Brecht the shift from the page to the stage was not simply a matter of the rendition of the poetic word on the stage, but meant defining the workings of the stage anew. In many ways, the whole epic tradition from Wagner to Brecht presents such an attempt to poeticise the stage. The transference of the textual poetic word onto the stage becomes no more than one element in a complex and challenging poetics of performance. For the epic tradition the problems of verse on stage cannot be tackled independently of all the other elements of performance. They are all structurally linked: actors, scenography, play-text, audience interact with each other. However, the ways in which these elements 'fuse' in order to create the desired performance poetics radically changes from Wagner to Brecht. The complete, synaesthetic ideal of the Wagnerian *Gesamtkunstwerk* and the totalising politics it implies is rewritten by the Brechtian principle of episodic fragmentation. Brecht writes about the *Songspiel Mahagonny* in 1927:

> ... so long as the arts are 'fused' together, the various elements will all be equally degraded, and each will act as a mere feed to the rest ... Showing independent works of art as part of a theatrical performance is a new departure. Neher's projections adopt an attitude towards the events on stage; as when the real glutton sits in front of the glutton whom Neher has drawn. These projections of Neher's are quite as much an independent component of the opera as are Weill's music and the text.[46]

In turn, this fragmentation proposes a new political framework, one that replaces totality with dialectics. It is part of Brecht's quest for an aesthetic rendition of dialectical materialism. As in most forms of poetic drama we have encountered, the philosophical drive hugely impacts on the thematic and formal experimentation. Again the use of poetry on the stage becomes a way of creating a philosophical theatre. However, this philosophical imperative has been held responsible for the 'unperformability' of some of the plays themselves. This may be the case with the Eliot dramas that 'fuse' Christian theology with modernist anxiety, while also resurrecting the fraught relationships between Christianity and theatre. For the epic tradition, on the other hand, this philosophical drive is quite deliberately used to create new performing conventions.

These conventions are directed against Wagnerian totality (and Naturalist totality) not against the stage *per se*. Indeed, it could be read as an attempt to retheatricalise the stage. The poetic word, the actor, the whole stage apparatus are reworked and rearranged. The poetry on the stage at any given moment forms part of the more general *gestus*; there to signify but also to comment. The notion of *gestus* for Brecht brings together the philosophical imperative of Epic Theatre (its meta-theatrical dimension) with the performative conventions of production. For Puchner, *gestus* 'is poised between a theatrical principle and an anti-theatrical one'.[47] I would claim that it is poised between a meta-theatrical drive and a theatrical one, constantly interacting between them. Hence Brecht's use of text on the stage is at once poetic (songs, lyric sequences, direct address and so on) and philosophical, commenting on the textuality of the actor's body, the stage, the reception and so on. Writing as a physical act, as intellectual labour, as phenomenological reflection: they all inflect the uses of poetry in the epic legacy. The apparently seamless surface that Eliot was after in his later plays where there would be no jolts and fragmentations and where the poetry would quietly but steadily take over stage and audience alike ('I, *too*, can speak poetry'), is blown up into its constituent parts.

Interestingly enough, while the poetic legacy is sometimes used to justify the 'unperformability' of the Anglophone dramas (that is, too poetic and so making them undramatic), it is the political dimension of the epic tradition that attracts similar criticisms. Indeed, in this critical tradition, from Martin Esslin onwards, the poetry (of Mayakovsky or Brecht) is used almost to excuse their politics. The separation of the poetic Brecht from the political and theatrical Brecht is some respects seen as his redeeming factor. However, in many respects, such a separation is not simply undesirable but also philosophically and practically untenable.

The epic legacy finds representatives in the Anglophone tradition in the theatrical works of W. H. Auden and Christopher Isherwood. Poet and novelist started writing drama in the 1930s, possibly in an attempt to fuse their left-wing political views with their broader literary projects. The theatre presented them with a model of reception that allowed for the fusion of pedagogy and aesthetics that they were after. Driven by their quasi-Romantic conviction, shared by the European avant-garde, that theatre almost *per se* both derived from and helped to create a sense of communitas ('Drama began as the act of a whole community', writes Auden), offering the ideal platform for formal experimentation in 'engaged art' and reception ('Ideally there would be no spectators. In practice every member of the audience should feel like an understudy,' continues Auden[48]), they wrote a series of plays together that may be read as the bridge between the experiments on the Continent and the more textually oriented Anglophone projects in poetic drama.

Auden wrote his first play, *The Dance of Death* (1933), alone. It started as a meditation on the Orpheus myth and ended as a *danse macabre* of capitalism. 'We present to you this evening the decline of a class,' it announced. The non-speaking dancer (capitalism) is surrounded by an announcer, a 'theatre manager', a chorus and a few characters who make non-scripted interruptions from the audience. The play itself combined influences from Berlin cabaret, popular music-hall traditions, Russian ballet, myth bound together in episodic form that used both verse and prose dialogue. Interestingly enough, the play was later produced as a double bill with Eliot's *Sweeney Agonistes* in 1934 at Rupert Doone's Group Theatre in London. The influential and inspirational Rupert Doone had danced with Diaghilev's ballets and had worked in the theatre with Tyrone Guthrie. It is fascinating that he would present these two markedly different plays as a double bill. That evening could be read as a showcase for the experiments in poetic drama in English at the time. Eliot's attempt bore all the elements that would be developed in his society dramas that were to follow: a transcendental quest for redemption blended through his fusion of Christian and ancient myth and imagery. Auden, on the other hand, presented a popular and deliberately 'crude' analysis of capitalism, through the blending of English popular performing traditions with those inspired by the European avant-garde. What both projects had in common was the insistence on the use of poetry on the stage.

The 1934 performance of *The Dance of Death* was also attended by Bertolt Brecht during his first visit to London. Auden, too, had attended the first production of *The Threepenny Opera* while in Germany in 1928. The relationships between Brecht and Auden continued for many years to follow, including the period of Brecht's exile in the USA.[49] However, the issue of influence remains a contested one although Brecht is usually cited as the source of the Anglophone epic tradition. Auden is also partaking in a local debate regarding the efficacy of poetry on the stage. For this he turns to the European avant-garde, and possibly to early Brecht, but also to Ernst Toller. Significantly, he is also heavily inspired by a home-grown epic theatrical tradition that includes popular performance, the folk revival, and experiments in dance.

Auden continued to write plays in collaboration with Isherwood throughout the thirties. These were mostly inspired by their communism and later dealt more directly with themes closer to home (empire, the English aristocracy and so on). *The Dog Beneath the Skin* (1936) finds a villager, Alan Norman, on a quest for the illusive aristocrat Francis Crewe. He is helped out by a talking dog (who turns out to be Crewe in disguise), while he trails through decaying Europe. The play proved to the writers the effectiveness of music hall and cabaret and also nods towards the more Futurist and Dadaist traditions on the Continent (for example, Alan's left and right foot hold a conversation). *The Ascent of F6* (1936), through the parable of mountain climbing (after the newsworthy loss of George Mallory on Mt Everest), examines the relationships between personal ambition, empire and class. By now Auden and Isherwood had worked out a formula for writing plays together:

> Our respective work on this play was fairly sharply defined. We interfered very little with each other's work. The only scene on which we really collaborated was the last. It was understood, throughout, that Wystan's speciality was to be the 'woozy' and mine the 'straight' bits.[50]

This sharp differentiation didn't always work, as the two modes interacted. The fact of co-authorship itself brings an interesting dimension to the whole debate about poetry on the stage. In a sense it might help to even further fragment the central 'poetic voice' of the author that Eliot was so concerned about transferring intact. Rather than simply distract, it helps add to the general drive to fragmentation, episodic narrative and multiple quotation that their work gestures towards. Auden continued to write for the stage, notably libretti for operas (Benjamin Britten had written the score for *F6* and the Cambridge production of Auden and Isherwood's *On the Frontier* (1938), and after his move to the USA he tried working with Brecht, some of whose plays he also translated.) The contribution of these two writers to the debates about poetic drama merits more discussion than this analysis permits. However, it is important to stress that the Anglophone tradition in poetic drama is not necessarily a unified one. In the works of Auden and Isherwood we encounter a 'home-grown' epic legacy that is in tune with the broader aesthetic and political concerns of the avant-garde but also filters them through local concerns and performance conventions.

Stages for Dancers

The double bill at Rupert Doone's London Group Theatre in 1934 (Auden's *Dance of Death* and Eliot's *Murder in the Cathedral*) also points towards the centrality of dance in much of the experimentation taking place at the time. As the title of Auden's early play indicates, the category of dance is crucial in most debates about the efficacy of the poetic word on stage and its relationship to the actor. Seen both as a form of *askesis*, able to carry the body of the actor beyond psychological and naturalistic representation, and as an aesthetically appropriate medium for the poetic word on stage, the movement that was to be later known as 'modern dance' was to have a huge impact on modernist performance experimentation. The triumph of the Ballets Russes in Paris over the twenty-year period of Sergei Diaghilev's inspirational direction (1909–29) posed a formidable challenge to any form of experimentation taking place on the stage at the time. Indeed, Eliot himself writes in 'A Dialogue on Dramatic Poetry' in 1928:

> But I blame Mr Diaghilev, not the ballet in principle. If there is a future for drama
> and particularly for poetic drama, will it not be in the direction indicated by the
> ballet? Is it not a question of form rather than ethics? And is not the question of
> verse drama versus prose drama a question of degree of form?[51]

This formal imperative is mainly aimed at the physicality of the actor's body. According to Eliot, the theatrical performer could learn much from the dancer. As Eliot himself concedes, however, this formal training carries with it a moral/ethical dimension as well. He continues:

> Apart from Stravinskii, who is a real musician, and from Cocteau, who is a real
> playwright, what is the strength of the ballet?
>   It is in a tradition, a training, an askesis, which to be fair, is not of Russian but
> of Italian origin, and which ascends for several centuries. Sufficient to say that
> any efficient dancer has undergone a training, which is like a moral training. Has
> any successful actor of our time undergone anything similar?[52]

The 'moral training' of the modernist performer informs most schools of actor training developed throughout Modernism, from Naturalism to Epic. The Ballets Russes, however, apart from the 'ethics' implied by the strict formal training of its dancers, also introduced a new image of the dancer's body with its own 'moral system'. The early productions with the central *femmes fatales* figures and their decadent *fin de siècle* sensibility (*Cléopâtre*, 1909; *Schéhérazade*, 1910; *La tragédie de Salomé*, 1913) all fed into a particular strand of Orientalism, already prevalent in nineteenth-century French visual arts. This, combined with the daring choreography of Michel Fokine and scenography by artists such as Léon Bakst, made the Ballets Russes a fine example of the 'total work of art' on stage. And it was a totality that was centred largely round and carried through the body of the dancer. The dancers of the Ballets Russes combined the 'ethics' of strict training, their *askesis*, as Eliot called it, with the 'ethics' of the heavily eroticised and Orientalised body of the dancer. Additionally, as dance historians today stress, Diaghilev's ballets centred primarily round the presentation of the male body. The heavily eroticised and sometimes Orientalised male body, especially in the figure of Diaghilev's primary dancer, Vaslav Nijinsky, becomes the main focus of many of these early ballets.[53] This spotlight on the male dancer has sometimes been read, especially in the early pieces, as constituent of their overall misogyne. The gallery of decadent *femmes fatales* that people the early productions would certainly invite such a reading.

However, as the dance historian Sally Banes has shown, this reading might be slightly schematic and does not take into account the totality of works spread over twenty years. In particular, she claims that the Stravinsky scores – *Firebird* (1910), *The Rite of Spring* (1913), and especially *Les Noces* (*The Wedding*) (1923) present an image of the female that is more ambiguous, sometimes fusing primitivism, Orientalism and traditions borrowed from Russian folklore. Either way, the issue of gender is central to the overall aesthetic proposed by the Ballets Russes. And the 'ethics' proposed by its dancers is highly eroticised, sometimes androgynous, always centred on the physicality of the body of the dancer.

As in the more strictly theatrical projects, this remoulding of the performer that takes place in ballet also involves a revaluation of gender and sexuality on stage. Although Diaghilev's productions have been hailed as essentially creating the notion of the modern male dancer, modern dance itself has been primarily the domain of female dancers and theorists. Ramsay Burt writes in *The Male Dancer*:

> The label 'modern dance' generally refers to the work of the pioneer dance reformers (nearly all of whom were women) who developed styles other than ballet, including Ruth St Denis (1879–1968), Isadora Duncan (1877–1927), Doris Humphrey (1895–1958), Martha Graham (1894–1991), Rudolph Laban (1879–1958), Ted Shawn (1891–1972) and Mary Wigman (1886–1973) during the first half of the twentieth century.[54]

In contrast with their theatrical counterparts the female dancers all seem to have created bodies of theoretical work as well as specific choreographies on stage. In other words, most of the women 'modern dancers', as many dance historians agree, had to substantially recreate the language of dance before they could find their place in it. Rather than simply embodying the experiments of many of the modernist male directors and playwrights (from Strindberg and Ibsen, through to Brecht) these female dancers created both the theory and the practice, as it were, of their artform. Possibly the ballet's reliance on the body of the dancer, in all its physicality, again brings to the surface the problems endemic to the relationships between gender and representation. The women dancers of this period, in addressing the issue of their own role in dance, created the template for what we now know as 'modern dance'. Although through the figure of Nijinsky the male dancer occupies a privileged position in modern dance, this needs to be read in conjunction with the steady influence of the women in modern dance. Interestingly enough, both the image of Nijinsky and the images of the female presented by the women dancers of the period, although not consistent, almost always problematise fixed gender roles and their position in their respective 'ethical' economies.

As Craig was quick to point out, however (in the following quotation), the phenomenon of the Ballets Russes fed into the existing experimentation of the period, much of which was pioneered by these 'dancing women', as Sally Banes calls them. Despite his usual patronising and slightly competitive tone, Craig rightly underlines the influence of 'the American'. One wonders why he doesn't name Isadora Duncan in his review of the Ballets Russes. He writes in an article entitled 'Kleptomania, or The Russian Ballet':

> But the Russians have done a clever thing: they have increased the value of their French Ballet by adding to it a few tricks stolen from other lands and other arts. This was clever of them, ... and highly reprehensible.
>
> ... While doing so they stole an idea or two from the only original dancer of the age, the American, and another idea or two from the most advanced scene designers of Europe and superimposed all these upon the wiry artificial framework of the old French Ballet.[55]

The eclecticism of the Ballets Russes is frowned upon in favour of the 'originality' of Duncan's work. Hers is a body of work, however, that is concerned with femininity, both its form and content. Most of her pieces, in all their neo-primitive and neo-classical splendour, are concerned with woman as nature and/or mother, with parallels in the anthropological and classical projects of the Cambridge Ritualists. This obsession with the female body both follows a nineteenth-century legacy (Bachofen's *Mother Rite* comes to mind) and a modernist experimental one. Perhaps the physical nature of dance and the absence of a play-text also helped to present a whole new emancipated image of the female body. And Duncan helps create this tradition. Craig's reluctance in naming her also somewhat betrays his own difficulties regarding the female performer.

The equivalent of Naturalism's obsession with the 'woman question' is reflected in modern dance through the constant revisiting of what Sally Banes calls 'the marriage plot'.[56] She posits this as central in both ballet and modern dance, providing the themes, the dancing conventions and even the interpretive framework for traditional ballet. Modern dance in turn engages with this in its desire to scrutinise it, to rewrite it, sometimes by turning it on its head, others by getting rid of it altogether. And this is a theme to which the Ballets Russes also made a valuable contribution. *Les Noces* (*The Wedding*) premiered at the Théâtre de la Gaîté-Lyrique in Paris on 13 June 1923. It was the third of the Ballets Russes works set to Stravinsky scores, and came after *The Firebird* (1910) and *The Rite of Spring* (1913). Choreographed by Bronislava Nijinska, Nijinsky's sister, and designed by Natalia Goncharova, this formidable piece was to radically rework the marriage plot. Like *The Rite of Spring* it results from Stravinsky's fascination with Russian folklore and for that reason has been mainly read as a companion piece to it. However, as Sally Banes claims, it is a crucial piece for the development of modern dance, not least for the central position it accords to women. *Les Noces* is not simply a dramatisation of a Russian Orthodox wedding; it is a complex piece that brings together the folk tradition, modernist experiment, the Orthodox liturgy, Marxist utopia, and filters all these through the 'marriage plot'. Stravinsky himself draws parallels between this work and another central text of Modernism: James Joyce's *Ulysses*:

> As a collection of clichés and quotations of typical wedding saying [*Les Noces*] might be compared to one of those scenes in *Ulysses* in which the reader seems to be overhearing scraps of conversation without the connecting thread of discourse. But *Les Noces* might also be compared to *Ulysses* in the larger sense that both works are trying to *present* rather than to *describe*.[57]

Joyce's interest in dance, particularly through his daughter Lucia, would substantiate Stravinsky's parallels. Indeed, Molly Bloom's closing monologue could itself be read as a variation on 'the marriage plot'. Either way it would be interesting to read *Les Noces* as occupying a similar position to *Ulysses* in the critical reception of modern dance and modernist performance.

Les Noces took over ten years to arrive on the stage. The period between 1912 and 1928 saw great changes in Russia, not least in the ways marriage, sex, and the rights of women were viewed. Although Nijinska had lived in Paris most of her life, she returned to Russia during the Revolution and the Civil War and finally emigrated to Paris in 1921. While in the Soviet Union she too shared in the initial utopian faith that the Russian avant-garde had in the possibilities presented by the Revolution. She ran her own ballet school in Kiev until 1919 and only left after suffering permanent hearing loss from a bombardment. While working on *Les Noces* she claims she 'was still breathing the air of Russia, Russia throbbing with excitement and intense feeling'[58]. This excitement included encounters with the revolutionary Russian avant-garde, particularly the constructivists. To this she added the fascination with folklore, as seen in the work of Vladimir Propp, and an equal fascination with the 'woman question', both high on the political and artistic agenda at the time (as the work of Meyerhold too exhibits). However, Nijinska's reading of the marriage plot, through the peasant Russian wedding, radically rereads it more in the tradition of the radical feminists like Alexandra Kollontai, who saw in the Russian Revolution not only the end of the class system, but also the potential end of patriarchy and the traditional family. Drawing on the analogies between the marriage liturgy and the funeral rites that exist in the Orthodox liturgy, and in the lyrics of folk songs that Stravinsky used, she creates a piece that is bleak and melancholy, where the brides again – as in the character of Marguerite Gautier – can be seen to function as symptoms of a decaying capitalism. It has been characterised by the dance historian André Levinson, disdainfully, as a 'Marxist choreography'; he also describes the ending as 'a sort of practicable stage property constructed with flesh and blood or an apotheosis of exhibition gymnastics'[59]. The debt to constructivism and probably directly to biomechanics becomes clear. At the same time, the piece exhibits a particular 'Marxist aesthetic' that arose out of the early period of the Revolution and the ways that utopian project was interpreted by artists all over the Continent of Europe at the time. Although *Les Noces* was in some ways quintessentially Russian, like the Ballets Russes, it found a stage in Paris (not Moscow) and, through an aesthetic that was now beginning to be recognised as cosmopolitan Modernism, presented the most radical and challenging reading of the 'marriage plot' that had appeared on the stages of Europe.

The choreography pays tribute to the tradition of folk dance but also to the new constructivist techniques being formulated in the Soviet Union at the time. The movements are strictly symmetrical, each dancer is almost always part of a group (the men or the women) and the only thing that separates the bride from the group is the impending wedding. David Drew, who worked with Nijinska in the 1966 revival of *Les Noces*[60] for the

Royal Ballet in London, comments that Nijinska cast the bride by asking the female dancers of the company to strike a particular pose, not by auditioning their dance skills. This formal emphasis on order, repetition and homogeneity is underscored by what Drew, in the same interview, called 'radically asymmetrical movements'. Similarly and despite the charge of 'exhibition gymnastics' the end result also aspires to a kind of spirituality. This is also apparent in the famous image of the pyramid of brides' heads, woven together with the new bride's braids. Nijinska famously wanted all the dancers' eyes (tilted sideways as the heads rest on the shoulders) to form a clear vertical line through the centre of this pyramid. This was formal comment, 'stage property constructed in flesh and blood', as Levinson claims, but, standing back, the final image could also be read as a version of the Orthodox marriage headdress or even as a mound of human skulls in a still picture that conflates the fertility rite of marriage with death ritual. It is this combination of formal and thematic experiment, energised by the radical sexual politics of the time, that makes *Les Noces* an 'iconic' modernist ballet, where the term also alludes to the connections with the orthodox tradition of iconography. Sally Banes writes:

> … as a new entry into a ballet tradition that had for the most part celebrated marriage as the ultimate desideratum for women, *Les Noces* made a radical statement not only in terms of its abstract form, but especially in terms of its sexual politics … *Les Noces* is a watershed work, obdurately shifting the terms of the ballet wedding's significance from the male to the female perspective.[61]

In pointing towards the ballet (and the Ballets Russes in particular) for potential models for 'the successful actor of our time', Eliot is engaging with a complex experimental tradition, one that was undergoing its own radical modernist reshuffling. As always, this involved a reconfiguration of the dancer/performer on stage and almost invariably by engaging the discourses of gender and sexuality. What begins to emerge from this process is something we would today understand as dance theatre, as seen in the work of Pina Bausch, for example. Eliot's reference to Stravinsky and Cocteau shows that he is aware that the ballet's strength lies in this very co-existence of music and poetry on stage. Crucially, what brings everything together on the stage is the performer. It is, however, a specific dancer/performer who embodies the possibility of a 'poetic drama' for Eliot in this context.

The Ballet Russes also had a huge impact on Cocteau, as Eliot knew well and as documented in the many drawings of the ballets Cocteau made throughout the height of their fame. Cocteau's *Les mariés de la Tour Eiffel*

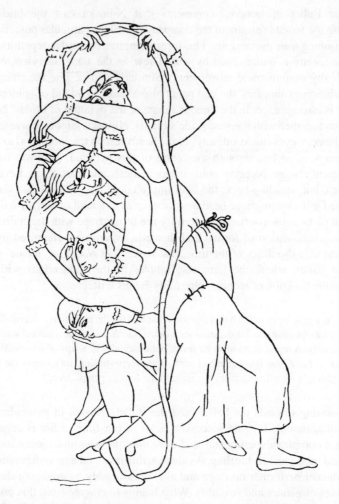

10   Natalia Goncharova, Drawing for *Les Noces*, 1923. Source: Henning Rischbieter (ed.), Art and the Stage in the 20th Century (Greenwich, CT: New York Graphic Society Ltd., 1968), p. 59.

(*The Marriage on the Eiffel Tower*), first produced by the Swedish Ballet in 1921, presents yet another take on 'the marriage plot', while introducing onto the stage Cocteau's idea of the actor as 'universal athlete'. This small piece combined poetry, dance and music – indeed no less than five prominent composers collaborated on this project: Georges Auric, Darius Milhaud, Francis Poulenc, Germaine Tailleferre and Arthur Honegger – and acts as a fine example of Cocteau's attempt at substituting 'poetry in the theatre' with 'poetry of the theatre'. The publication of *Les mariés* in 1922 was prefaced by his own manifesto for a poetic drama:

> Poetry in the theatre is a delicate lace, impossible to see at any distance. Poetry of the theatre should be a coarse lace, a lace of ropes, a ship at sea. *Les mariés* can have the frightening appearance of a drop of poetry seen under a microscope. The scenes are linked like the words of a poem.[62]

For Cocteau this poetry of the theatre is not simply a mater of transferring the poetic word onto the stage. It is the more a case of the word itself becoming part of the stage properties. 'Under the microscope' it is spatialised, physicalised, no longer able to provide the narrative lace of metaphor or even plot. Crucially this poetry of the theatre requires a new type of performer. Cocteau, again, acknowledges the contribution of Diaghilev and Rolf de Maré (the choreographer) in the creation of this dancer/actor. He states that the experiments with 'the fantastic, the dance, acrobatics, mime, drama, satire, music, and the spoken word combine to produce a new form; ... the plastic expression and embodiment of poetry itself.'[63] *Les mariés de la Tour Eiffel* was to be his contribution to this experiment. It is also the work that prompted him to formulate his notion of the performer as a 'universal athlete':

> A theatrical piece ought to be written, presented, costumed, furnished with musical accompaniment, played, and danced, by a single individual. This universal athlete does not exist. It is therefore important to replace the individual by what resembles an individual most: a friendly group.[64]

This fascinating formulation at once nods towards the constructivist manifestations of the actor as athlete, as acrobat, even as labourer (something that Cocteau would have been aware of through his connections with Nijinska and the preparations for *Les Noces*) and to the earlier symbolist versions of the same principle (as seen in Sologub's 'Theatre of the Single Will'). Interestingly, both the utopianism of the latter and the extreme individualism of the former are rewritten through the notion of the 'friendly group'. This 'friendly group' working in a studio space (equally championed by Cocteau) is for him the best vehicle for poetry of the theatre. It is no longer a matter of maintaining the clarity and integrity of the poet's voice, which constitutes Eliot's main concern. The poet himself is transcribed into this 'friendly group', which in turn stands in for the ideal of the 'universal athlete'.

In *Les mariés* Cocteau experiments with this idea of dispersal of poetry and the poet himself in the work of the 'friendly group'. Furthermore, this

11 'The Pyramid of Heads', Igor Stranvinsky/Bronislava Nijinska, *Les Noces* [1923], from the 1966 revival directed by Bronislava Nijinska, The Royal Ballet, Covent Garden

aesthetic is mirrored in the way the notion of dramatic character or even the individual human actor dissolves in favour of a fragmented representation, where the stage properties, animate or inanimate, happily occupy each other's place. The action is narrated or recited by two actors dressed as phonographs on either side of the stage 'half-hidden behind the proscenium arch'. This image of the phonograph, at once alluding to the uniqueness of the human voice (or the voice of poetry), and to a technology of reproducibility is to become very conspicuous on the modernist stage (see Walter Mehring's *Simply Classical* in Chapter 6 of this book). The characters enter and exit through a camera that 'opens like a door' and also helps to structure the action. This wedding party is trying to celebrate a marriage at the Eiffel Tower, which should culminate in a group photo, commemorating and monumentalising the event. However, every time one of the Phonographs shouts 'Watch the birdie', strange people and things appear out of the camera – A Bathing Beauty, A Fat Boy who proceeds to massacre the guests, A Lion. The movement is choreographed while the phonographs provide the narration and the voices of the actors, who wear masks. After a series of interruptions the wedding party manages to constitute itself as such and poses for the final photo. In the end, what creates the image of this marriage, what allows it to come together without further intrusions from the technological apparatus is the fact that it is turned into a work of art:

> SECOND PHONOGRAPH: Look. The wedding party and The Photographer freeze. The entire wedding party is motionless. Don't you think they're a little …
> FIRST PHONOGRAPH: A little wedding cake.
> SECOND PHONOGRAPH: A little bouquet.
> FIRST PHONOGRAPH: A little Mona Lisa.
> SECOND PHONOGRAPH: A little masterpiece.
> FIRST PHONOGRAPH: The Dealer in modern paintings and The Collector of modern paintings stop before the wedding party. What does The Dealer say?
> SECOND PHONOGRAPH: I've brought you to the Eiffel Tower to show you before anyone else, a truly unique piece:
> 'The Wedding Party'.
> FIRST PHONOGRAPH: And The Collector answers:
> SECOND PHONOGRAPH: I follow you blindly.
> FIRST PHONOGRAPH: Well? Isn't it lovely? It's a kind of primitive.
>
> […]
>
> SECOND PHONOGRAPH: … But look at that paint! What texture!
> Look at that style, that nobility, that 'joie de vivre'! It might almost
> be a funeral.
> SECOND PHONOGRAPH: I see a wedding party.
> FIRST PHONOGRAPH: Your vision is limited. It's more than a wedding. It's all weddings. More than all weddings: it's a cathedral.[65]

The wedding party, and indeed 'the marriage plot itself' is initially redeemed by turning itself into an 'experimental' work of art. However, in

Première page couverture :

DESSIN DE JEAN COCTEAU POUR « LES MARIÉS
DE LA TOUR EIFFEL » (original inédit)

Ci-dessus :

« LES MARIÉS DE LA TOUR EIFFEL »
VUS PAR MAURICE TAPIERO
(*voir suite des dessins page 6)*

12   Jean Cocteau, Design for *Les mariés de la Tour Eiffel*, 1922. Source: Théâtre: Spécial Cocteau, Paris: L'Avant-Scène, 1966, p. 2.

an almost Dadaist manner this greatness is also what turns it into a commodity. In the process the rituals of marriage and the funeral become interchangeable (as in Stravinsky's use of the same analogy in *Les Noces*). It is this fragmented, comic but also bleak image of the wedding party that the camera finally manages to capture. Even language starts to behave properly again. The final 'Watch the birdie' produces a dove from the camera. The metaphor is literally enacted rather than yielding strange and wonderful objects. With 'the camera working' and 'peace achieved' the characters all 'disappear into the camera'.

Cocteau rightly claimed that with this small piece he had 'already contributed a good deal' to the creation 'a kind of poetic spirit' on stage.[66] Equally intriguing is the footnote following that declaration which states that he is also 'perhaps' seeking to 'rehabilitate Wagner'. The hesitation and the use of the term 'rehabilitate' (that was to become notorious only a few years later in the Stalinist terror) show exactly how aware Cocteau was of the overall political dimensions of this debate. Cocteau approaches Wagner with caution. His poetry of the theatre was actively intervening in, or even correcting (rehabilitating) the Wagnerian ideal of the 'total work of art'. His version with its emphasis on 'the friendly group', stylised through the 'universal athlete', and narrativised through the fragment, is, I believe, a direct attempt at containing the totalising dimension of the Wagnerian aesthetic, while trying to maintain the radicalism of its formal experimentation. This critical engagement with the *Gesamkunstwerk* is very consciously continued by Brecht who, in equally deliberately Wagnerian terms, proposes the notion of a 'total work of art' that is based on the fragment.

In 1950, when Eliot is writing one of his final 'manifestos' on poetic theatre, it is Yeats's late play *Purgatory* that he puts forward as the paradigm of poetic drama. This small play, he claims, has 'laid all his successors under obligation to him'.[67] The impact of the Ballets Russes and Cocteau seems to fade away as in the end, for Eliot, it is primarily a matter of solving the 'problem of speech in verse'. However, this was not always the case for Yeats, as his so-called middle-period of *Plays for Dancers* clearly exhibits. Between 1915 and 1921 Yeats wrote four plays for dancers, which were based on the Japanese kyogen. The Orientalist dimension of these works will be examined in the following chapter of this book. Equally important is Yeats's fascination with the possibilities of dance on the stage. When he comes to stage one of these plays, *The Only Jealousy of Emer*, rewritten as *Fighting the Waves*, in 1929 at the Abbey Theatre, he too very directly draws on the experimentation with dance taking place at the time. In his experiments throughout the previous decade he had enlisted the talents of the Japanese dancer, Michio Ito; however, here he was working with actors, not dancers. Following Eliot's plea (of 1928) for the ballet to provide an *askesis* for the actor, he sets about creating the Abbey School of Acting (September 1927) *and* the Abbey School of Ballet (November 1927). This was run by Ninette de Valois, whose work as a choreographer Yeats had witnessed the previous year (1926) in a production of his own *On Baile's Strand*, directed by Norman Marshall at the Festival Theatre, Cambridge. Interestingly, the Festival itself had been inaugurated in 1926 with a production of *The Oresteia*, where Dame Ninette had eclectically used avant-garde abstract approaches to choreograph the chorus of the Furies. (The extent to which Yeats's *Plays for Dancers* partake in this neo-Hellenism is examined in Chapter 6 of this book.) Dame Ninette writes in her memoirs, *Come Dance with Me* (1957):

> The mind of Yeats was made up; he would have a small school of Ballet at the Abbey and I would send over a teacher. I would visit Dublin every three months and produce his *Plays for Dancers* and perform in them myself; thus, he said, the poetic drama in Ireland would live again and take its rightful place in the Nation's own Theatre, and the oblivion imposed on it by the popularity of peasant drama would become a thing of the past.[68]

The presence of Ninette de Valois and her group of dancers, as some contemporary scholars agree, forced Yeats to rewrite *The Only Jealousy of Emer* as a prose play.[69] This was *Fighting the Waves*, which was written taking the demands of dancers on board. For example, Ninette de Valois had great difficulty speaking on stage, especially when this involved verse. The end result could be compared to the production of Cocteau's *Les mariés*. It, too, used masks, borrowed from the Amsterdam production of 1922, a modern musical score for full orchestra by George Antheil, and relied on dance as the main narrative force. Famously, Cuchulain mimes a battle against a *corps de ballet* who represent the waves of the title. Even the mythological battle between the two 'brides' Emer and Fand, each claiming Cuchulain, could be read as a variation on the all-conspicuous 'marriage plot'. Here is how Lady Gregory recorded the event:

> I went to Dublin and saw *The Fighting of the Waves* – wild, beautiful, the motion of the dancers, the rhythm of the music, the scene. The words lost, the masks hideous – yet added to the strange unreality. We might all have been at the bottom of the sea.[70]

Indeed, the evocation of the 'Savage God' itself would not be inappropriate in this memory of the event that she records; itself, of course, echoing Yeats's own reminiscence of the first production of Jarry's *Ubu Roi*.

Yeats's *Plays for Dancers*, more than *Purgatory* (which was Eliot's model of poetic drama), exhibit a complex relationship to the notion of poetry on the stage. They also connect his work with the experiments of the European avant-garde at the time. The quest for poetry in, of or through the theatre almost always involves a similar quest for a poetics of physicality and embodiment. Dance is crucial in this context and has presented us with the most daring examples of modernist performance. Rather than reading these in opposition to the experiments in poetic drama undertaken in the Anglophone tradition, this analysis has hopefully pointed towards ways they could be read in conjunction. 'Words that shine' and 'bodies that move' on the stage need not allude to opposing conceptions of theatricality, but possibly different negotiations of similar problems. Through this brief presentation of examples from the theatrical works of Eliot, Yeats, Gertrude Stein, Auden and Isherwood, Cocteau, Brecht, but also from the modern dance, what emerges is a complex and sometimes contradictory engagement with the workings of the poetic word on the stage. In examining the possibility of a theatrical poetry, its creation, its transmission and its reception, all the playwrights mentioned above, whether consciously or not, *also* present us with theories of embodiment or in more direct terms, theories of acting.

5
Sada Yakko, Michio Ito and Mei Lan-fang: Orientalism, Interculturalism and the Performance Event

Whether witnessed in Yeats's fascination with the Japanese Noh or in Brecht's determining essay 'Alienation Effects in Chinese Acting', the encounter with the theatres of South East Asia, Japan and China plays a significant role in shaping the aesthetics of the theatres of Modernism. Much more than a matter of formal experiment or borrowing, this encounter impacts on the projects undertaken in a variety of ways: not only on their aesthetic but also on their political efficacy. Craig and Yeats's appropriation of the Japanese Noh and Kabuki theatres, Brecht's reworking of Chinese acting techniques, Artaud's entrancement with Balinese dance, the interest in the puppet theatres of the Japanese Bunraku and the Javanese Wayang all form a complex network of relationships that does not simply inflect modernist performance, bringing with it the sometimes surprising impact of the encounter with otherness, but, as this analysis hopes to show, in most cases is central to the whole process of the redefinition and retheatricalisation of the theatre. Furthermore, these encounters have helped to shape what would later be termed interculturalism: a trend that was to become all the more significant for the theatrical practices and theories of late modernity or postmodernity.

How are we to approach these encounters in the wake of Edward Said's *Orientalism* and almost thirty years of postcolonial theory? Are they restricted to specific contexts, like Artaud observing Balinese dance for the first time at the Colonial Exhibition in Paris in 1931, or Brecht and

Meyerhold observing Mei Lan-fang's performance at the Writers' Conference in Moscow in 1935? Are these contexts, always political and relational, to some degree formative and decisive of the aesthetic and philosophical experiments undertaken? And if so, to what degree? In other words, one of the main questions that the model of intercultural exchange poses is: how does culture travel? How do cultural forms migrate? As is the case with any other commodity, are they determined by history, economics and politics? And if those factors play a role, as they do in any economy of exchange, to what extent are they formative?

It is true that modernist performance partakes in the West's general fascination with the 'Orient', which is particularly striking in this period. For some the quest for a non-mimetic, non-psychological aesthetic that harbours abstraction and requires distance for appreciation finds something of a Holy Grail in the arts of the Orient. This Orientalist turn is, for example, clear in Wilhelm Worringer's *Abstraction and Empathy* (1908), which in many ways continues the binaries set up by Nietzsche in *The Birth of Tragedy*, where the Apollonian and Dionysiac are seen as analogous to 'the urge to empathy' or 'the urge to abstraction'. The latter finds paradigms in Byzantine and Oriental art forms. In the Anglophone tradition the works of Walter Pater, Arthur Symons and T. E. Hulme provide a similar context for the quest for an alternative to the anthropomorphism and the humanism of European classicism. Both within the aestheticist Anglophone legacy and within the fervour of the Continental manifesto, there is a move towards all things Oriental as part of a quest to rid Europe of the representational economies of classicism and the Enlightenment.

The very category of 'otherness' – the centre and kernel of much postcolonial thought – plays a constitutive role in the aesthetics and politics of most of the theatres of Modernism. As estrangement, alienation, as 'a slap in the face of public taste' or as the sacred, it informs the kinds of experiments undertaken and helps to shape the philosophical core of much of the theory. On one level, this encounter with the 'Orient' can be read as another useful distancing device that will help Europe become de-familiarised, unhomely, unsettled in its position of dominance. On another it relegates the 'East' as a screen, or as a process of mediation, existing to filter insight for the benefit of the European.

Otherness, involving either accusation or celebration, also forms a fundamental critical category within postcolonial studies. This is coupled with the equal validity offered to terms like hybridity, the intercultural, the 'in-between' and so on. The work of Homi Bhabha and Gayatri Chakravorty Spivak, and the late work of Edward Said, all move away from 'nativist' readings infused by notions of tradition and authenticity, or readings that rely on a centre–periphery dichotomy, to ones that privilege the in-between, the hybrid, the contrapuntal (the term that Said borrows from music),[1] while their work cannot be said to ignore specific historico-political contexts. The intercultural in this sense is read as analogous to the intertextual in literary theory. And in many ways, it is an attempt to bridge the opposition of history to textuality, while also creating space for the uniqueness of such encounters.

However, the problem of the particular relational – whether social, historical or political – nature of interculturalism persists. The Marxist-inflected critique of the readings that recycle otherness into the category of hybridity, ambivalence, fluidity have been voiced by Aijaz Ahmad[2] and in the context of performance studies more vocally by Rustom Bharucha.[3] Echoing Ahmad's *In Theory*, Bharucha states in *Theatre and the World* that interculturalism, like postcolonial studies, is mainly practised and theorised by Westerners, usually working within the safe parameters of educational institutions. He starts his critique with the emblematic modernist figures of Craig and Artaud, whose legacy, he believes, is continued by more contemporary theatre figures like Eugenio Barba and Peter Brook. He bases his case on Craig's and Artaud's combination of 'misunderstanding' and deliberate ignorance of historico-political contexts. He writes of Artaud:

> Artaud's writings on the Balinese and Cambodian dances are among the most alluring fictions of the 'oriental theatre' that have ever been written. Fictions, I emphasize, because Artaud's essays are neither historical accounts nor systematic descriptions of what he saw – they are his visions of an 'impossible' theatre that 'slumbered in his depths'. What concerned Artaud was not Balinese theatre as such but its connection with the 'oriental theatre', a magical storehouse of ancient rhythms and gestures, hieroglyphs and revelations, cosmic trances and metaphysics, mental alchemy and exorcism.[4]

And this accusation of 'getting it wrong' permeates much of the critique in this line of argument. Yeats, too, has been criticised for 'misreading' the Japanese Noh. Bharucha does concede, however, that this factual category is rarely high on the analytical agenda in such interactions. Like Susan Sontag, who urges us to read Artaud's work as part of the 'phenomenology of suffering', much critical engagement with these figures has tended to read them across an ahistorical trajectory that, as Bharucha claims, occupies the same Orientalist *topos* as their object of study (Yeats, Craig, Artaud).

The Orientalist 'problem' that figures like Yeats, Brecht and Artaud present us with is mirrored in their equally ambivalent and difficult relationships with orality and tradition. In turn their relationships with the theatres of the Orient on the one hand and with 'traditional theatres' on the other is both informed by and, crucially, helps to shape their overall politics. Interestingly enough, Brecht's explicit and somewhat creative use of Marxism has always been read as detrimental to the aesthetic process,[5] whereas the flirtations with fascism in Yeats, Craig and Artaud have been read mostly as aberrations. This reading posits Brecht at one extreme of completely compromised art and Artaud at the other expressing a project that is completely liberated from the political. It is commonplace for the Marxists to be accused of a specificity that results in mechanistic and propagandistic art, while the 'metaphysicians' (for want of a better term) are rarely read in relation to fascism, not as a facile accusation, but as a system of thought and political practice with which they had affinities of one sort or another. Still, this evocation of the political, while helpful in inflecting the nuances of the intercultural encounter, easily dissolves into an 'all is politics' rhetoric that has very little room or hermeneutic efficacy for the uniqueness of the creative event.

Insightful and in some ways corrective as these readings may be, they have little to say about the ways that context impacts on creativity; in fact, one neatly collapses into the other with little attention to what Peter Hallward has called the singularity of the creative event.[6] Hallward makes a decisive shift in his understanding of the postcolonial and it is one that might help us to further scrutinise these intercultural encounters between these charismatic Europeans and the theatres of East Asia. In his attempt to unlock the theoretical bind created by the oppositions between rhetorical – discursive and material – historical readings of intercultural exchange, Hallward proposes the category of the *singular*. This singularity of literature – and it is *literary texts* he is referring to – is different from its specificity that posits a relational identity, one that results from the multiple and complex negotiations of power and history. In this way aesthetic production is not slavishly determined by historical process, nor is it the result of the 'aesthetisation of politics', which according to Benjamin can only result in the totalising aesthetic of fascism. Nor is it to be confused with universality. This use of the singular – inflected by the philosophies of Gilles Deleuze as much postcolonial writing is at the moment – is not blind to the workings of history but, crucially, does not reduce the aesthetic encounter to a mere generative result of the historical and the political. The actual relationship itself, rather than being shaped by difference or otherness, is reconfigured through the category of sameness. It is predicated not by differentiation and individuation, but by the firm belief that the encounter with otherness is always an encounter with the same, or the Same, as Alain Badiou states:

> ... predication based upon recognition of the other must be purely and simply abandoned. For the real question – and it is an extraordinarily difficult one – is much more that of recognising the Same.[7]

This notion of sameness that is based not on a totalising universalism but on an immanent humanity (to borrow the term from Deleuze), allows us to move away from the politics of blame (*accusing* Artaud, for example, of Orientalism) and permits an engagement with the other, not as other, but as partaking in the same fundamental state of humanity. However, the complex and very specific workings of the historical contexts of these exchanges are far from ignored; they are formative but not determining. And this difference is not one of degree but one of *kind*. Possibly, this analysis claims, the singular that relies on sameness and not on difference could also be the sphere of literary and aesthetic production. In turn, it claims for this sphere an autonomous creativity that is not mediated through context, necessity or political pressure. Interestingly enough, as Hallward states, this sharp division between the political and the aesthetic finds its counterpoint in Brecht:

> However complementary their effects may be in certain situations, as a matter of principle political commitment and literary production should be treated as thoroughly distinct processes. No didactic, Brecht-like coordination of literature and politics should be granted the power to direct or predetermine the practice of 'legitimate' reading *in general* ... Every encounter with a literary text is precisely that – an encounter – and should be treated as such.[8]

This reductive reading of Brecht is not surprising, as from the debates between Benjamin and Adorno onwards Brecht's Epic Theatre has been used as a yardstick against which the autonomous artwork has been measured. This has been compounded by the equally enthusiastic adoption of Artaud by the thinkers of difference, deconstruction and poststructuralism, including Derrida and Deleuze.[9] Brecht's work is seen as restricted by context, whereas Artaud occupies that immanent singularity so cherished in these modes of thinking. However, as this analysis hopes to show, the encounter with the theatres of the Orient and their philosophies might open up an interpretive arena that no longer sees Brecht and Artaud occupying the extremes of a spectrum that has absolute commitment – dissolving into propaganda – at one end and total immersion in ritual and metaphysics – dissolving into madness – at the other. This study proposes to read Brecht's and Artaud's intercultural encounters as paradigmatic of their sameness and not of their contrasting difference. Brecht's involvement with East Asian theatre and Chinese literature and philosophy helps us to highlight the aspects of his work that sometimes remain hidden or obscure, such as his interest in death, in melancholy, in ritual and metaphysics, if we persist with the purely historical-political reading. The recent work of Anthony Tatlow and Fredric Jameson reads Brecht's philosophical theatre in relation to Chinese philosophy and in particular the Dao.[10] By the same token the intercultural encounter in Artaud situates his work historically, while not diminishing its transcendental dimension. To borrow a term from Edward Said, these two figures can be read as inhabiting a contrapuntal relationship: their reception within theatre theory has always relied on defining one against the other. This opposition, however, should not stop us from seeing the whole picture, despite the constant playing off each figure that occurs, as in music. In turn, their encounters with the theatres of East Asia and Japan also set up negatives and opposites, in a contrapuntal manner. The resulting 'polyphony' or 'organised interplay', as Said calls it, might expose more similarities than difference.[11] Again our interpretive arena will have to rely on a notion of sameness rather than otherness. So, this contrapuntal sameness is proposed as a way of bridging the great divide that separates the 'crude' readings of Brecht from the absolutely transcendent and ahistorical readings of Artaud. Both projects (and they are emblematic of most intercultural encounters during this period) are simultaneously specific – to their historical contexts – *and* singular as aesthetic events.

One way in which these intercultural encounters might be read as going beyond the rhetorical-discursive, material-historical divide may be by reading them, in Badiou's sense, as *events*. In fact, unlike the literary encounter, which might (mistakenly) be read as a *metaphoric* event, a performance constitutes a literal event. And, I believe, it is significant that most of these turns to the Orient resulted from very specific, situated events, and always in the presence of the actor's body. This body, usually male (although the case of Sada Yakko will be mentioned as well), becomes a type of lens through which the intercultural encounter is filtered but also magnified or distorted. In general the conspicuous presence of performers like Michio Ito, Sada Yakko and Mei Lan-fang makes the intercultural encounter and the performance event markedly different from textual forms of Orientalism. The materiality of the body at once points towards specific historical and political conditions (for example, the absence of female performers in most traditions mentioned; Stalin's role in the writers' conferences of the 1930s) but also, and crucially, might offer a channel into the interpretive arena of sameness rather than otherness, of singularity rather than specificity.

Yeats's encounter with Ito, as well as Meyerhold's and Brecht's with Mei Lan-fang, was not solely discursive and rhetorical; it was first and foremost an event in which the actor's body was conspicuous. Indeed, the impact and the inspiration (or the shock) were felt mainly through a reading of that body. As the word 'reading' implies, however, these encounters cannot be seen as unmediated, 'pure' exchanges, free of the workings of historical context and other specific demands. However, I believe that the fact that these encounters were part of broader 'theatrical events' involves its own methodological and theoretical constraints but also possibilities. The embodied aspect of these encounters makes them at once stubbornly historical and relational, but also singular and unique as artistic events. Indeed, if we read the aesthetic domain in the classical sense as primarily located in and mediated through the body, then these intercultural encounters may be significantly different from purely discursive or rhetorical ones. Their liveness at once situates the event historically, underlining the notion of otherness, but, at the same time, relies on a fundamental understanding of sameness. And this interplay between familiarity and distance becomes a formative category, inflecting both the politics and the aesthetics of modernist performance.

The notions of the 'intercultural sign' and the 'dialectics of acculturation' are formulated by Antony Tatlow[12] in his detailed accounts of the impact of East Asian theatre and philosophy, particularly on Brecht but also on other modernist directors. It is striking that Tatlow like Peter Hallward also engages comprehensively with Buddhism and Zen in his approach. What is striking in both cases is that these philosophies are read, more or less, as part of a materialist trajectory that finds analogies in the radical European tradition from Nietzsche (cited by Tatlow) to Deleuze (cited by Hallward). And predictably enough, Artaud figures majestically as one of the points of reference in this trajectory. Hallward writes:

> All of the otherwise incompatible conceptual personae that populate Deleuze's work (Spinoza, Nietzsche, Masoch, Proust, Kafka, Beckett, Bacon, Artaud, the nomad, the schizo, the dice-thrower, etc.) pursue a similarly singularising itinerary.[13]

The whole cast of protagonists mentioned above can be said to occupy a radical vitalist tradition, one that sits uncomfortably with Brecht's Marxism and dialectical materialism. Indeed, Brecht has been used as the yardstick against which the above tradition is measured. (Similarly, the Brecht/Beckett divide,[14] another inflection of the same binary opposition, has dominated theatre studies and literary theory more generally from the debates of the Frankfurt School onwards.) Tatlow's valuable contribution to this debate consists, among other things, of inserting Brecht into this trajectory, but not in a simple binary manner. With a thorough and comprehensive knowledge of both Brecht and East Asian theatre *and* philosophy, he approaches Brecht's encounters with the Orient as the 'same' as Artaud's, as occupying the same anxieties and concerns. That is, Brecht's encounter with East Asian theatre might offer ways of reading his work that do not confine it to the dictates of a narrowly defined ideology, bound by the specific and the relational. These encounters, again like Artaud's, are read as part of a radical break with mimetic representation and classical humanism. Tatlow writes:

> Buddhist dialectics are the starting point for an enquiry into the nature of subjectivity, for Zen contemplation of the self. Brecht called Hegel one of the world's great humorists, because in his system nothing ever stayed still, everything was continuously turning into its opposite. A comic catharsis through self-transcendence, the ability to be taken out of 'yourself', is available through Zen as well and can therefore become the basis of a clarified pragmatics, once you have seen the absolute relativity of your position. Zen seems to offer a more radical, but also a more rational, pragmatics, if we understand why it is absolutely possible for us to be 'descended', not from a god and trailing clouds of glory, but through transmigration, from a frog, since our destiny is linked to his. We have no claim to any special privilege.[15]

And it this lack of individuality combined with grace and stylisation that Brecht found attractive in Chinese acting. This emphasis on the body of the actor as both specific site and singular entity (through the function of *gestus*) is something that links Brecht with Artaud. Tatlow insightfully comments:

> Although they do this with decidedly different emphasis, both theories, and contrary to common belief also at times the practice of Brecht's theatre, advocate a gestural language that shuns or discounts representational convention, that comes from within the body, is expressed through it, and uncovers the forces that have structured it, and that is intended to create viscerally disturbing effects.[16]

In a sense, the body of the actor, inflected by this encounter with East Asian theatre, becomes, to use Deleuze's illuminating term, a 'single Body without Organs', unleashing all its creative power, undoing its relationships with specific historical structures. This is part of the great attempt to 'kill metaphor'. For Deleuze, the ultimate artwork is one that speaks 'literally, without metaphor ... to bring forth the thing in itself'.[17] This could also act as a working definition of Brecht's *gestus*. However, it is Artaud and not Brecht who is the inspirational figure here. Again, Brecht is consigned to the narrowly specific, caught in the bond of committed art, whereas Artaud transcends and enters that privileged domain of singularity. However, following the interpretive field mapped out by Tatlow, this analysis hopes to contribute to the thinking that firmly places Brecht's work within the same philosophical tradition, and does not confine it to the dustbin of dead ideology.

For Brecht, the stylisation, grace and control he witnessed in Mei Lan-fang's performance helped to establish the critical distance he was aiming for. However, this distance is simultaneously framed or even undermined by the aspects of ritual and the sacred that these conventions also draw on. As Tatlow states, Brecht is no stranger to the concept of ritual in acting:

> Spiritual. Ceremonial. Ritual. Actor and audience should not come closer to each other, they should move further away from each other. Everyone should move further away from himself. Otherwise we are deprived of the shock and horror which is a precondition for understanding.[18]

It is fascinating that the ritualistic quality evoked is called upon to provide distance, coldness, as it were, and not total immersion. Similarly Artaud's encounter with Balinese dance helps him to formulate not only a concept of acting but also something very close to a system of training for actors. Again pedagogy is something we tend to associate solely with Brecht. Artaud writes in 'On the Balinese Theatre':

> This may shock our European sense of stage freedom and spontaneous inspiration, but let no one say their precision makes for sterility or monotony ... Our theatre has never grasped this gestural metaphysics nor known how to make use of music for direct, concrete, dramatic purposes, our purely verbal theatre unaware of the sum total of theatre ...[19]

The evocation of 'shock' is a familiar image for the effect of the 'new' acting, deriving both from physiological definitions but also from that very emblem of modernity: electricity (unfortunately Artaud would later experience this shock in both these senses). In 1935 Artaud was to formulate more clearly his 'method' for training actors, which appeared under the title, 'An Affective Athleticism':

> One must grant the actor a kind of affective musculature matching the bodily localization of our feelings.
>
> An actor is like a physical athlete, with this astonishing corollary: his affective organism is similar to the athlete's, being parallel to it like a double, although they do not act on the same level. The actor is a heart athlete.
>
> [...]
>
> To use his emotions in the same way as a boxer uses his muscles, he must consider a human being as a Double, like the Kha of the Egyptian mummies, like an eternal ghost radiating affective powers.[20]

The first half of this quotation could easily have been written by the more materialist experimenters, like Meyerhold or Brecht himself. For Artaud's Double we can read Meyerhold's dialectical actor, who both embodies *and* demonstrates a role. In Artaud's 'gestural metaphysics' we can read traces of Brecht's *gestus*. Either way, the encounter with South East Asian, Chinese and Japanese theatre, far from being located on a purely metaphysical plain, is firmly located in the body. This body in turn becomes the key that unlocks both a metaphysical abyss *and* an historical negativity.

The European Tour

Much has been made in this analysis, thus far, of the presence of the body of the actor as the site on which these modernist intercultural encounters take place. Indeed, the specific performers, their histories as performers and the history of their reception is crucial in our understanding of the intercultural event. Sada Yakko and Michio Ito from Japan and Mei Lan-fang from China appear on the various European stages at a time when the role of the actor is being reconfigured. Their performances feed into preexisting debates and more often than not form a complex interaction of the familiar and the strange. At times they act as catalysts helping the amazed spectators to articulate their own thoughts, bringing them home, as it were. It is rarely the case that these performances remain completely strange particularly since most of the figures mentioned usually present a version of their 'traditional' acting that has already been adapted to meet the needs and expectations of their 'Western' audiences.

The case of Sada Yakko proves useful in tracing the significance of these tours as her presence impacts not only on theories of acting in general but also feeds into the anxieties and possibilities raised by the female performer. As we have mentioned throughout this book the actress emerges as one of the main protagonists of modernist theatre. The tours of Sada Yakko help to formulate a discourse on acting that engages with both gender and otherness, in a sometimes heady combination of both categories.

Sada Yakko was the cause one of Europe's first encounters with Japanese acting. She first appeared at the International Exposition in Paris in 1900 and then went on to England to perform before Queen Victoria. Ellen Terry herself claimed to have received 'a great lesson in dramatic art'.[21] Henry Irving was reported as saying, 'I never had an idea of such an acting.'[22] However, the truth is that Sada Yakko had never performed in Japan. Her acting career was prompted by her husband and manager Kawakami and only started once they had left Japan. Her training had been as a geisha, which meant she had mastered traditional Japanese arts like dance and song. The company she worked with had initially left Japan in order to study Western drama and acting techniques. However, their success prompted them to remain 'traditional', presenting traces of Kabuki mixed in with highly romantic stylisation, in an attempt to cater for the tastes and preconceptions of their audiences. As a result, Sada Yakko was hailed as the Japanese Sarah Bernhardt.

The analogy with the French actress is an interesting one, as Bernhardt is one of the actresses whose life and art embody many of the transitions and reformulations regarding the very possibility of the female performer within Modernism. In many ways, the idea of a specifically *Japanese* Sarah Bernhardt reads like a contradiction in terms, as this is an acting tradition that allowed for no female performers (although they did exist at one time, briefly, before they were quickly banned again). Indeed, it may have been the reason that Sada Yakko turned to the West in the first place. Training for actresses almost by definition could not exist in the theatres of China and Japan. In both there is a long tradition of female impersonators; and of course it is this glaring incongruity between performer and role that many Western modernists find attractive, relying as it does on stylisation, exteriority and artificiality rather than on psychology and verisimilitude. This is part of one of the most fascinating *topoi* of these intercultural exchanges. Modernity for the performers coming from China and Japan is seen as individuation and psychological character, nowhere more emblematically expressed than in the possibility of the female performer; while on the other side of this divide, the great modernist theatretheorists see abstraction and stylisation as the quintessential forms of modernist modes of representation. Individual psychology and mimetic representation are seen as part and parcel of an Enlightenment humanism that, if not dead, is at least in serious crisis.

In this sense the presence of Sada Yakko on the European stage points to the conflicts and contradictions in the representational systems of both Western and non-Western theatres. Those Europeans who were familiar with the classical theatres of Japan saw Sada Yakko as an aberration. Craig, for example, writes:

> Madame Sada Yakko was the first lady to go upon the stage in Japan. The innovation was a pity. She then went to Europe to study the modern theatres there, and more especially the Opera House in Paris, intending to introduce such a theatre into Japan ... it is to be presumed with the idea of advancing the art of the Japanese theatre. There can be no hesitation in saying that she is doing both the country and its theatre a grievous wrong. Art can never find a new way of creating better than the primitive way which the nation learned as children from nature.[23]

In a seamless combination of Orientalism and sexism Craig expresses very clearly and concisely the anxieties generated by the appearance of women on the stage. He continues:

> The introduction of women upon the stage is held by some to have caused the downfall of the European theatre and it's to be feared that it is destined to bring the same disaster to Japan since it is announced that Madame Yakko intends not only to use actresses for the female roles but to introduce other occidental customs upon her new stage.[24]

Craig's reading of the tradition of female impersonators remains firmly conservative, seeing in it a closed form that harks back to grand traditions and glorious pasts. This attitude may be balanced against the one expressed by the more materialist modernists like Meyerhold and Brecht, who see in it the possibility of de-naturalising representation and the workings of illusionism. However, as this analysis hopes to stress, both attitudes rely on the specific absence of the female body in representation. It may be simulated, metaphorised and so on, but it has no visibility or actual presence. In this sense the very physical presence of Sada Yakko on the stages of Europe helps to problematise and highlight the difficult relationships between

13   Sada Yakko, circa 1900

gender and representation on *both* the Western *and* non-Western stages. It becomes the kind of intercultural sign that Tatlow formulates in his approach; one that throws up the shortcomings of both representational systems.

Craig's friend and occasional collaborator W. B. Yeats was soon to engage with the Noh tradition in ways that prove provocative and challenging, creating one of the most fruitful and contradictory encounters between East and West on the modernist stage. Between 1909 and 1912 Yeats had collaborated with Craig at the Abbey Theatre, where Yeats first had the opportunity to put Craig's famous screens into practice. This scenic device itself, which was to both represent and conceptualise scenic space, can be viewed as in part Noh-inspired. (In general the influence of Craig's journal *The Mask* in initiating Western audiences to the highly abstract and ritualised Noh has been somewhat underestimated.)[25] Between 1913 and 1915 Ezra Pound was working on a translation of Noh plays based on the now famous Fenollosa manuscript. Ernest Fenollosa was a North American scholar and diplomat who played a crucial role in the introduction of Noh theatre to Western audiences and an equally determining role in the Americanisation of the Japanese economy. Again these two discourses have to be read in conjunction. After his death in 1908, his wife asked Pound to edit his manuscript of Noh plays and in 1916 *'Noh' or Accomplishment, A Study of the Classical Stage in Japan* appeared in London.[26] And this is the context that provides the inspiration for Yeats to write his *Four Plays for Dancers*. In writing these Yeats was, of course, greatly influenced by the Fenollosa manuscript, and one can say that in true Orientalist fashion his encounter with it was at this stage purely textual. He writes in the introduction to *Certain Noble Plays of Japan* (1916):

> In fact with the help of these plays 'translated by Ernest Fenollosa and finished by Ezra Pound' I have invented a form of drama, distinguished, indirect and symbolic, and having no need of mob or press to pay its way – an aristocratic form.[27]

The use of the term 'invented' is telling in itself, but equally significant in Yeats's demiurgical attempts is the presence of the performer Michio Ito. It is really through his engagement with the physical presence of Ito that his own aesthetic begins to take shape. He writes in the same introduction:

> My play is possible by a Japanese dancer whom I have seen dance in a studio and in a drawing-room and on a very small stage lit by an excellent stage-light.[28]

As was the case with Sadda Yakko, Ito was not performing traditional Noh. He too had come to Europe to study modernist dance but was urged to remain 'Oriental' for the aesthetic and other speculations of figures like Pound, Yeats and Edmund Dulac. The following extensive quotation from Liam Miller's *The Noble Drama of W. B. Yeats* throws light on this encounter:

> Michio Ito (1893–1961) came from a wealthy Japanese family and after a period spent in the study of the traditional dance forms of his native country

at the Mizuki Dancing School, where he graduated in 1911, he travelled to Europe to study European forms of dance and spent the following three years in Paris at the Dalcroze School. From Paris he went to London where he became a protégé of Ezra Pound's, and assisted Pound with his work of deciphering and editing the Fenollosa papers. Ito's study of Japanese dance forms was not related to the forms used in the Noh theatre, but he became interested in Noh forms when he came into contact with Pound in 1915, and in October of that year gave performances of Noh dancing for Pound and a group of friends in a costume specially reconstructed by Dulac and Charles Ricketts.[29]

This sketches a fascinating if somewhat disturbing image. It is not so much the charge of lack of authenticity that is of importance in the above context, but the fact that this encounter again helps to construct that all-elusive intercultural sign; one where the two cultures intersect, possibly throwing up representational 'crises' in both.

The image of Ito dressed in costume 'specially reconstructed by Dulac and Charles Ricketts' also feeds into the general anxiety that the modernist stage exhibits regarding the actor, the actress and the general representational

14   Michio Ito as the hawk in W. B. Yeats, *At the Hawk's Well*, 1916

efficacy of the human form. We saw how the case of Sada Yakko helps to bring this ambiguity to the surface and for Yeats and his aestheticist friends this also translates into the general aversion for the body of the actor. What Yeats finds attractive in Noh or Noh-esque acting is the ability of the body to behave like a puppet. He writes in the introduction to *Certain Noble Plays*:

> Therefore it is natural that I go to Asia for a stage convention, for more formal faces, for a chorus that has no part in the action and perhaps for those movements of the body copied from the marionette shows of the 14th century.[30]

This mechanisation of the human form, as we have seen earlier in this book, is not necessarily reflective of an anti-democratic and anti-modernist technophobia; it is multi-faceted and varied both in its aesthetics and its politics. However, in the case of Craig, Yeats and Pound, I believe, it informs the difficult position that the body of the actor and actress (or the impossibility of the actress) occupies in their work. Craig writes in a review of M. A. Hink's *The Art of Japanese Dancing* (1910), articulating what might be termed *somatophobia*:

> The fact that the body itself is never seen and that Japanese dancing is yet so fine a thing as it is and was dispels once and for all the illusion that it is necessary ... for the movement of the natural body to be seen ... The Japanese [style] with its strict ritual, its noble conservatism which still preserves traditional posture without change, or modification, its obedience to a fine tradition, its perfect control of its material ... that is the human body, approaches more nearly to the stately and splendid ceremonies of the past, of which, among us, some trace yet lingers in the symbolic gestures of the priests celebrating mass, and it thus partakes more nearly of the nature of an art.[31]

This spiritual annihilation of the actor's body at once relegates it to the realm of the transcendental, while appealing to the 'natural state of art'. Indicative of this tendency is Yeats's desire to have actors rehearse in barrels so they could concentrate on his words and not be distracted by their bodies. Of course, this type of anti-humanism need not necessarily derive from anti-theatricalism, but may in and of itself usher a new, modernist type of theatricality (one, after all, that was soon to be taken up by Samuel Beckett). However, in the case of Yeats, I do believe that it is just that, especially since it feeds into all sorts of other anxieties about the 'masses' and the potential democratisation that technology can bring to the stage. What Craig and Yeats find attractive in the Noh in addition to its purely formal qualities is its aristocratic dimension, one where the chorus, as Yeats states,

15   Michio Ito. Photo A. L. Coburn.

is separated from the action and that does not need a 'mob' for its audience. Hence the significance placed on small, intimate performance spaces, preferably living rooms and studios.

However, this desire may be said to sit uncomfortably with Yeats's (and Craig's) desire to help create a national Irish theatre. On the other hand, we could say that it inflects the kind of nationalism that Yeats formulates. Characteristically, while he is watching Ito perform in Dulac's and Rickett's Orientalist costume, he says, 'yet it pleases to think that I am working for my own country'.[32] This quest for universal or archetypal principles that, at times, lapses into a pseudo-anthropology, also evident in Craig's review above, is, I believe, part and parcel of the impact of Frazerian anthropology. As will be examined in the following chapter, the discourse on ritual introduced mainly by the Cambridge Ritualists allows for parallels to be reductively drawn between 'Oriental' arts and philosophy and Christianity. Thus Yeats is able to claim such an intercultural approach in his introduction to his and Shree Purohit Swami's translation of *The Ten Principal Upanishads*:

> But now that *The Golden Bough* has made Christianity look modern and fragmentary we study Confucius with Ezra Pound, or like T. S. Eliot find in Christianity a convenient symbolism for some older or newer thought.[33]

For Craig and Yeats, as for Pound and Eliot, the encounter with the theatres and the philosophies of India, China and Japan is always part of the general quest that seeks to rejuvenate Europe and it is usually conducted within an intercultural trajectory. This trajectory, however, remains stubbornly ahistorical, as it tends to read almost every form of religion and ritual (from Christianity to Zen) as occupying the same archetypal *locus*. As Yeats stresses above, much of this sensibility derives from the immense impact of *The Golden Bough* and tends to collapse difference and political specificity in the process. And it is this type of universality that postcolonial studies finds troubling. In the case of Yeats, Craig and possibly Artaud as well, this reading of interculturalism that they are directly or indirectly proposing, I would claim, feeds into the totalising aesthetics of fascism. In this sense their flirtations with fascism, conscious or not, need not be read as aberrations, but possibly as consistent with their overall philosophical and aesthetic projects. Characteristically, Craig writes in his review of Arthur Waley's *The Noh Plays of Japan*:

> These great plays, this great way of playing for a great audience! There is nothing to be said in a brief review about this sort of thing so good it is.
>
> What the No can be to us except something sad, I, after many years knowing of it and knowing what it stood for, dare not trust myself to say.
>
> In Italy, they will perhaps, make, one day, something heroic from the coming of Mussolini.[34]

The leap from Noh to Mussolini does not seem arbitrary, particularly if we bear in mind the close relationships between Zen Buddhism and Japanese militarism in the build-up to World War II.[35]

The case of Artaud and fascism is equally interesting and, I believe, both derives from and in turn helps to shape the type of intercultural encounter he embodies. Probably more than any other modernist, Artaud's fascination with fascism tends to be read in terms of personal pathology. This is either read as part and parcel of the creative process itself, as in Kristeva's primarily psychoanalytical interpretation of Artaud, which claims that 'poetic language is bordered by psychosis (as far as its subject is concerned) and by totalitarianism or fascism (as far as the institutions that it implies or proves are concerned)'.[36] In a somewhat worryingly cold-war turn of phrase that equates Mayakovsky's fate with that of Artaud, this reading reinforces a pathological interpretation of both the aesthetic event and its relationship to history. Naomi Greene writes in an illuminating study of Artaud and fascism:

> I would argue that to attribute the fascist impulses in his work solely to personal pathology means sidestepping the weight of history. Fascism may have appealed to Artaud, as to others, for psychological reasons but it was also a complex social, economic, and historical phenomenon ... In the end, the argument that only 'special' reasons (that is, illness) could have propelled Artaud into this orbit ignores the widespread enthusiasm generated by fascism.[37]

Against the nostalgic, quasi-romantic reading of fascism that groups together very diverse cultural influences in its quest of universals that will revive a dead or dying Europe, the plea to see fascism as a specific historical phenomenon may also allow for other historical specificities to surface. However, this reading does not imply that these modernist theatremakers themselves read fascism in this way. Their attempt to universalise fascism is parallel to the ways they encounter other cultures. The reductive impulse present in their encounters is, I believe, heavily inflected by their readings or misreadings of fascism. In turn the intercultural text/event that results from such encounters only serves to heighten their fascination with fascism.

Mei Lan-fang in Moscow

The figure of the Chinese actor Mei Lan-fang has become almost emblematic of the intercultural encounters on the modernist stage. Indeed, as his very successful tours world-wide prove, Mei Lan-fang created a huge impact on the Western stage from the USA to London, via Central Europe and Moscow. Unlike the performers we have concentrated on so far, Mei Lan-fang was a star in his homeland before he decided to tour abroad. Indeed, he very consciously toured the West with the aim of introducing audiences to the classical Chinese theatre. He showed no fascination with Western acting techniques and when he made minor adjustments to his performances for the sake of the audience's comprehension it was not in the name of 'fusion'. Here was a star, already a national treasure in his homeland, someone who had already been credited with 'modernising' Chinese classical theatre.

The encounter with Mei Lan-fang was to prove formidable. Here was someone who could not be simply read within the context of an 'Orientalist' encounter, framed by empire or otherness. He posed a different challenge to that presented by Sada Yakko or Michio Ito. More than any other performer he demanded to be interpreted in his own terms. Of course, this does not make these encounters more or less 'authentic', as those terms were usually way beyond the reach of the audience. Clearly, however, appearing as *the* representative of Chinese theatre, past and present, positions Mei Lan-fang somewhat differently from the others, infusing the whole intercultural event with something that approximates equal weighting of terms, or balance. His towering presence is impossible to avoid in any study of Chinese theatre, intercultural or not. Writing on the subject as recently as the 1980s, Jo Riley bases a whole book on the 'empty centre': that is, Mei Lan-fang:

> Mei Lan-fang, and all that he once represented, the mythical jingju that I never experienced in the 1980s, has become the empty centre of this study. He is the one figure that unites all kinds of theatrical performance occurring in China; elements of his art are reflected in all theatrical events, from puppet theatre, mortuary ritual and nuo masked theatres, and I found that the examination of all these other performance events illuminates, reflects and fulfils the image of the great master.[38]

Reading this book and many others, like the work of the more traditionalist Orientalist A. C. Scott, one gets the impression that Mei Lan-fang's relationship to Chinese theatre is comparable to that between Shakespeare and the English theatre. In a mixture of awe that combines cultural tourism with actual depth the figure of Mei Lan-fang, in both Western and Chinese eyes, it seems, comes to represent Chinese theatre itself. What is fascinating in this parallelism is that such a position should or could be occupied by an actor. From Aeschylus to Shakespeare to Ibsen to Brecht, great theatrical traditions are identified with playwrights. The modernist canon may also reserve some places for directors, but never has such an emblematic position been occupied by an actor.

I believe that every encounter with Mei Lan-fang carries with it the full weight of his determining presence. And it is something that his performances in Moscow help highlight. Mei Lan-fang's appearance there in 1935 and its impact on Meyerhold, Tretyakov, Brecht and Eisenstein occupy a very privileged position on the intercultural stage, not least because each one of these very vocal artists recorded and appropriated the encounter – for his own purposes perhaps, but almost consistently with the starry-eyed amazement of sheer awe and wonder. A revisit to the event might help us to scrutinise how the more materialist modernists conceptualised and practised interculturalism.

A. C. Scott's description of the Russian tour reads like an introduction to a great Romantic novel:

> On February 21st 1935, the Chinese party, which was led by the Chinese Ambassador to Russia, W. W. Yen, left Shanghai. Miss Butterfly was accompanied by five senior members of the Star Picture Company, to which she was under contract, while Mei Lan-fang had a group of about twenty stage people. It was the first time that either a Chinese actor or film star had visited Russia.[39]

Furthermore, the tour itself arrived at a crucial moment within the experimental fervour of the Soviet avant-garde. Sergei Tretyakov, one of the leading figures of the Soviet theatre scene who had already visited China, was instrumental in setting up this tour and making sure the eager Soviet avant-gardists got as much exposure as possible to this style of acting. In the spring of 1924 Tretyakov taught Russian literature for a year at the University of Peking and studied Chinese culture. The result of this encounter was his agitational play *Roar, China!*, which has been hailed as part of the initial experimentation with creating a 'theatre of attractions', the stage equivalent of Eisenstein's 'Montage of Attractions' in *The Battleship Potemkin*. Both productions opened in 1926, heralding a new era for committed art on both stage and film.

The point that needs to be highlighted at this juncture is a simple one: Mei Lan-fang's arrival on the Moscow theatre scene was already read within a specific context and fed into preexisting formal experiments. The reactions of Meyerhold, Tretyakov, Eisenstein and Brecht were not simply awestruck Orientalist misreadings but possibly helped to initiate a more complex and subtle encounter, one that we could possibly read today under the aegis of the intercultural sign or event.

The other point that prompts discussion in A. C. Scott's introduction to the Russian tour is the mentioning of Miss Butterfly. As was known at the time,

16   Mei Lan-fang as the fisherman's daughter in *The Fisherman's Revenge*, 1930s

classical Chinese theatre does not employ actresses. Indeed, Mei Lan-fang himself was famous for playing female parts, the *dan* roles. And this incongruity between performer's body and role is one of the things the audience found so striking. Miss Butterfly, however, was a representative of the new generation of actresses who had re-emerged since the arrival of film. Film as a medium was seen to be the more 'natural' home for female performers than the stage. The emphasis on verisimilitude, on psychology and external appearance made film appear to be a more modern medium, able to cater for female psychology better than the stage. But the stage itself by about 1912 had begun to accept actresses. However, after hundreds of years of stylised *dan* roles the female actresses had to be taught how to play these roles. Some were fortunate enough to be taken on board by masters like Mei Lan-fang:

> One of them, Hsueh Yen-chin, attracted the attention of Mei Lan-fang and he agreed to take her as his pupil and so become one of the first great actors to accept the actress on equal terms. Other men followed his example and several other actresses began to study under well-known actors.[40]

This was arguably the start of the modernisation of Chinese classical theatre. Interestingly enough, Mei Lan-fang is once again the champion of such changes. And it is in the midst of all these changes and experiments on either side of this encounter that the visit to Moscow takes place. Carol Martin calls Mei Lan-fang a 'bridge figure':

> Mei was in Moscow at the same time as Brecht and others not only because he was a great classical Chinese actor but also because he was a bridge figure who was interested in connecting traditional Chinese acting to what were for him newer Western ideas about acting.[41]

Part of this modernisation process was the arrival of the female actor on the Chinese stage. Indeed, as Carol Martin claims, the *xin nuxing* (new woman) movement was having a decisive impact on Chinese theatre, challenging established forms, particularly the tradition of men playing women. Drawing on the work of Katherine Hui-ling Chou,[42] Martin's analysis claims that there was a climate of modern theatrical experimentation at the time, fuelled by the *xin nuxing* movement that had already tapped into 'the political potential of Chinese acting'. However, it is Mei Lan-fang's impersonation of a female role, and not Miss Butterfly's, that was for Brecht to typify the possibilities of the *gestural* type of acting. This refusal to engage beyond the formal aspects of this 'impersonation', as Carol Martin succinctly puts it, is itself not very 'Brechtian':

> Brecht's emphasis on the form of Chinese acting at the expense of its interior processes, and his choice to ignore the significance of men playing women, could only have occurred because he ignored two of his own main concerns: an understanding of the historical conditions that produced traditional Chinese acting, and an inquiry into the assertion that the actor could and should quote the character played.[43]

Although Brecht was not familiar with the particular philosophical workings of the *dan* roles, it would be fair to say that he was aware that such formal sophistication had to be underpinned by a philosophical dimension of some sort. The 'blind spot' that he exhibits towards the workings of gender in this philosophical/aesthetic system is not untypical of the rest of his work either. Again, the notion of the 'intercultural sign' as formulated by Tatlow may help to highlight the shortcomings in the representational economies of both Brecht and Chinese traditional theatre. This 'intercultural sign' is made visible through the actor Mei-Lan-fang as 'bridge figure'.

This was not by far Brecht's first encounter with Chinese and Japanese theatre and philosophy. He had translated Chinese poetry and with the help of Elizabeth Hauptmann wrote two versions of the Japanese Noh play *Taniko*. These were the *Lehrstück*, learning plays, *He Who Said Yes* and *He Who Said No*. These were written in the mid-1920s and the interaction was purely textual, for, as far as we know, Brecht had not witnessed any live performances of either Japanese or Chinese theatre. They were based primarily on Hauptmann's translation of Arthur Waley's *The Noh Plays of Japan*. In this sense, what he was about to witness in Moscow in 1935 already fed into his concerns, writings and experiments with theories and practices of acting. In other words, Brecht was able to 'read' Mei Lan-fang's performance in familiar as well as in extraordinary terms. At the same time, the experimental context he was moving about it in was one of the Russian Formalist and the Soviet avant-garde artists; they had already equipped him with such terms as estrangement, literariness, fabula and *sujzet* (that is, story and narrative). So Mei Lan-fang's performance enters a preexisting interpretive field and does not simply arrive as a finished product, awaiting praise or miscomprehension. What Brecht witnessed in this performance was not necessarily a precursor to epic acting but an art that is parallel to it. He had already been thinking and writing with some clarity about his ideas on *gestus* and epic acting in general before this meeting. In his notes to the production of *Mann ist Mann* at the Staatstheater in 1928, defending the acting style that audiences had found difficult to appreciate, he writes:

> … it may be that the epic theatre, with its wholly different attitude to the individual, will simply do away with the notion of the actor who 'carries the play'. Against that, the epic actor may possibly need an even greater range than the old stars did, for he has to be able to show his character's coherence despite, or rather by means of, interruptions and jumps. Since everything depends on the development, on the flow, the various phases must be able to be clearly seen, and therefore separated; and yet this must not be achieved mechanically.[44]

And this is how Jo Riley reconstructs Mei Lan-fang's performance:

> Mei [Lan-fang] has entered the stage as the concubine Yang Yuhuan. His appearance at this one moment embodies the content of the piece from the point of entry

to the point of departure as empress/not-empress (concubine), dignified/not-dignified (drunk), beauty/not beauty (chosen and rejected) ... Moreover the deliberate and carefully chosen signs Mei Lanfang adopts to appear as Yang Yuhuan invite the initiated spectator to penetrate the layers of meaning from the outside to within – right up to the perception of the male body of the performer Mei Lanfang. The body of Mei Lanfang, the actor and his heritage, is also open to the spectator. The spectator's gaze is directed towards the separate elements of articulation of Mei Lanfang's body underneath (and through) the costume: the movement of the hand, finger, eye or foot.[45]

This is probably similar to the kind of performance that Brecht witnessed. And if this is the case, then it is strikingly similar to the formulations on epic acting that he was gesturing towards in the late twenties and early thirties. His desire for the episodic narrative of writing to be transferred to the actor, bodily not textually, finds an unlikely correspondent in the acting he witnesses by Mei Lan-fang. According to Riley, as previously mentioned, the emphasis on breaking up and putting together again is firmly located in the actor's body:

> The performer is trained (prepared) to dissect parts of his corporeal body in performance as separate units of articulation – hand, eye, finger, foot. The Chinese performative body recomposes itself as marionette and marionette master.[46]

And it is such a dialectical breakdown into marionette/marionette-master that Brecht finds immensely attractive, as it parallels the breakdown between being a character and demonstrating one; a centre and kernel of the alienation technique. In the Brechtian world this dialectic is never fully resolved and points towards an endless 'changeability' as the actor's body denotes 'this way of changing'; in the Chinese context, as Riley points out, 'the congruence of the performing body, and the space around it [results in] a mathematical, spatial, temporal matrix of *creation*, the Luo diagram, the key to understanding the source, control and articulation of *presence* by the actor on the Chinese stage'.[47] In both cases a different kind of presence is being articulated through the actor's body and unlikely parallels are being drawn between the materialism of the Brechtian body and the transcendence of the Chinese's actor's body. And in both cases the performing body is put together again in the context of what Artaud would call the 'communal sacred'. In the case of Chinese theatre, that is Luo philosophy, and in the case of Brecht, dialectical materialism.

This positioning of the actor also implicates the audience in new ways. The art of being a spectator was something that Brecht was interested in throughout his life. Again the Chinese theatre provides parallels if not direct paradigms. Jo Riley writes:

> The performer's movements, as the manifestations of presence, or life, serve in the Chinese theatre to designate and connect, *articulate* and create the fictive, theatrical world. In doing so, the performer's body ... is the locus of theatrical representation; the *incorporation* of another world. In this, the Western idea of the spectator as witness to the theatre event is challenged ... This body of performance knowledge means that the Chinese spectator *participates* in the reconstruction of the fictive world. The Chinese spectator goes to the theatre to be part of the represencing of the other world.[48]

If the Chinese spectator goes to the theatre to help make the other world present, the Brechtian one helps construct the 'new world'. The transcendent dimension lies less in the Marxism – however schematic and dubious – employed and more in the purely *utopian* aspect of Brecht's project. The above description of the performer's body could also double as a cursory sketch for the body politic. As this is read in the Chinese theatre it is redeemed and reconstructed within the framework of Luo philosophy. Within the Brechtian project, I would claim, and despite his proclamations, the Brechtian body never fully resolves the contradiction between its materialism and its transcendence, leaving that space endlessly open for rewrites, appropriations, changes and so on. However, mentioning transcendence in the same sentence as the Brechtian performer might already appear to be blasphemous. The parallels with Chinese acting might be one way of reintroducing this category of analysis. It may also present us with a way of reading both the work of Brecht and this intercultural encounter less mechanistically, not overdetermined by historical context.

At the same time, Brecht himself was acutely aware that the two worlds mentioned above could not be substituted for each other in this model of transference. Indeed, his reading of Chinese acting technique seems to be aware of its social context and of the inextricable relationship that it bears to theatrical form. He writes:

> It is not easy to realise that the Chinese actor's A-effect is a transportable piece of technique: a conception that can be prised loose from the Chinese theatre. We see this theatre as uncommonly precious, its portrayal of human passions as schematised, its idea of society as rigid and wrong-headed; at first sight this superb art seems to offer nothing applicable to a realistic and revolutionary the-

atre. Against that, the motives and objects of the A-effect strike us as odd and suspicious.[49]

Here Brecht is tapping into one of the great debates with modernism: the relationship between form and content/context. Indeed, while he was writing the above piece he was already partaking in heated debates with Georg Lukács and Walter Benjamin, defending the experiments that Lukács had branded as Formalist. Within this context the notion of 'a transportable piece of technique' acquires added significance, as it implies the relative autonomy of artistic forms. However, Brecht himself grounds this concept of form within its broader socio-historical context and wonders about the radical potential of such a form as the A-effect (alienation effect), as it seems to derive from a world-view utterly removed from his own, and from his ideal one. After a detailed analysis of Mei Lan-fang's acting technique and its parallels to his notion of *gestus*, he concludes:

> In point of fact the only people who can profitably study a piece of technique like Chinese acting's A-effect are those who need such a technique for quite definite social purposes.
>
> The experiments conducted by the modern German theatre led to a wholly independent development of the A-effect. So far Asiatic acting has exerted no influence.[50]

Hastily trying to resolve the above conundrum, Brecht answers both yes and no to the problem he sets himself. This is not mere rhetorical sophistry but in some ways exemplifies the very process that Brecht was trying to formalise and render aesthetic: the famous 'not but', the ability of the performer to exhibit one view while always hinting at all the other possibilities. So, according to Brecht, Chinese acting technique could be transportable, put to use towards very different social and political ends. At the same time, however, and in contrapuntal relationship to this statement, he puts forward a genealogy of the A-effect that sees it as developing independently from Chinese acting. So in a sense they are both the same and different.

This co-existence of familiarity and strangeness, I believe, is compounded by the fact that Brecht's experience of Chinese acting technique is not simply textual but mediated through the performing body of the actor. The kind of presence that Mei Lan-fang was creating involved embodiment, reconceptualising the audience, fragmentation and resolution within a broader philosophical system: all elements that pointed towards a radical conception of acting. Indeed, what Brecht witnessed in Mei Lan-fang was the possibility of the *actor-philosopher*. Here was a model of acting that was anti-Platonic *in extremis*. It posited the possibility of what Brecht was to later call a 'philosophical theatre'.

The vision of Mei Lan-fang performing a female role presented for Brecht and his companions a way of reconciling theatre and philosophy. The ways the actor embodied and enacted a philosophical world-view, creating absolute presence, underlined the physicality of the body and its interconnectedness with the spectators. It presented a type of embodied philosophy, again a contradiction in terms according to Western metaphysics. Jo Riley writes of this performing body:

> Not only the pose alone, as pattern or form of life, creates the theatre world. The Chinese performer *moves* to manifest the presence of life within. Moreover, the movements of passage that the Chinese performer makes across the stage designate and connect – *articulate* – or create the theatre world in the present, real world. The performing body connects planes of meaning with his corporeal body; positioning himself as the axis of time and space, he mediates the other world of theatre in this world. All times and all spaces are brought together by the articulate(d) performing figure.[51]

This is a tall order that the performing body is asked to fulfil, and one that can only fully be accomplished with the help of a philosophical system. And the system in the case of Chinese theatre is available; it is there to fragment, dismember this body and put it back together again. Indeed, this is the transcendental body *par excellence*, one, however, that is steeped in materialism. This kind of materialism, if not exactly absent from Western metaphysics, is at least highly heretical, as the works of Nietzsche and Deleuze exhibit. It is, though, central to our understanding of the relationship between theatre and philosophy. The separation of the two – the original debate between Plato and Aristotle about the efficacy of mimesis – is predicated on a reading of the actor's body. For Plato this can only be the bearer of distortion and disease; for Aristotle it becomes the form for the humanist subject.

What Brecht witnessed through the presence of the performing body of Mei Lan-fang was the possibility of resolving that contradiction. Anthropomorphic humanism might not be the only way to portray the 'real', and mimesis might not lead directly to distortion and the 'decadence' of the body. Mei Lan-fang presented these materialist modernists with the possibility of an embodied philosophy. And this is the trope that Brecht rewrites for the purposes of Epic Theatre, highlighting its oxymoronic nature and never really resolving the ultimate contradiction on which it is based: the actor-philosopher.

The emphasis placed on the presence of the performing body in these modernist intercultural events may offer ways of reading them that at once accord significance to specific socio-historical contexts but, and importantly, do not reduce them to a simple generative outcome. The ways the body of the performer achieves presence in the non-mimetic traditions of acting we are dealing with also engage with broader issues of representational efficacy. Never a direct and seamless representation of the inner workings of character/soul/consciousness but always exhibiting its modes of production, the body in traditional Asian theatre is always a body in process: one that is endlessly de-composing and recomposing itself, exhibiting the very mechanism that constitutes presence itself. Hence it is simultaneously steeped in its materiality and embodying transcendence. And it is this double movement, one that is never fully reconciled, that makes these projects attractive to the innovators of modernist theatre.

The encounters with the theatres of South East Asia, Japan and China prove crucial in our understanding of modernist performance. Neither a case of simple misunderstanding nor Orientalist appropriation, although usually entailing elements of both, these encounters feed into preexisting experiments, inflecting their aesthetics but also their politics. Through the interaction with specific performing bodies these intercultural events are specific to their contexts but in the very event of cultural interaction point towards a singularity that makes a plea for the autonomy of the aesthetic event. Whether this event is then reconstituted within Brecht's utopian Marxism or Artaud's sacred/mystical domain remains, again, a matter of specificity. What has possibly been gained in the process is a series of moments that gesture towards singularity, a singularity that does not schematically dissolve into its socio-historical context nor is recuperated solely through the metaphysical. Through the force of the performing body it becomes an embodied, materialist transcendence. And it is this performing body that creates the space – literally not metaphorically – for the intercultural event to take place.

In its urge to retheatricalise the stage, to make it both spectacular and philosophical, modernist performance finds parallels in the theatres of the East. More specifically, this rejuvenation of the theatre is centred on the body of the performer. This is no coincidence as it is precisely the site that needs redefinition, since in the Platonic anti-theatrical legacy it is also the site of contamination and disease. If the long anti-theatrical legacy initiated by Plato is located in the performing body of the actor, then any attempt to reconcile theatre and philosophy would also locate itself in the body of such a performer. The fascination exerted by the bodies of these touring performers is not only an aesthetic one, but also an epistemological one: one where the aesthetic and the philosophical do not negate each other, as Plato would have it, but rather co-exist in all their splendid unresolved contradiction. Through the notion of the intercultural event, once again, the body of the actor becomes the quintessential site of modernist experimentation in performance.

6

Greeks and Other Savages: Neo-Hellenism, Primitivism and Performance

When I read your pamphlet, I saw that you weren't committing murder, but were simply observing that the classics were already dead. But if they are dead, *when* did they die? The truth is, they died in the war. They are amongst our war victims.

> Bertolt Brecht, 'Conversation
> about Classics' (1929)[1]

You advertise 'new hellenism'. It's all right if you mean humanism, Pico's *De Dignitate*, the *Odyssey*, the Moscophoros. Not so good if you mean Alexandria, and worse if you mean the Munich-sham-Greek 'Hellas' with a good swabian brogue.

> Ezra Pound, letter to Margaret C. Anderson,
> *The Little Review* (1917)[2]

Brecht's and Pound's respective assessments of the significance of the classics for the modernist project in general touch upon the ambiguities, the complexities and the sheer richness of the fraught relationship between the ancients and these 'new' moderns. For all the heated, manifesto-style proclamations of 'newness', Modernism, particularly modernist performance, exhibits a profound and passionate attachment to the classical European tradition, especially in its various Greek-Hellenistic-Hellenic guises. From Brecht's rather crude confirmation of their death to Pound's more meticulous categorisation, the engagement with classicism forms one of the main agonistic sites of modernist performance. In what amounts to a radical reading at the time, most schools of performance from Wagner and Nietzsche onwards engage with the classical tradition and mainly as performance. Breaking away from the predominantly German philosophical tradition that viewed drama as philosophy, modernist performance starts to view classical drama – especially Athenian tragedy – as a form of *praxis* that presents both a model of performance and a model for the relationship between theatre and society. In other words, modernist theatremakers saw in the Athenian model of drama a form of total theatre. This totality was sometimes seen as a prototype to be emulated (Craig, Italian Futurists, Reinhardt) or, contra Wagner (as is the case with Brecht), it was seen as instigating a parallel political totality and, therefore, was to be avoided. In this sense, the modern theatre – the Epic Theatre for Brecht – could only come to life after the death of this classical tradition. Indeed, his Epic Theatre defined itself against this reading of the Athenian model.

I hope to show that this engagement with the classics was more fraught and contradictory than the scheme proposed above suggests. In the first quotation Brecht, in a radio conversation with Herbert Ihering (who had published a book called, *Reinhardt, Jessner, Piscator or the Death of the Classics* [1929]), and in line with the argument that he pursues in his early theoretical writings, counts the classics amongst the casualties of the First World War. For him at this date, classicism is implicated in the failures of the Enlightenment. According to this reading of Modernism, the First World War is seen as the culmination of the discourses of the Enlightenment, and Modernism in turn as the aesthetic response to the sense of loss, despair and betrayal that ensued (especially in Germany). Seen as the cornerstone of humanism and enlightened reason, Athenian drama for Brecht is at the heart of the problem. His vehement attacks on the Athenian model of drama, crude and somewhat mechanistic as they are (conflating Aristotle with subsequent Aristotelianism), have at their source this disenchantment with Enlightenment thinking and the humanism it presupposes. His quest for a 'modern' humanism and a new realism had no place for such a classical tradition. For Brecht, this tradition was already dead; it died in the First World War. Cronos-like, he suggests, this legacy devours its own achievements. Much later in his life, when he returned to Germany after the Second World War and exile in 1948, and around the same time he is putting together his *Short Organum for the Theatre*, he writes a version of Sophocles' *Antigone*, based on Hölderlin's translation of 1803. This version portrays a more complex relationship with Athenian tragedy than he ever articulated or possibly even intended.

Pound's dissection of the 'new Hellenism' manages to combine philological rigour and modernist iconoclasm. He approves of the Hellenism in Pico della Mirandola's fifteenth-century oration *On the Dignity of Man* (c. 1486) and in the *Odyssey*. (Very soon afterwards he was to start his epic *Cantos* with a reworking of a Renaissance version of an episode from the *Odyssey*.) The reference to the Moscophoros (c. 570 BC) is intriguing. It is an archaic statue found in the area of the Acropolis of a young male, a *kouros*, bearing a calf around his shoulders. It is a 'Male Dedicant Statue' dedicated by the tyrant Polyzelus. This reference to the preclassical aesthetics of the statue itself and to the fact that it relates to sacrifice is a nod to a growing body of scholarship at the time, namely the work of the group of classicists called the Cambridge Ritualists. The influence of this group of scholars cannot be overestimated as recent studies show.[3] Jane Ellen Harrison (1850–1928), Gilbert Murray (1866–1957), Francis M. Cornford (1874–1943) and to a lesser extent Arthur Bernard Cook (1868–1952) created a new approach to the 'Greeks' heavily influenced by Darwin's evolutionary theory and 'Frazerian' anthropology, framed by their liberal/socialist politics. Indeed, this approach, focused as it was on archaic notions of ritual, the sacred, magic and sacrifice, is what is being alluded to in Pound's reference to the Moscophoros. In the Christian version the Moscophoros is the good shepherd:

> What man of you, having an hundred sheep, if he lose one of them, does not leave the other ninety-nine in the wilderness, and go after that which is lost, until he find it? And when he has found it, he lays it on his shoulders rejoicing.
>
> (*Luke* 15: 4–5)

In an evolutionary link that could have been sketched out by the Cambridge Ritualists themselves, the sacrificial beast of preclassicism is 'saved' by the Christian shepherd and reinstated within the collective flock, rather than presented as a scapegoat on the altar. This imagistic conflation of the preclassical with the Christian forms an aspect of Pound's new Hellenism. For his friend T. S. Eliot, this Moscophoros-emblem could prove very pertinent as it might be read as also preechoing Eliot's attempts to reconcile his classicism with his Christianity, as in his experiments with Christian tragedy. The work of the Cambridge Ritualists and Sir James Frazer's *The Golden Bough* provide the theoretical framework that will enable such stage experiments to take place, and they propose the type of Hellenism, mostly preclassical, that Pound approves of. What he doesn't seem to approve of is the so-called decadent Hellenistic period, centred around Alexandria (where the *Odyssey* declines into the *Argonautica* and the 'Moscophoros' into the 'Laoköon'), and like Brecht he has even less of a taste for the German Romantic and Idealistic view of 'Hellas'.

Pound's Munich-sham-Greek 'Hellas' conjures images of the sculpture galleries of the Munich Glyptothek with their Greek remains 'completed' by Danish neo-classical sculptor Bertel Thorwaldsen and their famous Alexandrian 'Sleeping Faun'. The monumental Hellenic architecture of Gottfried Semper[4] also comes to mind. Semper designed the aborted Festspielhaus at Munich, which it was hoped would stage Wagner's works. Semper's monumentality was compounded by his theatricality. This is so much the case that Henry Francis Mallgrave proposes 'the Semper-Wagner-Nietzsche triangle of ideas' as a precursor to the 'much branded notion of a Wagnerian *Gesamtkunstwerk*'.[5] Semper writes specifically on theatre and monumentality and his notion of 'architecture as something that must appeal to the higher laws of humanity, as something to be directed toward the national consciousness of a people'[6] is what makes his brand of Hellenism 'sham-Greek', according to Pound. On the other hand, the same monumentality in mind and matter is what makes Semper attractive to a Wagnerian reading of Hellenism. In either case the reference is a spatial one and an urban one at that. This physical and spatial dimension of the new Hellenism will prove crucial in redefining theatricality. The tensions between monumentality and embodiment – especially in theories of acting and dance – will regularly draw on this new Hellenism in search of models for the performing body and its relation to theatrical space. It is fascinating that Pound's reflections on the new Hellenism are framed by these two physical presences: the Moscophoros at one end and the monumental Munich-sham-Greek on the other. Instead of referring to Hellas in terms of great ideas, indeed in terms of the great German tradition in classical scholarship (the famous and allegedly conservative classicist Ulrich von Wilamowitz-Moellendorff[7] would have made a suitable target), Pound in typical imagist style bases his argument on a group of startling images.

Pound's distaste for sham-Greek 'Hellas' is not unlike Brecht's. It is the same sham-Greek tradition that for Brecht died in the First World War. They share too a distaste for the totality of this aesthetic as it appears in its Wagnerian ramifications. Pound, however, manages to recuperate his Hellenism through his sometimes fraught relationship with the Cambridge Ritualists. It was in particular his friends Yeats and

Eliot who had an intense involvement with Ritualist ideas, especially in their quest for models of poetic drama. In general the Anglophone tradition in modernist drama seems to have had as much time for the classics as the classicists did themselves. In some cases it seemed as if they were almost part of the same project. The famous classicist Gilbert Murray, who had translated Euripides for the contemporary stage, confesses to Yeats in a letter in 1903 that he, too, was in search of a modern theatre:

> I feel quite at a loss about the proper form for a modern play ... and the proper sort of representation, too. The *Hippolytus* seems to me right, for one style; and your three especially perhaps *The Land of Heart's Desire* strike me as right for another. I used to believe in a sort of Ibsen-Dumas form of prose play, but it now mostly seems to me ugly and all wrong; a form created to suit a bad style of representation.[8]

Murray's work on classical tragedies made him reconsider the whole 'style of representation'. True to the evolutionary model, the engagement with the classical sources throws up questions about modern performance. This points to another reason why this group of scholars was so influential: through varying applications of anthropology, classics, religion, evolutionary theory, the social theory of Émile Durkheim and (in the case of Murray and Cornford) practical theatrical involvement, they were creating links between the past and the present. It was a heady cocktail of ideas infused by their general liberalism. Even more appealing was their insistence, through the work of Harrison, on the primacy of ritual over myth. This emphasis on the *dromenon*, rather than narrative or text as the origin of aesthetic practice, posits theatre as the foundational art form. This ritualistic reading of theatre proved very attractive to both Eliot and Yeats, as we shall see.

The model of Hellenism proposed by the Cambridge group is a very specific one. Focusing as it does on the preclassical period and concerning itself with origins and ritual, it tends to blend in very neatly with another of the fascinations of the period: primitivism. Indeed in most cases the anthropological, Cambridge-inspired take on Hellas folds over onto the rediscovered fascination with Africa (tribal art and ritual) and the 'Orient'. In this sense Hellenism fuses with primitivism. It is not its other, there to provide the civilising and humanising discourses that will rid the past of savagery; it is itself savage. Robert Crawford writes of Eliot's interest in anthropology:

> Anthropology for Eliot did not remake the myths, but showed how they had, while becoming the possessions of high culture, transmitted and not transmuted

primitive origins. By purporting to deinterpret them by removing the excrescences of later interpretations it made possible a reinterpretation which allowed mythology to be seen again as something that while still existing on the level of the most civilized and polished communication kept speaking of what it had sprung from – men's basic needs and desires.[9]

The same could be said of Eliot's being influenced by the Cambridge group, particularly Jane Ellen Harrison. Their reading of classical drama, while philologically sound and rigorous (according to the German tradition), also constantly foregrounded its preclassical, ritualistic and anti-humanist side. Robert Ackerman usefully summarises the Ritualists' theories on the origins of drama:

> On the basis of comparative anthropology and the study of 'primitive religion' they concluded that drama evolved from certain magical fertility rituals performed in the worship of a deity who died and was reborn. Dionysus was the Greek exemplar of this class of gods, called by Jane Harrison 'eniautos-daimons' or 'year-spirits'.[10]

For Pound, Eliot and Yeats this was classicism as primitivism. This was definitely not the classicism of Semper and Wilamowitz. Nor, however, was it the classicism of Wagner. This kind of classicism-primitivism found correspondences in the ritualistic theatres of the Orient. Eliot maps out his sources for 'Sweeney Agonistes' to a potential American director of the play:

> In 'Sweeney Agonistes' the action should be stylised as in the Noh drama – see Ezra Pound's book and Yeats' preface and notes to 'The Hawk's Well.' Characters *ought* to wear masks; the ones wearing old masks ought to give the impression of being young persons as actors and vice versa. Diction should not have too much expression. I had intended the whole play to be accompanied by light drum taps to accentuate the beats (esp. the chorus, which ought to have a noise like a street drill). The characters should be in a shabby flat, seated at a refectory table, facing the audience; Sweeney in the middle with a chafing dish, scrambling eggs. (See 'you see this egg.') (See also F. M. Cornford: 'Origins of Attic Comedy', which is important to read before you do the play.)[11]

In drawing on all these sources, Eliot is looking mainly for modes, forms, conventions of performance; for ways of making his play a *dromenon*, in Harrison's terms. Again the Ritualists presented a mode of embodiment, or rather presented an embodied view of the Greeks. It is this that is attractive for the purposes of performance. The drum beats accentuate the significance of rhythm – a primal force of ritual according to Harrison. Eliot's essay 'The Beating of A Drum' (*Nation and Athenaeum*, 6 October. 1923) analyses the relationships between rhythm, movement, dance and narrative and explicitly engages with Cornford's book on Attic comedy. The beating of a drum becomes a permanent fixture in many of these plays. For Crawford the chorus sounding 'like a street drill' is an example of Eliot's 'uniting the noises of primitive and metropolitan life'.[12]

Cornford's *The Origin of Attic Comedy* had been published in 1914; it read Aristophanic comedy in terms of fertility ritual and was to have a huge impact on Eliot. Cornford's scheme of the parts of comedy is roughly followed by Eliot, who transposes the central ritualistic elements of comedy according to Cornford ('Fight', 'Cooking', 'Feast', 'Sacrifice', etc.) into a domestic, urban setting. Again the kind of classicism invoked here is very close to primitivism.

For Martha C. Carpentier,[13] when this primitivism also conflates nature with the 'female principle', it becomes particularly attractive for Eliot. She claims that it is Jane Harrison's work that had the strongest influence:

> Her emphasis was not on the phallic energy of Dionysus, nor on the material renewal of fertility ritual, but always on the mysticism and communal worship of the matriarchal *daimones*, among which he is preeminent. This predilection is unique to her among the Cambridge Anthropologists, and because Eliot was also influenced by French sociology, his dramatic theory is closer in spirit to Harrison than to Cornford or Murray. He shared her desire to evoke a collective spiritual experience through resurrecting the ancient ritual 'mould' inherent in Greek drama, not only in theory but on the modern stage.[14]

However, as the above analysis proceeds to show, that is where the similarities end. The works of Bachofen and Engels, for example, participate in the nineteenth-century fascination with matriarchal theories of origin and social development. The work of Harrison could be read as inflecting such a tradition and proposing as a result new models of gender politics for Modernism. And this is what made her work attractive for many women modernist writers like Virginia Woolf and H.D. For Eliot, however, this fascination with the female principle is punctuated by a more complex love-hate relationship, which, according to Carpentier, is turned into a ritualistic misogyny on the stage. From 'Sweeney Agonistes' through *The Family Reunion* to *The Cocktail Party*, the concept of death/resurrection/salvation/renewal involves the actual or imaginary murder of a woman. Eliot's version of Harrison's *daimon* is the Fury, the witch, the castrating female who nevertheless carries within her body the possibility of renewal. And according to this reading, the tension created by viewing the female body as the site of both possible redemption *and* death helps to create the disturbing gender politics of these plays. Sweeney proclaims:

> I knew a man once did a girl in
> Any man might do a girl in
> Any man has to, needs to, wants to
> Once in a lifetime, do a girl in.
> Well he kept her there in a bath
> With a gallon of Lysol in the bath.[15]

And continuing the 'cooking' references to Cornford, started by the egg, Sweeney says to Doris, 'I'll convert *you*! / Into a stew. / A nice little, white little, missionary stew'. Eliot will continue his quest for a drama that mixes Christian and preclassical Greek ritual in the later plays which display similar difficulties with the 'female principle'. It is fascinating to note that his initial attraction to such a 'female principle' should come from Jane Harrison, who was to be later adopted as an emblematic figure by feminists across the disciplines of literary studies, classics and anthropology.

It is the conflation of Hellenism and primitivism that allows for such complex and contradictory readings to surface in the first place. For some, this return of the savage via the Greek presented a quintessential modern sensibility and allowed for possibilities of emancipation and critique (hence the adoption of Jane Harrison by Virginia Woolf). For others, this return signalled a type of return-of-the-repressed whose presence marked the impossibility of knowledge, progress or salvation. For Yeats, the encounter with the new Hellenism fuelled a fascination with the Celtic Twilight. If Eliot could find links between the ritualistic aspects of Greek drama, Noh drama, Christian liturgy and mumming plays, then surely there was a place for the Irish oral tradition. Yeats's late play *Purgatory*, with its *Oresteia*-type theme and its ritualistic murder, could be seen to bring these influences together. Its use of a single tree for its basic stage design was to be immortalised in Beckett's *Waiting for Godot*.

Much earlier in his life Yeats had had formative encounters with the Cambridge group. Gilbert Murray in particular was a great admirer of Yeats and had created with him and others (Edith Craig and Arthur Symons amongst them) 'The Masquers Society' in 1903 'to give performances of plays, masques, ballets and ceremonies'.[16] This active participation in contemporary concerns about theatre made Murray very attractive to Yeats. Although like Eliot and Pound he did not fully approve of his translations, the value of Murray's work as a Hellenist was never doubted. Eliot writes in his essay 'Euripides and Professor Murray' (1920):

> And it must be said that Professor Gilbert Murray is not the man for this. Greek poetry will never have the slightest vitalising effect upon English poetry if it can only appear masquerading as a vulgar debasement of the eminently personal idiom of Swinburne ... As a poet Mr Murray is merely a very insignificant follower of the preRaphaelite movement. As a Hellenist he is very much of the present day, and a very important figure in the day.[17]

The debate here seems to be between the poet and the scholar and Eliot naturally sides with the former. However, in his case, as with Yeats and Pound, his own excursions into poetic drama are fundamentally linked to Murray's project *and* to his translations, particularly of Euripides.[18] For Murray, the academic and the poet-translator could not be separated. He had himself written an original drama called *Andromache* (1901), which had been produced at the Royal Court. His translations also presented his personal views. For him, the emphases on ritual, dance and collectivity were what made Athenian drama modern, not primitive. In an evolutionary model he could see his world-view reflected in the Greeks. He wrote to Yeats in 1905:

> I shall translate some Aeschylus some day when I feel I can do it, but really I can, as a rule, only work at the people who have got my own religion. And Sophocles hasn't. (The said Religion is not perhaps very visible in the *Hippolytus*, but it is there. And it is plentiful in the *Troades* and the *Bacchae*.)[19]

The religion, as it appears in the Euripides plays mentioned, includes ritualistic dismemberment, critique of empire and war, an insistence on the voices of women, slaves and foreigners, and a triumph of Dionysus. And it is this preclassical (and anti-classicist) reading of Euripides that Murray finds attractive and appropriate for the modern age. His translations of Euripides (*Hippolytus, Elektra, Trojan Women, Medea*), produced by Harley Granville-Barker for the Royal Court, helped to create the 'classical revival' in the first ten years of the twentieth century. In turn this 'revival' had a huge impact on modernist notions of performance.

Despite not sharing the same 'religion' as Sophocles, Murray was responsible for the translation of *Oedipus Rex*, staged by Max Reinhardt at the Royal Opera House, Covent Garden, in 1912 (a production that was to play a significant role in the history of censorship and the British stage, as the play had been previously banned by the Lord Chamberlain).[20] This was already a famous production on the Continent. Reinhardt had produced Hugo von Hofmannsthal's translation at the Festhalle in Munich in 1910: after Vienna and Budapest it was performed in the Circus Schumann in Berlin and continued with a successful tour of Europe. This was not, however, a Munich-sham-Greek production, although it still maintained aspects of Wagnerism (particularly in its use of space); famous for its direction of crowd scenes and for its abundant use of extras, the production caused a sensation in London. Reinhardt brought to his productions of Greek plays an expressionist perspective coupled with a desire to make the plays 'modern'. His eclectic use of theatrical conventions borrowed from various performing traditions throughout Europe also helped to create the types of quasi-anthropological links made by the Cambridge Ritualists. After all, this was the same director who had also 'revived' the medieval morality-play *Everyman*, also adapted by Hofmannsthal. Criticising this aesthetic, one review at the time in the *Telegraph* stated that, 'After all, we do not want pageantry intruding into Sophocles.'[21]

It was this very intertextuality in performance conventions that Murray found attractive in working with Reinhardt. The production proposed a reading of the Oedipus story that was collective and grand, relying heavily on the physicality of the actors. Indeed, according to more recent scholarship, this was one of the first productions that posed the problem of how to perform Athenian tragedy taking on board modernist experimentation.[22] This attempt was met with both admiration and scorn. Nevertheless, it did propose a scenic solution to the problem. Instead of relying solely on the text, it was one of the first performances of tragedy to ask a wide audience to examine problems of staging and performance and not simply the ideas of a particular classic. It is this approach that appealed to Murray, making him depart from his favourite Euripides and turn to Sophocles, although he had earlier proclaimed of the play that 'it has splendid qualities as an acting play, but all of the most English-French-German sort: it is all construction and no spirit'.[23]

Reinhardt's production, on the other hand, did not appear to be in the least 'German' to Murray. The reference to the 'English-French-German sort' of classicism that centred on the idealisation of Sophocles is at once a comment on the classical scholarship associated with that tradition and on the model of Hellenism it proposes. For Murray, this was equivalent to the Munich-sham-Greek that Pounds derides. For both men, Sophocles was identified with Enlightenment humanism and as such could not really form part of the modernist exploration into performance. Indeed, as Murray states, Euripides proved more useful for modernist aesthetics and politics; and this is possibly what he means when he states that he shares the religion of Euripides but not that of Sophocles. Pound had also proclaimed that 'it would probably be easier to fake a play by Sophocles than a novel by Stendhal'.[24] Pound revises his views later in his life when he comes to translate Sophoclean tragedies. His translations are very close to what we would understand today as radical adaptations. Murray, on the other hand, seems to have approached Sophocles through the possibilities presented by Reinhardt's innovative staging. And this staging brought with it a type of eclectic cosmopolitanism that we would today associate with 'world theatre'. In turn, this cosmopolitan Hellenism blended with Murray's own ideals, as Edith Hall and Fiona MacIntosh claim.[25]

Hall and MacIntosh claim that 'London audiences were overwhelmed'[26] and particularly impressed by the performances of Martin-Harvey and Lillah McCarthy (as Oedipus and Iocasta). However, as they too state, the main criticism voiced in the press at the time concerned the 'authenticity' of the performance, its 'Greekness'. Adapting Richard Bentley's criticism of Pope's *Homer*, a review in the *Morning Post* stated: 'It is a pretty performance, Herr Reinhardt, but you must not call it Sophocles'.[27] For Murray, though, this reading of Sophocles was exactly what made the production successful:

> By 'Greek' we normally mean classical or fifth-century Greek. Now the *Oedipus* story itself is not Greek in that sense. It is preGreek; it belongs to the dark regions of preHellenic barbarism. It struck one of the ancient Greek commentators, for instance, by its 'senseless and bestial cruelty'. Oedipus is preHellenic; Sophocles is Greek. In the production ought we to represent the age of Sophocles or that of Oedipus? The point is arguable, and I have my own view about a middle course; but he who insists on keeping to the age and style of Sophocles must also insist on dressing Macbeth in Elizabethan ruffles.[28]

By reading the Oedipus story not as the fundamental cornerstone of classicism and humanism but as part of a 'preHellenic barbarism', Murray manages to reconcile his brand of Hellenism with Sophocles while also co-opting the playwright to his particular model of origins. It is almost as if the story of Oedipus was attractive to Murray despite the classicism of

Sophocles. This was as close to reading *Oedipus* 'against the grain' as any modernist director had attempted. And this preHellenic, almost anti-Sophoclean, reading of *Oedipus* also presented modes of performance and presentation that offered scope for experimentation on stage. Murray continues his championing of Reinhardt's production:

> Professor Reinhardt was frankly preHellenic, partly Cretan and Mycenaean, partly Oriental, partly – to my great admiration – merely savage. The half-naked torch-bearers with loin-cloths and long black hair made my heart leap with joy. There was real early Greece about them, not the Greece of the schoolroom or the conventional art studio.[29]

This was the new Hellenism as primitivism for Murray (Dionysus as the Savage God). The Greece of the 'schoolroom' and the 'conventional art studio' Greece had run their course. As Pound and Brecht would clearly articulate a little later, this Greece was seen as part of the problem. If Modernism in the theatre meant an attack on Enlightenment and humanist modes of representation, the classical notions of Greece would have to form part of the same ideological and aesthetic trajectory. How useful could they be for any project that was trying to redefine the relationships between theatre and society, theatre and the sacred, while searching for a language to channel its newly found theatricality? This other Greece that Murray unearths, however, presents many possibilities for such experimentation. With its emphasis on ritual, collectivity, physicality and embodiment, this savage (Cretan/Mycenaean/Oriental) Greece also appears strangely modern. It is what makes Murray's heart 'leap with joy'. It is also what links his theories on origins of drama with evolutionary theory. What for Murray creates the strongest emotional response *in the present* is the very *primitivism* of the performance. Replacing the human in us all (and humanism) with the savage in us all (and primitivism), this new Hellenism transpires as modern, engaging, critical and, despite its proclamations, very theoretical and sophisticated. Significant as it was, the Reinhardt production of *Oedipus Rex* would have been even more intriguing had the original designer stayed on board. That was Edward Gordon Craig. Reinhardt had been trying to set up collaborations with Craig since 1904 at the instigation of his friend Count Harry Kessler, the great patron of the period.[30] For a number of reasons (mainly to do with Craig's personality) none of these reached fruition, but between 1904 and 1910 Reinhardt and Craig held many planning meetings. Amongst the plays Reinhardt asked Craig to work on (scenery and costumes) were Shaw's *Caesar and Cleopatra* (1905), *King Lear* and the

Oresteia (1906), and *King Oedipus* (1910). Craig suggested *Hamlet*, *Macbeth*, and *The Tempest*. Craig was gaining quite a reputation throughout Europe at the time and was also involved with Stanislavsky in their famous production, the Moscow *Hamlet* (one of the few collaborations entered on by Craig that actually materialised). He had already written his manifesto *The Art of the Theatre* (1905) and after 1908 launched *The Mask*, the first modernist journal to address theatre as performance. Partly due to his insightfulness and talent and partly due to his charm and relentless self-promotion,[31] Craig was able to enter into a series of negotiations with Reinhardt over a number of years without their ever mounting a production together. It needs to be acknowledged that Reinhardt was extremely tolerant of Craig's demands. His brother and producer, however was not and failed to meet Craig's financial demands.

The problems were not solely financial. The main issue seemed to be one of 'authorship' of the performance as both Craig and Reinhardt went to great to pains to delineate their roles. In a letter to Craig, Kessler reassures him:

> You would make a *complete scheme* of the whole of the movements and actor's [sic] positions and gestures *on paper* and explain this to Reinhardt (for the Oresteia) and to whoever [sic] undertakes to help you in Shaw's play, *showing* them besides yourself exactly the gestures and movements you want, as you would to an actor.

> Thereupon, Reinhardt, or in Shaw's play, his proxy, would go through the parts with the actors, *impressing your intentions on them* as nearly as possible and you would *be present* at the rehearsals.[32]

One wonders what would be left for Reinhardt to do in this scheme of things! The image suggested – a favourite of Craig's – is that of the relationship between the puppet and the puppet-master. And it is one of the ways in which Craig deals with the tensions between the author, actors and director. When dealing with animate creatures, however, such a scheme proves problematic. The reasons for the failure of Craig's collaborations are too many and varied to list here, but regardless of the outcome Reinhardt's Greek productions were influenced by his encounters with the charismatic yet elusive Englishman. In turn, Craig's vision for a 'new theatre' was also heavily inflected by his own brand of Hellenism.

Craig saw in the Athenian model of drama a form of total theatre. In particular the use of scenic space, architecturally conceived in relation to the human form, also derives from his understanding of Hellenism. Michael

Walton claims that Craig, more than most of his contemporaries, understood Athenian tragedy and this had a determining impact in his own
aesthetic. Craig, the Arts and Crafts engraver, the young actor, the theatre
theorist, the designer, the 'director', found, through his Hellenism, a
channel for his combined talents. Walton underlines this:

> Craig himself worked on this association between engraving and the art of the
> stage and produced thereby a vision of Greek drama which, probably for the first
> time since the Hellenistic period, addressed the way in which Greek tragedy was
> created as a masked performance with all that that implies for stage movement,
> for *cheironomia*, the language of stage gesture, and in the crystallising of emo-
> tions into concentrated sculptural forms.[33]

It is this 'crystallising of emotions' into material form that we find in the
designs for *Elektra* that Craig did for the Italian actress Eleonora Duse. He
started working on these in 1905, the same time when he was in discussion
with Reinhardt. In general Craig's influence on the Reinhardt productions
was to be seen not only in the architectural sense of space but also, and
slightly surprisingly, in the way Reinhardt's Greek productions conceptualise the human form in that space, particularly in the famous chorus and
crowd scenes. Writing of Craig's attempted collaboration with Reinhardt,
L. M. Newman makes a similar claim:

> Nevertheless, some elements in Reinhardt's production may well derive specifi-
> cally from the Englishman – for instance, the outstretched arms of the crowd in
> *König Ödipus* come straight from a design for *The Masque of Hunger* reproduced
> in *Deutsche Kunst und Dekoration*, published in October 1905 when their mutual
> interest was at its peak. And the open stage of the *Theater in der Redoutensaal*,
> attributed to Copeau, actually sprang from Craig's model for the *St Matthew
> Passion*, which he had shown to the Frenchman in 1915.[34]

We can understand Craig's influence on the visual conception of the stage,
but on *acting*! However, this stylised sense of stage gesture, with its 'crystallising of emotions' that blends into a more general architectural sense of
theatricality, is also a hallmark of Craig's designs for the stage.
Unfortunately most of these designs never actually materialised on the
stage. Apart from his work with Stanislavsky on the Moscow *Hamlet*, Craig
was not able to work fruitfully with any director. Instead, through the pages
of *The Mask* and under the guise of numerous pseudonyms, Craig mounted
attacks on his contemporaries. Reinhardt, of course, became an obvious
target. He calls Reinhardt's company a 'firm' and castigates them for their
tightness with money. The main thrust of his claims was that he, Craig, had

'got there first'. 'What Craig dreams Reinhardt practises' says a 'reviewer' in *The Mask* and sets the record straight: 'Craig began by *doing* the thing in 1900 before anyone else, and damme if he isn't called a theorist', in the same stroke refuting the accusation that he never puts his ideas into practice.[35]

Despite his unpractical attitude, or perhaps because of it, and in spite of what might seem at first glance his rejection of actors in favour of marionettes, Craig's designs for the stage portray a deep interest in the presence of the human figure and its relationship to scenic space. The monumentality of his designs for Eleonora Duse and for Isadora Duncan is always underscored by the vitalism projected by the human form. It is a combination of elements that Reinhardt was able to experiment with more efficiently and successfully than Craig. Craig's vision of theatre, whether on paper, in discussion or in practice, had an undoubted impact on Reinhardt's productions. This vision, as Walton claims, is in part shaped by Craig's understanding of classical Greek drama. It is the same sense of theatricality that Craig brings to his collaboration with Yeats on *The Hour Glass*, where he designs sets, costumes and masks. Although there is no specifically 'Greek' aspect to this project, the blending of these stage elements and the sense of theatricality that results could be said to derive from Craig's new Hellenism.

Although Craig admired Murray's translations he may not have been as impressed with Murray's 'savage Greece'. His Hellenism was initially more of the classical, quasi-monumental strand. This was to be moderated later in his life through his encounters with Isadora Duncan,[36] and her explorations in dance. Isadora Duncan's Greece had more in common with the vitalist, primitivist strand of the Cambridge group and indeed she had plans to work with Murray. Her experiments in dance presented a vision of Hellenism that fused with her modernist notions of the body. Her actual performances in the ruins of ancient Greek theatres were seen as creating a physical and organic relationship with the past. It is this vitalism the permeates Craig's designs as well, where the human form is not overwhelmed by the monumentality of the set, but organically merges with it. Curiously, through this brand of Hellenism, influenced by his encounters with Duncan, Duse and the Cambridge group, Craig also addresses the problem of the human form. His designs for classical plays exhibit a sensitivity to and an awareness of the dynamics of the human form on the stage. Looking at these designs today one sees the tension between the monumentality of the set and the humanism of the actor. Yet these designs remained for the most part on paper; beyond the personal and biographical reasons, another reading could propose that this 'utopian vision' never reached the stage because it never successfully resolved this tension between the two Hellenisms. The monumentality of the Hellenism that inspired his total vision of theatre had to be confronted with the humanism implied in the very physicality of the actor's presence. Craig's designs for Duse and Duncan begin to explore such issues. However, the realisation of these designs would

The Mask
1 9 0 8

17 Edward Gordon Craig, *Isadora Duncan Dancing*. The Mask, Vol. 1, No. 6 (1908), p. 126b.

require an utterly modernist concept of acting, one that Craig was unable or unwilling to consider.[37]

For Pound and Yeats this modernist concept of acting would result from the encounters between their own 'new Hellenism' and the theatres of the Orient. Both offered models of 'grand theatres' of the past, and models for acting. The theatres of the Orient seemed to offer practical solutions to many of the issues explored by the primitive Hellenism of the Cambridge Ritualists. At the same time, the Noh, in particular, was aristocratic and philosophical enough to cater for the exclusive and sometimes totalising aesthetics of many modernists. In other words, the Oriental and Orientalist traditions in theatre could be read as reflecting both the monumental school of Hellenism *and* its modernist, primitivist counterpart. For Pound, it is this combination that proves useful when he attempts to translate Sophocles. He writes in his Preface to his *Women of Trachis*:

> The *Trachiniae* presents the highest peak of Greek sensibility registered in any of the plays that have come down to us, and is, at the same time, nearest the original form of the God-Dance.
>
> A version for KITANO KATUE, hoping he will use it on my dear old friend Michio Ito, or take it to the Minoru if they can be persuaded to add it to their repertoire.[38]

As his translation was first performed on radio, on the BBC's Third Programme, Pound did not get the opportunity to put his ideas into practice. Although this translation appears quite late (1954), the reference to the God-Dance echoes the terminology of the Cambridge Ritualists. In the same gesture he remembers his old friend, the dancer, Ito, who first inspired him and Yeats. For Pound, it is this combination of a ritualistic Hellenism, as seen in the figure of the God-Dance, with the conventions of stylised embodiment presented by the Japanese Noh that offers ways of approaching Greek tragedy. A modernist theatre aesthetic would combine both these sources in a manner that is clear, hard, concrete, and in all other ways imagistic.

Despite his initial irreverence ('I think, it would probably be easier to fake a play by Sophocles than a novel by Stendhal'), Pound had already engaged with Sophocles in his translation of *Elektra*. Once again this exercise proved to be an eclectic mixture of sources and references. It contains transliterated Greek, various forms of English (Black American, Scots, archaic English lyrics, Cockney); the stage directions again are Noh-like and demand the appropriate reverence; and it includes 'a wild Sioux injun war dance with tommy hawks'. No doubt the Sioux dance would provide the desired 'primitive' affect and prove the equivalent of the God-dance. The translation ends with Orestes saying, as he leads Aegisthus to his death,

> No, but you aren't dying for pleasure
> You've got to go thru with it ALL.
> It's a pity you can't all of you – die like this
> And as quickly, everyone like you
> It wd/save a lot of unpleasantness.
> Chorus (sings)
>   O SPERM ATREOS
>   Atreides, Atreides
> Come thru the dark,
> (speaks)
> my god, it's come with a rush
> (sings)
> Delivered, Delivered,
>   TEI NUN HORMEI TELEOOTHEN
> Swift end
>   So soon.[39]

This extraordinary translation acts as a fine example of Pound's new Hellenism. Faithful to his imagistic notion of poetry, it combines meaning, language and rhythm in very strong images, where an ' "Image" is that which presents an intellectual and emotional complex in an instant of time'.[40] Time, of course, is provided by the ritualist's notion of rhythm and not by the concept of linearity. In this instance it fuses with the rush (HORMEI) that gushes from the sperm of Atreus and wreaks its revenge. It is this wonderful blend of meaning and form, typically imagist, that marks his translation. As a result, the play ends in a dark, pessimistic, violent and vengeful tone. The image of Hellenism that Pound presents us with here is ritualistic, repetitive, virile, violent and death-driven, and his language enacts these qualities. It is these elements that Pound as a modern finds attractive, not the classical humanist or monumental ones. He explains:

> My pawing over the ancients and semi-ancients has been one struggle to find out what has been done, once for all, better than it can ever be done again, and to find out what remains for us to do, and plenty does remain, for if we still feel the same emotions as those which launched the thousand ships, it is quite certain that we come on these feelings differently, through different nuances, by different intellectual gradation. [...] ... yet a man feeling the divorce of life and his art may naturally try to resurrect a forgotten mode if he finds in that mode some leaven, or if he thinks he sees in it some element lacking in contemporary art which might unite art again to its sustenance, life.[41]

In a sense this is the most 'classical' of neo-classicisms. It claims that we share the same human substance *and* that we can regain that organic unity of art and life lost to the moderns. However, it does offer one significant variation: what it claims to reunite us with is the ritualistic, primitive, disruptive side of that Hellenism. Rather than the reconciled, identified, organic relationship to life, Pound's new Hellenism is all about promoting the inorganic, the distant, the savage and the strange. His encounter with Athenian tragedy offers him the same formal solutions it offered Yeats. Parallel to or even in place of Eliot's 'mythic method' (outlined in his assessment of Joyce's *Ulysses*),[42] the Cambridge Ritualists proposed a *dramatic method*, based on the *dromenon* and the *eniautos-daimon*. These notions proved very influential, particularly since they asserted the precedence of ritual over myth.

Pound's hailing of Ito as the ideal performer for his *Trachiniae* underlines the parallels that were drawn at the time between the *dromenon* of the Greeks and the ritualistic aspect of Noh drama. Yeats's *Plays for Dancers* can also be seen as influenced by this new Hellenism. Yeats had already used Craig's screens in *The Hour Glass*. These presented a non-representational way of conceptualising scenic space; they were indeed monumental but always exhibiting an interesting tension between the monument/screen and the human form. Yeats's use of stylised movement was inspired by the Noh, but it also fed into all the experiments with movement and dance going on at the time. Some of these, like Duncan's, had a distinct Hellenic quality. The use of masks, chorus, music, stylised gesture and the genre's structural relationship to philosophy, could all equally have derived from Athenian drama.

Hellenism, in its various guises, not only looks towards the Orient for parallels and counterparts, it also turns towards Alexandria. In Pound's initial categorisation of the types of Hellenism, Alexandria appears as a site of a Hellenism he finds disagreeable. For Pound, as his translations clearly show, the new Hellenism was to be hard, virile, clear and masculine. The Alexandrian, Hellenistic model that relies on diffusion, diaspora, influence is considered to de decadent and effeminate. The modernist poet who adopted Alexandria as her literary and nostalgic home was H.D. (Hilda Doolittle) who had a long association with Pound and whose whole career can be read as attempting to forge a modernist Hellenism that has Alexandria rather than Athens as its base and symbolic home. The attempt to revive a new Hellenism for the moderns posed a number of problems for H.D. In as much as this revival was based on patrilinear lineage and ideas of reason and progress it was seen as lacking. In turning towards Alexandria, H.D. was searching for alternative models of Hellenism. She quite consciously aligns herself with this alternative genealogy of Hellenism as Eileen Gregory writes in *H.D. and Hellenism*.[43] Like her contemporary, C. P. Cavafy, H.D. finds attractive those very elements of decadence and fusion that make Alexandria a 'corrupt' form of European Hellenism.

In this light the appeal of Euripides for H.D. makes good sense. Whereas Yeats, Pound and Eliot are concerned mainly with Aeschylus and Sophocles, H.D. turns to Euripides in her attempt to forge an aesthetic that is subversive politically and more experimental formally. H.D.'s long association with the works of Euripides spanned her whole career. Between 1912 and 1919 during the First World War she translated choruses from *Iphigeneia at Aulis* (1915) and *Hippolytus* (1919). During the late 1920s she wrote a long lyric poem, *Hippolytus Temorizes* (1927). She continued writing essays and translating plays (*Helen Ion, Bacchae, Hecuba*) throughout the 1920s and early 1930s. Between 1933 and 1934 – a period some scholars mark as a turning point in her life and work[44] – she engaged in psychoanalysis with Freud. Throughout this period H.D. continued her involvement with Euripides, which culminated in the composition of *Helen in Egypt* in the early 1950s. This is a long lyric poem that brings together and rewrites five Trojan plays of Euripides.

The kinds of Hellenism that H.D. engaged with bear striking parallels to the work of the Cambridge Ritualists and Jane Ellen Harrison in particular. As Eileen Gregory states, there are no direct contacts here, as with Virginia Woolf, but it would have been almost impossible for H.D. not to have been aware of Harrison's work, or not to have read her books. H.D. would have found the anthropological take on the origins of religion quite appropriate to her Alexandrian model. In addition, she shares with Harrison the desire to construct a matrilineal model of genealogy. Gregory writes, 'like Harrison, H.D. attempts to reassemble from its refractive facets in Greek cults the occluded image of the divine mother'.[45] And this attempt always bears with it the marks of nostalgia, a characteristic of the brand of Hellenism that Pound and Eliot had found sentimental, unreliable, feminising and verging on the pathological. For H.D., however, this nostalgia towards the Greeks presented a way of reviving the past for the purposes of the present.

Unlike Brecht, H.D. saw in the classics a possible cure for the ills of modernity and particularly the catastrophes of the First World War. 'My work is creative and reconstructive, war or no war, if I can get across the Greek spirit at its highest I am helping the world, and the future.'[46] In this sense, and especially in relation to war, the classics transpire as both the poison and the cure, as the ultimate *pharmakon*. For some, the Great War marks an indelible end, as the classics can no longer offer a remedy for the ills of the world; for others, and through the act of 'reconstruction', as H.D. calls it, the new Hellenism is proposed as the ultimate remedy. Significantly, in this latter case, the stress is placed on the term 'new'. The act of reconstruction itself is seen as partaking of a received classical heritage though one that is reconfigured according to the aesthetic and political demands of modernity. For H.D. this double-edged process pays homage to the classical tradition while also making it relevant for the project of modernity. Like her reworking of Helen it is both *'phantom and reality'.*[47]

The tension between reconstruction and subversion becomes particularly striking in the ways the European avant-garde confronts classical Hellenism. Although the main thrust of the approach is vehemently anti-classical, a gesture of defiance against an established tradition (in the manner of Duchamp's moustached Mona Lisa), it still springs from a complex and contradictory relationship to the models it tries to subvert. The Dadaist performance piece *Simply Classical! An Oresteia With a Happy Ending* by Walter Mehring with music by Friedrich Hollaender was written as a puppet play for a Dada Soirée at Max Reinhardt's cabaret in Berlin in 1919. It is typical of the Dadaist disdain and mockery of the classics while exhibiting profound knowledge of the workings of the plays and their mythological contexts. It is full of topical references, mainly to the war and its aftermath. It utilises a range of techniques that were to become stock – classical almost – within avant-garde performance.

The play is divided into three sections: (1) Agamemnon in the Bath; (2) The Dawn of Democracy; (3) The Classic Flight from Taxation. Agamemnon appears as the representative of the old guard 'commanding general in his best years'. Aegisthus and Clytemnestra appear as the bearers of democracy, not Orestes, who appears as an officer of an Attic Free Corps. Electra is 'of the salvation army'. Apollo is Woodrow (Wilson) Apollo, having an 'unmistakable similarity to President W ...', the text claims. In general all the characters allude to contemporary figures. The chorus is made up of newspapermen, representing various political affiliations. The path to democracy, which the original trilogy charts, is transposed onto the events surrounding the War and the founding of the Weimar Republic.

Aegisthus and Clytemnestra are standing in while his Royal Highness, Agamemnon, fights the war. The light from Troy that the night watchman sees in the original, announcing the victory of the Greeks, is here turned into a telephone. The all-embracing light that permeates the trilogy, which announces the end of barbarism and prefigures the dawn of democracy, is turned into an equally significant modernist emblem. Telephones are conspicuous in avant-garde drama. They allow for all sorts of comedic stage business to take place, while also underlining the function of the voice. They offer a way of dissociating voice on the stage from the body of the actor, apt for an aesthetic that so heavily relies on fragmentation. Its use in this play also acts to underline the connections between theories of light (Enlightenment) and theories of technology. The light of the original that signifies progress, democracy and humanism is here turned into a technological gadget. It is a gadget, however, that is at once ironic and auratic. The telephone in this play is still a 'new' object, containing all the promise and hope inspired by a new technology. It is this fusion of the auratic and the functional that underpins these props on the stage and does not allow us to simply read them as ironic or subversive. Here is how the return of Agamemnon from Troy is announced:

> (*The telephone at the column rings like crazy.*)
> CLYTEMNESTRA: The telephone, the telephone. I have an idea …
> AEGISTHUS: (*In a rage.*) Women always have ideas.
> THE TELEPHONE: (*In the most beautiful dark voice.*) Here is Agamemnon.
> CLYTEMNESTRA: Who? Wrong connection. This is …
> AEGISTHUS: (*runs around, pulling his hair.*)
> I am a moralist, an anti-militarist.
> I am against duels, I cannot stand seeing a fly in rage.
> I cannot look at a uniform or blood.
> That woman has seduced me and I am done for.
> CLYTEMNESTRA: Darling, where shall I hide you in a hurry?
> THE TELEPHONE:
> I am coming directly from the trenches
> And look forward to a solemn luncheon!
> CLYTEMNESTRA: (*Runs around.*) O, my nerves, I'm losing my mind.
> AEGISTHUS: (*Likewise.*)
> This damned telephone.
> Spoils my favourite position.
> And now I can start writing poetry again.[48]

Here the voice of Agamemnon is not simply mediated through the telephone, it/he *is* the telephone. This fusion of human and machine is something that avant-garde performers, especially the Futurists, were constantly experimenting with at the time. It is interesting to note how this fascination with technology is filtered through the classical legacy, as it is here, where the debates about technology are superimposed and read through the main concerns of the *Oresteia* about light, progress and democracy.

Simply Classical does not hesitate to poke fun at Reinhardt himself, who presumably hosted the event at his cabaret. Mehring and Hollaender would have been aware of Reinhardt's large-scale productions of Greek plays, famous for their crowd scenes:

> If only Aeschylus were to know
> With happiness he would overflow
> A bit of classicism in a modern way
> Redoubles the humour, he would say.
>
> [...]
>
> Go to Reinhardt when he curses,
> It is classic how he rehearses.
> Smoothly runs the Oresteia
> All with his machinery.[49]

This criticism echoes Craig's disputes with Reinhardt, according to which his staging of classical plays seems to be possible through the application of a huge production 'machine'. It is odd, however, coming from the Dadaists, who were far from technophobic. Indeed, the operative word here is 'machinery', which to the Dadaists is retrogressive. For them, this was a nineteenth-century use of 'machinery', that is, as a hidden means to an end. The end result, as in the Reinhardt Greek productions, seemed to cover up the process that created it. The 'machinery' helped to present a seamless result, whereas the use of technology for the Dadaists helped to fragment the creative process itself. The telephone does not simply convey the message; it is the message. It becomes a character in a way that was inconceivable even a generation earlier.

The Pythia section appears as a 'Filmic Interlude', Orestes is a 'Bolsheviste' and, as we've seen, there is a Woodrow Apollo 'always in Yankee clothing, [who] lives only in higher spheres'. Full of contemporary references and rooting for the modern, the play really only uses the *Oresteia* as a springboard to comment on its present time. At the same time, however, it does display an intimate knowledge of the dynamics of the original. Although it skips the gender politics altogether, omitting Athena from the trial scene, it reads the Aeschylus as basically a 'traditional' play about empire: one which needs to be turned inside out. However, this blasphemous reading of the play only interacts with it at the level of ideas, themes, ideology and politics. That is, it approaches the *Oresteia* as a body of knowledge, and not as a play with its own conventions of performance. This Dadaist version, with characteristic avant-garde flair and obsession with fragmentation, has little time for the idea of totality that emerges from reading classical drama as performance.

The same principle of the fragment, the ruin, can be said to fuel Brecht's attitude towards the classics. However, his aphoristic proclamation after the First World War, listing them amongst the fatalities, is somewhat modified after the Second World War and his return to Berlin after exile. His engagement with Sophocles' *Antigone* in particular acts as a fine example of his difficult but ultimately passionate and creative relationship with the Athenian model of tragedy. Significantly his adaptation of *Antigone*, while definitely rewriting the narrative, is *also* concerned with creating models of performance. He writes in the Foreword to the *Antigone-Model*:

> As it is not so much a new school of playwriting as a new way of performance being tried out on an old play, our new adaptation cannot be handed over in the usual way to theatres to do what they like with. An obligatory model production has been worked out, which can be grasped from a collection of photographs accompanied by explanatory instructions. […] The idea of making use of models is a clear challenge to the artists of a period that applauds nothing but what is 'original', 'incomparable', 'never been seen before', and demands what is 'unique'.[50]

The influence of his friend Walter Benjamin can clearly be felt here. It might also be partly responsible for Brecht's reappraisal of the ruin, the fragment, as something through which the past can be redeemed rather than simply laid to waste. His revaluation of the classics, particularly of Athenian drama after the Second World War, brings with it the melancholy nuances of a Benjaminian sensibility. The ruin is not mere rubble, or a vehicle for subversion and ridicule; it also becomes the locus of historical memory. The ruin as a template for a modern theatre, especially an epic post-war theatre, proves particularly demanding. Brecht writes:

> How can such a theatre be created? The difficulty about ruins is that the house has gone, but the site isn't there either. And the architects' plans, it seems, never get lost. This means that reconstruction brings back the old dens of iniquity and centres of disease. Fevered life claims to be particularly vital life; none steps as firmly as the consumptive who has lost all feeling in the soles of his feet. Yet the tricky thing about art is that however hopeless its affairs may seem, it has to conduct them with complete ease.
>
> Thus it may not be easy to create progressive art in the period of reconstruction. And this should be a challenge.[51]

This extraordinary scheme that links the past with the future through the ruin sounds more like Artaud than Brecht. The architects' 'plans' that survive from a classical tradition appear to surface as 'centres of disease' that produce a 'fevered life'. Like Artaud's plague, this poison may also contain within it the possibility of a cure. However, the 'tricky thing' for Brecht is to maintain the distance, the strangeness, that at once acknowledges the 'fevered' yet 'vital' life but can formally channel it. And it is precisely this challenge that his version of *Antigone* addresses; it is an exercise in form, as some critics acknowledge, but it is a quest for an appropriate form that would contain a 'fevered life' with 'complete ease'. The reference to a 'progressive art' can only refer to the debates about realism and the accusations of 'formalism' aimed at Brecht. In effect, it is a response to Adorno's claim of the impossibility of poetry after Auschwitz. However, in the same breath, and writing against Brecht, Adorno continues that 'it is now virtually in art alone that suffering can still find its own voice, consolation, without immediately being destroyed by it'.[52] In many ways, it is this formal challenge that *Antigone* is addressing. It is part of Brecht's search for an aesthetic that would be appropriate for a post-war, post-fascist Europe. This reconstructive project also contains within it Brecht's particular version of Hellenism.

The original in this case is Friedrich Hölderlin's 1803 version, on which Brecht relies very heavily. Significantly, Brecht seems to skip a generation of German Hellenism to go back to Hölderlin, whose translations were ridiculed when published and had a reputation for being particularly obscure. Of course, Brecht found this difficulty attractive as it compounded his desired effect of estrangement. On his return to Berlin, his encounter with Hölderlin also offered a type of German classicism, indeed Hellenism that had not been tainted by Nazism. In returning to Hölderlin he was performing two acts of recuperation, one for Germany and the other for the whole of Europe (through ancient Greece). At the same time he was working on collecting his theoretical writings for the theatre in the *Short Organum for the Theatre*. 'One must imagine him working simultaneously on these projects,' as the editors of Volume 8 of Brecht's *Collected Plays* suggest.[53] This *Antigone* offers a platform for Brecht to reassess the role of art in the post-war era *and* to carve out a role for himself as a 'progressive', committed artist of the era. And the event of staging this production helped to create what was to become the hallmark of the Brechtian project: the Model. With designs by Caspar Neher and photographs by Ruth Berlau, he produces the *Antigone-Model*, which in many ways can be read as a speculative proposition for the engaged work of art. The fact that he chooses to do this through a German Romantic version of an Athenian tragedy is highly suggestive.

In reworking Hölderlin's translation, Brecht himself could be seen as elaborating on a certain German Romantic sensibility that saw in Sophocles not the lyrical, measured poet of Athenian democracy but the Oriental, wild Dionysian version of the same project. Writing in the historical context of a new order, which would be republican and vital, he was all the more interested in making his adaptations relevant to his historical moment. David Constantine, Hölderlin's and Brecht's translator, writes:

That is the chief interpretative tendency in Hölderlin translations: to bring the ancient texts home in such a fashion that they will quicken hearts and minds in the torpid present. In translating like that, serving, as he thought, the present needs of his own countrymen, Hölderlin put himself ever more at risk. Always choosing the more violent word, so that the texts are stitched through with the vocabulary of excess, of madness, rage, he was also voicing those forces in his own psychology, which very soon would carry him over the edge.[54]

This fusion of the personal and the political makes Hölderlin a very intuitive reader of the classics for Brecht. The madness, violence and rage that permeate Hölderlin's translation is, in a way, historicised (or 'rationalised' as Brecht claims) and becomes part of the political fibre of the play. Rather than reading the story in the familiar Hegelian terms[55] of the individual against the law of the state, Brecht, following Hölderlin's lead, sees *Antigone* as a tale of destruction. He writes:

In *Antigone* the violence is explained by inadequacy. The war against Argos derives from mismanagement in Thebes. Those who have been robbed have to look to robbery themselves. The undertaking exceeds the strength available. Violence splits the forces instead of welding them together; basic humanity, under too much pressure, explodes, scattering everything with it into destruction.[56]

Admittedly Brecht makes major changes and additions: he exaggerates the role of Haemon's brother Megareus (offstage), and disposes of the mother, Eurydice, altogether; the war with Argos gets a 'realistic' sheen and is fought over mineral wealth; Creon has total and absolute power and no rightful claim whatsoever. However, despite these attempts at 'rationalisation', which, some critics contend fail anyway, I would argue that the text's main concern is with charting the 'scattering of destruction' mentioned above. This fascination with catastrophe that attracts Brecht to Hölderlin in the first place is, I believe, the main structuring force of the adaptation. In a sense, the whole project is about finding a form to accommodate historical catastrophe.

The role of Antigone is radically rewritten to blend with this aesthetic. Rather than presenting the moral and heroic character (usually female as suited Brecht's own formula) as the antidote to the extreme and total power of Creon, she appears to be rather more implicated in the violence she supposedly opposes. 'She ate bread baked in servitude, she sat comfortably in the shade of the strongholds of oppression. Only when the violence dealt out by the house of Oedipus rebounded on that house did she awake.'[57] So, this 'rationalisation' does not involve a transposition of the conflict into the present in terms of right and wrong, moral and immoral, state and natural law, man and woman, and all the usual binaries that the play is read as enacting. Rather, this reading of Antigone presents her as inextricably linked to the power structures she is trying to resist. For Brecht, the interest in the play lies not so much in how one system of values can triumph over the other as in how both systems might be implicated in the violence of war. It also helps excavate the tensions in the original play between law and lawlessness, between civilisation and barbarism. Hence the emphasis placed in his production on the aesthetic of barbarism:

> In modelling the set Cas [Caspar Neher] and I stumble on an ideological element of the first order. Should we place the barbaric totem poles with the horses' skulls at the back between the actors' benches, thus indicating the barbaric location of the old poem which the actors leave in order to act (the de-totemised version)? We decide to place the acting among the totem poles, since we are still living in the state of totemic class war. [...] *Antigone* in its entirety belongs with the barbaric horses' skulls.[58]

His own *Antigone*, however, firmly located between the old and the new, among the totem poles, was to underline the structural, dialectical relationship between the two. Like Hölderlin before him, Brecht sees in the 'Greeks' not the taming, civilising *gestus* that leads to progress and civilisation but the barbarism that results from empire and war. Or rather he sees them both bound together, implicated in each other's narratives, like Creon and Antigone. Rather than a paean to humanism, his *Antigone* is about the violence that it potentially engenders. Sophocles' famous 'Ode to Man', rather than charting man's progress, is turned into a catalogue of catastrophes framed by the word 'monstrous' at the start and the end of the ode. This is Hölderlin's translation, which Brecht maintains, of the term *deinon* in Sophocles. It is a notorious term that has inspired much philosophical reflection,[59] which roughly translates as awesome, wondrous, extremely able, but also as strange, other and monstrous. It is significant that Brecht, following Hölderlin, highlights this bleaker aspect of the humanism that the ode celebrates. By the end of the ode the subject of this humanism that Brecht, quoting Hölderlin, explores becomes a stranger to himself:

ELDERS:
Monstrous, a lot. But nothing
More monstrous than man.

[...]

A measure is set.
For when he wants for an enemy
He rises up as his own. Like the bull's
He bows the neck of his fellowmen but these fellowmen
Rip out his guts. When he steps forth
He treads on his own kind, hard. By himself alone
His belly will never be filled but he builds a wall
Around what he owns and the wall
Must be torn down.
The roof
Opened to the rain. Humanity
Weighs with him not a jot. Monstrous thereby
He becomes to himself.[60]

This is a particularly melancholy reading of the 'Ode to Man': an ode that has been read as charting the development of man's mastery over nature, his ascent to reason, the development of the state and democracy. The reworking is so extreme that Brecht himself is forced to provide an explanation in his 1951 'Notes on the Adaptation'. (*'First Chorus*: Human beings, monstrously great when they subjugate Nature, become great monsters when they subjugate their fellow men'.)[61]

This reading of *deinon* as both wondrous and monstrous punctuates the whole adaptation. It informs Brecht's decision to place the horse skulls amongst the actors and not behind them. In this way, rather than gesturing towards prehistorical ritual, these horse skulls become the emblems of historical violence. Although the adaptation uses ritual and although the discourse in the *Antigone-Model* is full of ritualised and medicalised language (fevered life, the consumptive), this ritual is never really conceptualised within a primitivist framework. The violence in the text and on the stage is not a reference to any anthropological, prehistorical ritual that stands in for humanism in crisis. For Brecht, as he clearly states in the *Model*, his adaptation of *Antigone* is a study of state power in crisis that 'only becomes aware of its own laws of motion in a catastrophe'.[62] The reading of humanism proposed through this interpretation of *deinon* allows for both the wonder and the catastrophe to surface. Although it uses ritual, this is never seen as prehistorical but rather as the bearer of historical catastrophe. The primitive, the barbarian is not something that forms part of a humanist evolutionary trajectory. For Brecht, as was the case for Walter Benjamin, it has always run parallel to the movement for progress, light, reason and civilisation and the two cannot be structurally separated. Hence the decision to place the actors amongst the skulls.

Brecht was working on *Antigone* and the *Antigone-Model* while was he was compiling what was to become the *Short Organum for the Theatre* in the late 1940s after his return to East Berlin. It is fascinating to read these two projects in tandem. His manifesto for a new theatre, after the war and after fascism, is mirrored in the most unlikely of sources, a classical Athenian play. True, he views it as a ruin, as a fragment from a grand tradition. Yet it is one that contains for him the possibility of redemption but also, and crucially, the possibility of critique. This reading of *Antigone* through Hölderlin proposes a version of tragedy that is very close to Epic Theatre. Yet at first sight this appears as slightly out of kilter for a theorist so closely associated with the anti-Aristotelian movement in the twentieth century, especially since it could be argued from his *Poetics* that Sophocles was Aristotle's favourite dramatist.

Brecht's vehement attacks on the Aristotelian model of theatre mainly concern modes of reception (i.e. the history of *catharsis*) rather than theatrical production and performance. As he states, 'Stylistically speaking, there is nothing all that new about the epic theatre.'[63] His somewhat schematic readings of Aristotle (usually conflating it with Aristotelianism)[64] and the fevered, manifesto-style of much of his writings have earned him a dubious position in contemporary critical theory, particularly regarding the classics. However, when Brecht specifically describes the modern, Epic Theatre, he is mainly writing against Wagner and the idea of the *Gesamtkunstwerk*. Against the idea of synthesis he underlines the importance of fragmentation:

> So long as the expression 'Gesamtkunstwerk' (or 'integrated work of art') means that the integration is a muddle, so long as the arts are supposed to be 'fused' together, the various elements will all be equally degraded, and each will act as a mere 'feed' to the rest. The process of fusion extends to the spectator, who gets thrown into the melting pot too and becomes a passive (suffering) part of the total work of art. Witchcraft of this sort must of course be fought against. Whatever is intended to produce hypnosis, is likely to induce sordid intoxication, or creates fog, has got to be given up.[65]

It is the idea of totality, itself a particular interpretation of the Athenian model, that Brecht finds problematic. In a discourse that refers to cannibalism, ritual and intoxication, the spectator for this kind of theatre becomes the scapegoat. This attack on the Wagnerian view of totality in the 1930s is also aimed at the Hellenism it reconfigures. And it follows Brecht's announcement of the 'death' of the classics after the First World War. However, by the end of the 1940s his approach to *Antigone* proposes another type of Hellenism. This one relies on the fragment, the ruin rather than on totality. This fragmented Hellenism (via Hölderlin, but also via the two world wars), seen as both the poison and the cure, becomes for Brecht a constituent element of his Epic Theatre. What remains from this encounter – the *Antigone-Model* – can itself be read as such a fragment. More so than the textual reworking – which heavily relies on Hölderlin – the Model with its designs and chiefly its photographs acts as a gestural and speculative paradigm of the relationship to theatre of the ancients *and* as a somewhat utopian proposition for the theatre of the moderns.

The encounter with Hellenism proves a formidable one for modernist schools of performance. Whether sacred, totalising or critical, the relationship

18   Brecht-Neher, *Antigone-Model 1948*, photos Ruth Berlau

19   Brecht-Neher, *Antigone-Model 1948*, photos Ruth Berlau

to the Athenian model of drama enables modernist theatremakers to articulate their own ideas and formulate experimental stage practices. As totem, monument or rubble, the Athenian stage constantly resurfaces on the modernist stage. It is there as part of the battle between the moderns and the ancients, one of the first debates to highlight the significance of historicity in matters of aesthetic form. This new Hellenism, reconfigured through the work of scholars such as the Cambridge Ritualists, and through the

20   Brecht-Neher, *Antigone-Model 1948*, photos Ruth Berlau

21   Brecht-Neher, *Antigone-Model 1948*, photos Ruth Berlau

experience of two world wars, proposes a relationship between past and present that is embodied, situated and historical. This proves particularly pertinent for the heated discussions at the time on form and content, aesthetics and politics, commitment and autonomy. Significantly, in all these debates modernist performance features as a key paradigm.

7

'The Revolution said to the theatre ...': Performance and Engagement

The Revolution said to the theatre:

'Theatre I need you. I need you, but not so that I, the Revolution can relax in comfortable seats in a beautiful hall and enjoy a show after all the hard work and battles ... I need you as a helper, as a search light, as an advisor. I want to see my friends and enemies on your stage. I want also to study them through your methods.'

(A.V. Lunacharsky, 1938)[1]

The tension between innovation and tradition is recast dramatically in the debates about engagement and autonomy. The seventeenth-century *Querelle des anciens et des modernes*, which probably for the first time read formal matters in conjunction with issues of historicity, is restaged within the context of modernity. The debates within Modernism and the avant-garde that raise the issue of the political in the theatre all rely on an assortment of readings of a 'classical tradition'. The conspicuous presence of performance in all these discussions further stresses this dynamic. The early debates on expressionism and realism voiced mainly by Bloch and Lukács, the 1930s discussions elaborated on by Adorno and Benjamin[2] and the more recent approaches[3] all privilege the notion of performance in the exemplification and explication of their argument. The manifesto, so beloved a format of the period, can also be seen to highlight – indeed embody – this performative dimension of the avant-garde.

The ability of theatre not only to represent, reflect or abstract reality while standing apart from it, but also to *stand in* as a model of society, now receives its most radical reworking since the Athenian model proposed by the Greeks. Theatre is seen as the civic space that not only partakes in but also, crucially, provides the conceptual and practical tools for 'world-building'. Not since the 'golden moment' of Periclean democracy had such an all-encompassing mission been assigned to the theatre; and it is this 'golden moment' that is constantly revisited in the various new Hellenisms of the period. The work of Brecht can be seen as addressing the fundamental premises of this Athenian model of the fusion of art and politics. In this context, it is no coincidence that the work of Brecht features prominently in all the theoretical debates of the period (and in subsequent contemporary ones) on the politicisation of art. Whether as the modernist exemplar *par excellence* of the successful fusion of art and politics or as the failed outcome of such an attempt, the almost total identification of the modernist artefact with a theatrical project needs highlighting. As in Aristotle's *Poetics*, against which much of Brecht's work is addressed, 'art' and the aesthetic/poetic really stand in for the *dramatic*. It is an interesting conflation, one which modernist performance constantly revisits, revitalising this 'world-building', almost foundational aspect of theatre.

This performative imperative is, I believe, crucial to our understanding of these debates. The collective, civic dimension of performance together with its institutional dimension make it particularly attractive for any modernist project that is concerned with reconfiguring the relationships between the political and the aesthetic. The situated, embodied experience of performance also offers ways of renegotiating the individual and the collective, while looking towards new definitions of authorship. The stage itself becomes a utopian space, which might become the site of fusion of the great disjunctions experienced by the advent of modernity. Based as it is on various forms of labour, both aesthetic and non-aesthetic, it is seen as the appropriate *locus* of the healing of the great divisions between manual and intellectual labour, high and low art, and might finally reconcile theatre with the world at large. Such reconciliation, however, can no longer be achieved by any form of 'organic art'. Performance, with its emphasis on bodily experience and collective reception, offers the possibility of such reconciliation through fragmentation rather than identification and wholeness.

This new 'wholeness' is partly achieved through the 'integration of art and life'. This principle seems central both in theories of the avant-garde and in the ways the avant-garde presents itself. From Walter Benjamin's early formulations of his 'aestheticisation thesis' (1936) to Peter Bürger's now classic recuperation of the avant-garde within the radical politics of the late 1960s and Boris Groys'[4] more recent critical reinterpretation, the principle of the separability of life and art is highly contested and always politically charged. All accounts stress the difference between this avant-garde immersion of art in 'the praxis of life' and the previous century's aestheticist concept of *l'art pour l'art*. 'What distinguishes them from the latter [*l'art pour l'art*] is the attempt to organise a new life from the basis in art',[5] states Bürger. Günter Berghaus, in the most recent and comprehensive study of the historical avant-garde to date, stresses that this conflation of art and life also (and somewhat paradoxically) relies on the principle of autonomy. He writes:

> The avant-garde concept of autonomy: artists aimed at establishing a critical distance to social determinism and to the affirmative role of art in capitalist society. They offered a critique of the ideology of bourgeois society and demonstrated an awareness of the institutionalised conditions of artistic production. The avant-garde anticipated a society in which the instrumental rationality of the capitalist system would be eradicated. Art served as a model for a liberated future and anticipated a non-alienated existence to be accomplished through creative art/life praxis.[6]

As Berghaus stresses, this autonomy – creating a utopian space outside the workings of capitalism – also fed into 'its [capitalism's] constant drive to renew and advance itself',[7] and in many ways to the subsequent institutionalisation and canonisation of the historical avant-garde. More emphatically, Boris Groys believes that this 'aestheticisation' thesis that confuses the categories of the aesthetic and the political, rather than being a critical or emancipatory project leads directly to totalitarianism, and in the case of the Russian avant-garde this led directly to socialist realism. Although this seems rather a damning account of the history of the Russian avant-garde, it does raise the problems associated with the 'aestheticisation' thesis. In its extreme rendition the loss of this separation allows it be completely appropriated by state power and turned into propaganda. Although this may appear oxymoronic for an aesthetic that initiates a fractured and fragmented reconciliation to the world, nevertheless, as Groys shows in his *The Total Art of Stalinism*, the total integration of the avant-garde work may lead to its total appropriation. The political efficacy of this *gestus*, from nineteenth-century aestheticism to twentieth-century Nazi and Stalinist propaganda, is still contested and will mark most schools of performance within the avant-garde.

There is a sense in which the conspicuous presence of performance in this context can further inflect and refine these debates. It is characteristic of modernist performance-pieces that they set up a relationship between performer and audience that does not so much reflect reality as reconstitute it anew, as if it were a work of art. This kind of artistic practice demands a new relationship to the world not only in terms of content (indeed in some instances the politicisation of content becomes taboo), but mainly in formal terms. These terms are in many ways determined by the practices of performance. The 'total' involvement of the artist, body and soul, required an equally radical reimmersion of that artist in society. So radical was this that many avant-garde artists ended up victims of the very reality they were trying to reconstruct.

To speak of the 'failure' of the avant-garde seems to be endemic to most theoretical approaches to its demise. These also almost invariably end up 'blaming' the avant-garde artists themselves for these failures, since, the argument runs, an engaged avant-garde puts itself *ipso facto* into an impossible position. From the initial attacks by Lukács and Adorno to the more recent ones by Groys, it seems that the avant-garde is judged according to the inadequacies of a world it failed to reconstruct. This issue of 'failure' casts a shadow over every discussion of the avant-garde, so much so that it might be said to form part of its aesthetic. The fascination with total destruction permeates every aspect of the avant-garde artwork. More than a disgusted gesture of defiance, this aesthetics of catastrophe becomes a cognitive category as well, explicating Adorno's belief that 'art is the negative knowledge of the actual world'.[8] Catastrophe, however, also conjures up images of apocalypse,[9] underlining the force of a metaphysical strand in the avant-garde. This metaphysical current sometimes gets subsumed under the categories of political commitment and engagement. It is fundamental, however, to the thematic and formal experiments of the avant-garde.

The remainder of this chapter will focus on a series of performance events in an attempt to tease out some of these concerns. Some of these, like the Italian Futurist *serate* and 'First Dada International Fair' or the Soviet Blue Blouse movement, have been firmly located by historians and critics within the avant-garde. Others, like the Federal Theatre Project (FTP) in the USA, are not usually read within this context, but will hopefully provide useful insight into the complex relationships between the avant-garde and state power. The FTP case also acts as a bridge between the concerns of the historical, European avant-garde and those of the avant-garde groups of the USA, foreshadowing the fate of the whole project in the post-Second World War period.

The Futurist *Serate*

With the publication of the *Foundation and Manifesto of Futurism* on 20 February 1909, Futurism was blasted onto the European scene and its charismatic front man F. T. Marinetti proposed his own version of the fusion of art and life. As that early manifesto clearly states, the modernist overhaul of artistic media demanded an equally revolutionary stance towards Italian bourgeois society. Marinetti himself had already had a considerable political education through his encounters with anarchism and communism and to these he added his fascination with technology, violence and war, making his Futurist movement nothing less than a revolutionary attack on Italian culture and society. His early play *The Electric Puppets* (January 1909) had caused a stir in Turin where it premiered and encompassed many traits that would later form the hallmarks of Futurist performance: the biting critique of the bourgeoisie, a fascination with technology and puppets and an underlying misogyne. Futurism was to be virile, vital and male, a cathartic force that was to purge Italy and subsequently the whole of Europe from decadence, feminisation and corruption. Also, it underlined the strong attachment that these early Futurist pieces had to the written word. Like Jarry, Marinetti's early work engages with the classical traditions of European theatre, albeit in a blasphemous and subversive manner. And like Jarry, he too writes his 'Ubu-play', *Le Roi Bombance*, also produced at the Théâtre de l'Oeuvre and directed by Lugné-Poë (3 April 1909) with an equally scandalous reception.

However, it was the establishment of a series of performance events, the *serate*, that was to combine the Futurist fervour for revolutionary action with their equal investment in formal experimentation. These combined lectures, poetry, painting and music in what, for Günter Berghaus, proposed a new form of Performance Art, encompassing Marinetti's ideal of 'Art as Action'. Berghaus writes:

> The *serate* were a weapon in the political and artistic fight for a total renewal of Italian public life. They were an all-round attack on the cult of the past and the social forces that sustained it. Not only did they serve to glorify war and revolution, they *were* an act of insurrection, 'like the throwing of a well-primed grenade over the heads of our contemporaries'. But they were also a medium of artistic expression, and it was in this combination of art and politics that the anarchist tradition of 'generative violence' found its concrete application. The Futurist *serata* was a vehicle through which art and life could be joined together into a compact union.[10]

The 'scandalous' impact of these events was in a sense preinscribed and provoked by Marinetti himself and used as a propaganda tool for the Futurist movement. The fusion of art and politics proposed was to be achieved through this 'generative violence'. However, as far as their actual 'participation in the political life of the country was concerned, the erection of a Fascist State prevented them from fulfilling their sociopolitical program of action',[11] as Berghaus clearly states. He also draws parallels between their project and that of the Russian avant-garde, where again the clash between the utopian politics of the Constructivists and the very real politics of the Soviet state had dire consequences. Once again the 'aestheticisation thesis' is severely tested when it is applied to state power.

Walter Benjamin, writing later and in the context of the rise of fascism, returns to the Italian Futurists in his crucial essay 'The Work of Art in the Age of Mechanical Reproduction' (1936).[12] For him this glorification of war and violence isn't simply a heightened gesture of defiance against bourgeois society, but both results in and helps to construct a specifically fascist aesthetic, where 'Fascism is the introduction of aesthetics into political life'.[13] Indeed, this spectacularisation of political life is something that the later fascist state of Italy will heavily draw on in disseminating its propaganda and in the interpolation of its citizens,[14] sometimes by adapting experimentation introduced by the Futurists (in a move mirrored by the Soviet state's appropriation of its avant-garde). Benjamin then proceeds to differentiate between this form of aestheticisation of politics (which he considers to be fascist) and that of communism, which responds by 'politicising art'. Are the two really so different, however? Boris Groys does not seem to think so, and in his assessment of the Russian/Soviet avant-garde it is this very identification of art and life, politics and art that allows him to read the Russian avant-garde as a precursor to the totalising aesthetics of Socialist Realism. In both cases it seems that reading the Italian Futurists and the Russian Constructivists (for whom Marinetti and his followers were an inspiration) as 'failed' attempts at the great modernist project of aestheticising politics, overlooks their radical potential, their formal innovation, and co-opts them as instrumental for a *realpolitik*, sometimes overlooking the fact that many of them fell victims to the political systems that they are seen to propagate.

The early Futurist *serate* broke all the rules about what was considered a theatrical event. They proposed new relationships between the stage and the audience and amongst aesthetic media. They were shocking and scandalous, where the idea of 'shock' is itself aestheticised, part of the theatrical event, and often advertised and preplanned by Marinetti himself. However, as Berghaus claims, Marinetti, at this early stage 'tended to adhere to a literary conception of theatre';[15] the word was still the main structuring discourse in these events. This was to change significantly with the rise of the painter Giacomo Balla in the Futurist movement. This, for Berghaus, radicalised Marinetti's concept of theatre and introduced the concept of 'art performances'. These brought together the dynamism of Futurism and a spatial/material (not necessarily linguistic) concept of art. Balla and Depero's manifesto *Futurist Reconstruction of the Universe*[16] went even further in its aspirations to transform life into a work of art. With its proposition of 'Dynamic Plastic Complexes' it offered ways of such integration through abstract 'force-lines', dramatic/kinetic sculptures that at once exerted an atmosphere of almost mystical aura *and* nodded towards the Futurist fascination with technology. Significantly, this new development in Futurism also shifted the performance event outside any recognisable 'theatrical space' and into the spaces of fine art galleries, stressing the crucial roles played by the visual and plastic arts at both this early stage and in the later developments of the avant-garde. The Dadaists were to continue this exploration of new performance spaces, in their attempted integration of artistic media into a totality that aimed to recreate the work of art, the artists and life itself.

'First International Dada Fair'

Two rooms on the ground floor of a five-storey apartment building in Berlin provided the venue of the 'First International Dada Fair' from 1 July to 25 August 1920. There had been previous Dada events and smaller exhibitions; most famously the Cabaret Voltaire in Zürich under the mesmerising Tristan Tzara had started to create a tradition of performance events that combined text, dramatic and visual art in a scandalous and provocative manner. The Berlin event was one of the first to proclaim its internationalist character, one that could in the same breath celebrate fascinations with Americana *and* communism. It proved to be the main forum that brought together the Dadaists and the Soviet constructivists. Amongst the artists who took part were the influential satirical artist George Grosz (Marshal), the photomontagist John Heartfield (Dadamechanic) and the poet Raoul Hausmann (Dadasoph). The presence of Hans Arp from Zürich, Francis Picabia from Paris, Walter Serner from Genoa and Ben Hecht from Chicago (amongst others) increased the international dimension. Indeed it was a formidable line-up, helping to form one of the almost mythical avant-garde epiphanies that have fuelled both artistic and critical imaginations.[17]

A crucial factor is the reliance on performance to structure and present the event. In her documentation of Berlin Dada, Hanne Bergius makes a general claim about the 'nature' of Dada:

> The fundamental ideas and attitudes of the Dada movement were theatrical and performative; they were purposeful, playful productions that engineered

effects. Relating negatively to stage and audience, the artist nevertheless needed spectators, whom he despised, in order to present the Dadaist spirit of negation and revolt, of shock and scandals. He transformed his stagings into poetical activity, detonating the traditional dramatic unities of place, time and action.[18]

These unities had been safely dissolved and the International Fair, with the nod towards the market in its very title, was forging a new aesthetic where these elements would now be read in terms of the everyday, the material (preferably used and discarded) and the spontaneous. The two rooms were packed with over seventy works of art, all of which experimented with collage, montage, photomontage and typography, culminating in an aesthetic we today would identify as performance art, happening, installation, or any combination of those categories. There was an emphasis on the presence of the artists, as in Heartfield's self-photo-portrait screaming, 'Some day photography will supersede and replace all of painting' (1920). Many of George Grosz's paintings depicting Germany in the aftermath of the First World War appeared at this fair (*Germany, a Winter's Tale* (1917); *Germania Shirtless* (1919)). The Russian Constructivists were heavily referenced, with particular homage paid to Vladimir Tatlin, whose *Monument to the Third International of the Communist Party of the Soviet Union* – the unfinished spiralling tower – was presented as an example of the utopian unfinished project of socialism. Its combination of apocalyptic vision and constructivist technique made it particularly attractive to the Dadaists, though interestingly enough, Tatlin's tower is read by the Dadaists (and by Grosz in particular) not as a monument of reconstruction and creation, but as a ruin, as a spiralling heap of fragments. This interface between the Dadaists and the Constructivists was to prove crucial, making Berlin Dada, as Hanne Bergius claims, open to the 'double draft', blowing from the USA and the Soviet Union.

A central piece of the Fair was *The Great Plasto-Dio-Dada-Drama* by Johannes Baader (Super-Dada, President of the Earth and the Globe, Chair of the Last Judgment), subtitled *Germany's Greatness and Decline at the Hands of Schoolmaster Hagendorf, or the Fantastic Life Story of the Superdada* (1920). This was an installation that dominated the second room. It was appropriately ambitious and aimed to encapsulate the spirit, but mostly the material, of Dada. Termed by some art historians as 'one of the great assemblages in art history', it combines all the Dadaists' techniques of montage, collage and fragmentation into a great Dadaist monument. Johannes Baader, who was also an architect, created an artwork where the monumental was replaced by the everyday and the theatrical. It gathers together materials from Baader's life, preferably used objects (tickets, programmes, pieces of metallic rubble, wires, a male dummy, and so on), which are arranged over four floors: 'The Steps of the Overman', 'The Preparation of the Superdada', 'The World War' and 'World Revolution'. The ascent follows the initiation of the Superdada and his final propelling into the ether, where his message will be broadcast 'by radio'. In a mixture of the metaphysical and the political, theosophy and communism, Baader's *Dada-Drama* rewrites the total work of art as the total work of destruction.[19] As a constructivist work of destruction, however, it enacts rather than portrays the apocalypse it thematises. It is dynamic, hopeful even and, importantly, it relies on the presence of an audience. Although it is an assemblage rather than a 'drama', it invites, indeed requires, audience participation. This use of architectural space and the human figure points towards Kurt Schwitters' *Merzbaus*, the first of which he began in 1923 (making the last in 1948, in, of all places, the English Lake District).[20] According to the classical tradition, architecture as either paradigm or metaphor is supposed to provide order and linearity, ideally within an overall humanism that accords the human figure centrality. Here, it is used as the motor of destruction; the individual can either be turned into one of the raw materials of this performative architecture, or, at the other extreme, can become its main agent, a prophet, a dictator, the Superdada. Hanne Bergius writes:

> Here the Superdada buries his past as architect and master builder, so as to share in the beginning of a new epoch by way of an intensification of life – turned against himself. For him, the 'moments of destruction' and 'dissolution' are 'the preconditions for the formation of a completely new age, which will grow out of the clear, science-based consciousness of the unutterable greatness and force, which every single human being represents in reality'.[21]

Accordingly every single human being can become a Superdada in a scheme of things that dissolves the distinctions between aesthetic and non-aesthetic activity. Pushing this thinking to its logical if extreme conclusion, the avant-garde claims (as this Dada drama does) that the only thing separating art from everyday activity is its *institutional* dimension; and this institutional life of art and the artist (according to the Dadaists) is always determined historically and politically. For some critics, like Peter Bürger, therein lies the main contribution of the avant-garde: its challenge to the very institution of art. He writes:

> The European avant-garde movements can be defined as an attack on the status of art in bourgeois society. What is negated is not an earlier form of art (a style) but art as an institution that is unassociated with the life praxis of men. When the avant-gardists demand that art become practical once again, they do not mean

that the contents of art should be socially significant. The demand is not raised at the level of contents of individual works. Rather it directs itself to the way art functions in society, a process that does as much to determine the effect that works have as does the particular content.[22]

This attack, Bürger believes, possibly constitutes the truly original *gestus* of the avant-garde. Although it is not the first time newness and innovation in aesthetic movements has been called upon as a way of rewriting the past and creating new forms, the historical avant-garde is possibly the first instance in the European tradition where art and artists want to negate themselves and their creations. This is much more than the continuation of an ancient quarrel; it challenges the very existence of art by demolishing the historical institutions that have helped to create it. The Dadaists' attacks on the museum, the academy, the gallery and on the cult of the artist himself, are not merely melodramatic gestures of disgust (a slap in the face of public taste), they are acts of catastrophe and self-annihilation. Herein also lies, according to some critics (such as Groys), one of its main problems: the essentially undialectical nature of this attack. Such radical polarisation, apocalyptic and total as it presents itself, is in danger, the analysis claims, of reproducing the very structures it is trying to destroy. Hence the Superdada can transform from everyman to prophet, to dictator, to revolutionary, with the term 'artist' tagged on.

This negativity towards the institution of art is itself somewhat historically grounded and not identical in the various tumultuous lives of the historical avant-garde. The relationship between the Russian avant-garde and institutional power changes drastically when members of the artistic avant-garde are given political positions, and are 'permitted' to shape policy. The Dadaists involved in the 'First International Dada Fair' also helped to stage the 'First International Dada Trial', when they were officially charged and called upon to explain themselves and their work. The trial itself shows how seriously the Dadaists were taken *and* provides them with yet another forum to stage their Dada drama.

The trial was organised by the Ministry of the German Military. On 20 April 1921 Baader, Grosz, Herzfelde, Schlichter and Otto Burchard (the gallery owner) had to appear before the First Criminal Division of District Court II, Berlin. They were accused of severe defamation of the Reichsheer army. Rather than defend their actions by denying the power of art, the Dadaists' lawyers based their defence on the very separateness of art that the Dadaists themselves were trying to dissolve. The main thrust of their defence was based on the very conventional generic categories of irony and satire, which they claimed, in this instance, were directed against 'the excesses of militarism' in general and were not a specific attack on Germany. This discourse in many ways undid what the Dadaists were trying to achieve. However, it probably needs to be balanced against the behaviour of the Dadaists themselves during the court proceedings. Bergius writes:

> This was a public trial, and the Dada friends, among them Hausmann and Höch were missing, used the occasion to stage a little spectacle. To start with, they attempted to dodge the court's orders by letting a guard, a 'Cerberus in uniform' (Herzfelde), throw them out at one door of the courtroom, only to enter again through the other until finally all the benches were 'filled tightly' and 'people were laughing and grinning'.[23]

Baader, Grosz and Herzfelde staged defences mostly relying on the separability of art from life, peppered with irony and satire. In effect they tried to turn the courtroom into a Dadaist event and that would have happened had they been able to produce a 'reconstruction' of the fair as the court demanded. This proved difficult, although the prospect is highly seductive. To the purists, the posthumous 'reconstruction' of a Dadaist exhibition is betrayal enough. A Dadaist courtroom drama would have been fascinating, not simply as an act of defiance but as a test of the whole aestheticisation thesis. In this case the institutional inappropriateness of the original fair kept it outside the courtroom. As a performance event, it was ephemeral, situated and embodied but not easily reproducible. The prosecution had to rely on a portfolio of works submitted. The irony that the whole event could be reproduced in a format that allowed it to be interpreted as part of historical and institutional trajectory was not lost on the Dadaists themselves. It was the same ability to interpret the event as ironic and satirical (Baader's defence was based on humour) that led to the acquittal of most and to the fining of others. Indeed, it was the reinterpretation of the whole fair within an institutional framework that allowed both the trial to take place *and* the defendants to mount a case on the basis of artistic licence. Similar strategies of deception will be applied a few decades later in the USA by Brecht in his appearance before the House Un-American Activities Committee.

The trial was one of the last public appearances of these Dadaists as a group. With the advent of National Socialism the Berlin Dadaists either went into hiding or emigrated, as did Grosz, Heartfield, Herzfelde, Hausmann and Mehring. Most went to the USA, taking with them their mythical version of an Americana that had previously fuelled their avant-garde manifestos. The portfolio from the First International Dada Fair, constructed for the purposes of the court, was expanded on with the addition of Grosz's fifty-five political drawings of 1921 entitled *The Face of the Ruling Class (Das Gesicht der herrschenden Klasse)*. This portfolio appears again, after most of the artists have emigrated, as part of Hitler's exhibition of Degenerate Art (*Entartete Kunst*) in Munich in 1937.[24]

This extraordinary journey from the 'First Dada International Fair' to the exhibition of Degenerate Art takes in all the contortions and appropriations that the event had to undergo in order to be constructed and interpreted as an aesthetic commodity. Interestingly enough, this occurs initially within a legalistic discourse, as the notion of the portfolio first appears in the proceedings of the Dadaist trial, and the process of defining the event through the workings of censorship continues right up until the exhibition of Degenerate Art. This is not the kind of destruction that the Dadaists originally had in mind. Equally, it could be claimed that what eventually ended up at the Degenerate Art exhibition was in no way the Fair itself in all its spatial/physical dimensions, but an already institutionalised version of the event. The ephemeral quality of the Dadaist event actually resists total appropriation, while also raising serious questions about documentation and critical assessment. The Dadaist moments in the trial, for example, are not forged by the infamous portfolio, but by all the interactions taking place between the Dadaists, the representatives of power *and* the portfolio. Again performance is crucial in both constructing the Dadaist event *and* resisting its appropriation. Also, reflecting Benjamin's formulations, this immediacy and ephemerality of the performance event creates an interesting chasm between reproduction, as such, and reproducibility. The inability to reproduce the Fair as an aesthetic commodity was not dependent on its aura and uniqueness (although these were used in its defence). Rather, the principle of reproducibility itself, as the main force that created the event, obscures mechanical reproduction and allows a space for the continuing existence of the ephemeral event beyond the confines of the courtroom, the gallery or the academy, as the case may be.

The issue of reproducibility, and how it pertains to matters of politicisation, reception, audience or construction of the masses and to the general 'world-building/destroying impetus' of the avant-garde, is in many instances worked out, exemplified and tested on models that are essentially theatrical. Benjamin's championing of Epic Theatre is not coincidental in this context. Neither are his frequent references to Dada. The Dadaist use of the ready-made, the everyday, the discarded and used material helps to tease out some of the issues surrounding Benjamin's crucial essay.[25] As Eduardo Cadava claims, Benjamin is less interested in the empirical fact of reproduction, or in mere 'mechanical reproduction' (which is not particularly new or modern), but in 'reproducibility as a mode of being'.[26] The principle of reproducibility becomes a formal quality that impacts on the making of the work of art itself, and not simply on its circulation and reception. The Dadaist use of real materials and the 'liveness'[27] and ephemerality of the performance events they presented heavily inflect this principle of reproducibility. In fact, events like the 'International Dada Fair' cannot be reproduced, as the attempted transference to the Degenerate Art exhibition (or indeed to later reconstructions) indicates. However, in the actual construction of the Fair the concept of reproducibility was vital. Ironically, this fascination with reproducibility as a mode of production and reception might possibly be what in the end deters total and mechanical reproduction in the form of an aesthetic commodity. The Dadaist moment is *par excellence* not reproducible, and part at least of this may be connected to the performance dimension of much of this experiment.

The Blue Blouse (1923–28)

Just two years after the 'Dada International Fair', the 'First Russian Art Exhibition' was mounted at the van Diemen gallery in Berlin in 1922.[28] This featured amongst others the montages of Aleksandr Rodchenko, who was very impressed by the work of the Dadaists. Mayakovsky was also in Berlin at the time and so was El Lissitzky (1890–1941), who wanted to publish a magazine with Housmann, called *qngE*. Throughout the course of planning this, he had to differentiate between the positions of the Soviet avant-garde and the Dadaists. Lissitzky was no stranger to little magazines, as he was already publishing another with Ilya Ehrenburg (1891–1967), characteristically entitled *Object (Weshtsch – Object – Gegenstand)*, which was being published, interestingly, by a Berlin publisher (Skythen). Here he differentiated between the goals of the Dadaists and those of the Constructivists:

> We believe the negating tactics of the Dadaists are anachronistic. It is about time to build on ground laid open ... We believe that for our time the triumph of constructive matter is fundamental. We find it in economics, in the industrial development, as in the psychology of our contemporaries, and in art. The *Object* will stand up for constructive art whose job is not to adorn life but to organise it.[29]

This shift from the work of destruction to a work of rebuilding and construction is characteristic within the Russian avant-garde after the Revolution of 1917. The momentous event of the October Revolution and the two years of civil war that resulted presented for the Russian avant-garde the moment of apocalypse itself. The total negation that the Dadaists desired had for the Russians occurred in empirical reality. Everything was reduced to rubble from the workings of the state machine to people's every-day lives. As Andrei Belyi succinctly put it, 'the victory of materialism in Russia resulted in the complete disappearance of all matter'.[30] The effects of shock and estrangement that the Russian Formalists had induced only a few years previously were now part of daily reality. Groys states:

> Since it seemed that the apocalypse had come and that things had been displaced to reveal themselves to the apocalyptic vision of all, the avant-gardist and formalist theory of the 'shift' that lifted things from their normal contexts and 'made them strange' by deautomatizing perception and rendering them 'visible' in a special way was no longer merely the basis of avant-garde art but an explanation of the Russian citizen's everyday experience.[31]

In other words, out of the rubble of the Revolution everyone emerged as an avant-garde artist. Art itself no longer needed to stand back, as the whole of life had been enveloped by strangeness. In the same stroke the avant-garde both celebrates and loses its autonomy. It renders itself autonomous in the sense of a non-mimetic, non-representational relationship to the real. At the same time, it wilfully sacrifices that highly contested formal autonomy by merging itself heart, soul and most importantly, body into the workings of politics. The aesthetico-political project of destruction of the Dadaists becomes one of construction for the Soviet avant-garde. Groys continues:

> The constructivists themselves regarded their constructions not as self-sufficient works of art, but as models of a new world, a laboratory for developing a unitary plan for conquering the material that was the world. Hence their love of hetero-geneous materials and the great variety of their projects, which embraced the most diverse aspects of human activity and attempted to unify them according to a single artistic principle.[32]

This shift from the avant-garde proposing art as the 'negative knowledge' of the world to an almost 'organic' integration of the work of art into the rebuild-ing process is made even clearer with the introduction of the NEP (New Economic Policy) in 1922. This marks for many scholars 'the beginning of the end' of the Soviet avant-garde. As a result of the NEP many avant-garde artists became part of state organisations, were given official positions and invested with the power to help 'construct the new soviet individual'. One of the most notable was the journal *Lef* and then *Novyi Lef*, which brought together some of the most charismatic figures of the Russian and Soviet avant-garde: Aleksandr Rodchenko, Vsevolod Meyerhold, Aleksei Gan, amongst others. The journal charts the shift from the fascination with material to an emphasis on production, process and function. Early on, the contemplative work of Malevich, Kandinsky and Tatlin is seen as embodying an almost mystical fascination with material. (Rodchenko called his former friend Tatlin a 'typical Russian holy fool'.) But the somewhat utopian and metaphysical strands that fuelled many of these projects begin to give way to more functional, pedagogic approaches. Although Shklovsky, the great Russian Formalist theorist and poet, starts objecting in the early 1920s, asking the artists to reject political commitment, he is given the answer that 'Communist power, the Third International, and so forth were as much a fantasy as the art of the avant-garde and could therefore be considered avant-garde materials and used as elements in avant-garde constructions'.[33] It is not as if the avant-garde was specifically propagating 'political' art in a directly mimetic, quasi-realist mode. Sometimes the direct political 'message' was subsumed under the overbearing attention paid to formal matters. However, in as much as art had immersed itself in the workings of reality, it is the whole

A skit in the interest of industrialization.

22   The Blue Blouse, A Skit in the Interest of Industrialization

A poster composition: **New and Old Holidays.**

23 The Blue Blouse, A Poster Composition: New and Old Holidays

A dance of the machine, entitled **Ford and Us.**

24 The Blue Blouse, A Dance of the Machine entitled 'Ford and Us'.

of art that gets subsumed and not only its political dimension. Everything is political because everything is art, seems to be the implication. Hence around 1922 the total work of destruction of the Dadaists (despite all their tributes to the Russians) turns into a total work of construction.

It is in this climate that the Blue Blouse (*Siniaya Bluza*) (1923–28) theatre movement appears. This was an extraordinary project that at its peak probably played to over 100,000 people, achieving an international reputation. It also exemplified some of the policies of the NEP, relying heavily on avant-garde experimentation but filtering this through a more accessible 'popular-ist' aesthetic. Against some of the charges of elitism and formalism that were already beginning to be levelled against the previous generation of avant-garde artists, the Blue Blouse was deliberately direct and agitational, more concerned with communicative efficacy than formal experimentation. Although they built on the achievements of the avant-garde and mainly utilised agit-prop techniques and the 'living newspaper' format, at the same time they borrowed heavily from the popular and oral performing traditions and relied on the structures of amateur club theatre for their tours and their audiences. On 3 March 1928, the Moscow correspondent for the *Christian Science Monitor* reports after viewing a Blue Blouse performance:

> They sing, dance, play the accordion, declaim, act and transform costumes on the stage with sleight-of-hand rapidity. If they are still inferior to the 'Chauve-Souris' in finesse they possess more agility. Their handsprings, somersaults, and balancing features of their production ... One of their most effective skits is entitled 'Industrialization'. One after another the actors come out in fantastic costumes, adorned with symbols indicating factory buildings, installation of electrical sta-tions or other items in the program of industrialization ... The theme of one of their satirical pieces is the unfortunate plight of a poor Soviet Citizen whose existence the bureaucrats in various institutions refuse to recognise, because he has somewhere mislaid his indispensable 'document' or passport ...
>
> A piano furnishes a brisk accompaniment, usually jazz, to most of the per-formances, and snatches of Russian songs and melodies, played on the accor-dion, are interspersed.[34]

As we can see from this account, the aesthetic of the Blue Blouse managed to strike a balance between the formal experimentation of the Russian avant-garde and popular performing traditions. The 'skits' are structured round techniques borrowed from the circus, the cabaret and the review, all adapted and rewritten. The fascination with the circus is typical of the period; the circus itself is viewed as a carnivalesque site that offers non-psychological ways of presenting the human body, and models of collectivity for the audience. The circus becomes another famous 'laboratory', to borrow a term so prevalent at the time. Its techniques are analysed and dissected as part of the project of constructing the new Soviet individual. Its emphasis on the physicality of the body rather than its interiority offered ways of turning the actors into raw material, highlighting once again the desire to break everything down into its material components and construct it anew. Circus offered such a conceptual and practical space. From Marinetti's influential manifesto 'The Variety Theatre' (1913) to Eisenstein's seminal 'Montage of Attractions' (1923) the circus features as a key site that will help to reconstruct the new theatre. Eisenstein's 'Montage', which appears at the same time as the Blue Blouse takes off, could be seen as an attempt to expand the 'laboratory of the circus' to include the whole of theatre production. In particular the notion of the 'attraction' itself, so crucial to the agit-prop nature of the Blue Blouse, relies on such a fascination with the physicality and the immediacy of the circus:

> An attraction (in relation to the theatre) is any aggressive aspect of the theatre; that is, any element of the theatre that subjects the spectator to emotional or psychological impact, experimentally regulated and mathematically calculated to produce in him certain emotional shocks which, when placed in their proper sequence within the totality of the production, become the only means that enable the spectator to perceive the ideological side of what is being demonstrated – the ultimate ideological conclusion. (The means of cognition – 'through the living play of passions' – apply specifically to the theatre.)[35]

Rather than rely on spectacle, this radical reworking of the idea of 'attractions' posits them as modes of critical intervention, rather than mind-numbing aestheticisation. These attractions in the Blue Blouse productions are mainly achieved through the highly skilled use of the actor's body, both the central medium and the raw material. S. Yuzhanin writes, 'the actor of the Blue Blouse is synthetic; he is a singer, sportsman, and transformer'.[36] These actors wore a blue worker's blouson and trousers. This basic costume was augmented with details, collars, pockets and so on, but the main material of the Blue Blouse remained distinct and clear, allowing the actor to transform effectively in front of the audience. One could push the laboratory analogy even further and tentatively claim that the actor's body itself was being turned into a type of laboratory.[37] The actor in this scheme of things acquires a privileged position in the great work of 'constructing the new soviet individual'. All that the Blue Blouse needed, in effect, was well-trained actors:

> The Blue Blouse makes no special demands on space or conditions; any stage and any premises fit its requirements. The performances do not need decorations; the entire work of expression and form is fulfilled by the actors.[38]

Note how Yuzhanin stresses the concept of the 'entire work', highlighting the integration of 'expression and form'. The Blue Blouse actor becomes such a locus of construction, uniting 'expression and form', popular entertainment and avant-garde experiment, and through touring, Moscow (the centre) and the outskirts (the peripheries) of socialism. Rather than being a psychological actor, he or she becomes a type of acting machine: a Bauhaus-related mechanised eccentric, there to shape, filter and disseminate the models for the new world that was in the process of being constructed.

This was not to remain the case for long, as the notion of the 'typical hero' to be put before the proletariat changed dramatically throughout the 1920s, together with whatever liberalism remained in the NEP. Towards the end of the 1920s, the Blue Blouse is dismantled, and with the steady imposition of Socialist Realism the notion of the typical hero is yet again reconfigured. The days of the actor as gymnast, juggler, clown and all-round entertainer, a mechanised eccentric, are over; the 'typical' hero is now sought in the acting theories of Stanislavsky rather than in the work of Meyerhold or the Blue Blouse. A commentator from the period writes:

> The typical hero should possess a striking, vivid personality. Sometimes it seems that not only the spectator but even the artist has no really clear idea of the heroes of a work – their desires, their aspirations, their character traits, why they are where they are or where they are going. I think that here our artists could learn a great deal from Stanislavski, who demanded that his actors express each separate personality even in crowd scenes; even if they uttered only two or three sentences they were required to embody a specific personality.[39]

Gone is the emphasis placed on the materiality of the body. This typical hero is described in terms of an inner life, in terms of 'character traits'; in fact in terms which quintessentially characterise the bourgeois subject. The reference to 'aspirations', 'desires', the questioning of motivation, direction and so on (where, why) is a direct application of some of Stanislavsky's techniques for actor-training that would later evolve into his formidable system. The adoption of these techniques is rather ironic in this context, as Stanislavsky himself had mostly kept away from direct political involvement after the Revolution. Meyerhold, his close friend and sometime collaborator, had immersed himself in the great work of constructing a new future. In another bitter twist, Meyerhold is the one who is judicially murdered during the Great Terror,[40] while Stanislavsky continued to work for the rest of a long life. 'After decades of bloody struggle with formalism', as Groys says,[41] the end of the twenties saw a resurgence of a kind of heightened realism, one that initially saw analogies in Stanislavsky's method, but later was to abandon those as well for the starker, less subtle forms of Socialist Realism.

By 1928 the Blue Blouse movement had been dismantled and the next decade was to see the systematic and brutal elimination of the avant-garde project and its main protagonists. However, to view this outcome as a direct result of the internal logic of the avant-garde itself seems somewhat deterministic, ahistorical and in the end insensitive to historical loss. As with the critique against the Dadaists, this failure of the avant-garde is attributed to its undialectical nature. The passionate attachment to utter destruction or total immersion in a project of construction elicit equally total and totalising responses. Groys develops this thesis:

> Because the avant-garde took an undialectical view of its own project as absolutely opposing or directly negating the past, it was unable to stand up against the total dialectical irony of Stalin's negation of the negation, which in the practical language of dialectical materialism signified a dual destruction – the unending destruction of the destroyer, the purge of the purgers, the mystical sublimation of human material to distil from it the new 'Soviet individual' in the name of Stalin's superhuman, transcendent, transhistorical 'new humanism'.[42]

This is a damning assessment of the historical significance of the avant-garde that in the end reads it simply as a prelude to Stalinism. It seems that the harshest critiques of the revolutionary avant-garde, as is the case with the critique of Brecht, are the Marxist ones.

The Blue Blouse had a curious life after the 1920s. Following Groys' logic, it would be equally undialectical to assume that its banishment led to its total annihilation. The strange reincarnation that it was to undergo was due to a number of factors ranging from influence, to inspiration, to personal and political investment, to historical context, and above all to the workings of the ubiquitous dialectic. This new life was to take shape in the USA. This may seem like an unlikely alliance, but the Russian avant-garde, particularly before the 1930s, was fascinated with the USA. It was seen as the perfect site of modernity. Its advances in technology were envied and its new modes of production (particularly Fordism) copied. In a famous Blue Blouse skit called 'Ford and Us' the principles of fragmented, broken-down labour are transferred to the artistic process. The avant-garde were cosmopolitan Westernisers (something which was held against them later), whose vision of America was to have a huge impact in the creation of the new Russia.

The pr-1930s cosmopolitanism of the Blue Blouse was also reflected in their numerous international tours. According to Robert Leach, Blue Blouse companies toured England, France, Czechoslovakia, Latvia, China, the USA and Germany.[43] By 1929 Blue Blouse companies had reached Japan where they inspired local versions organised by Seki Sano.[44] Both

Seki Sano and John Bohn, director of The Proletbühne (a German Blue Blouse-inspired workers' theatre) were to seek refuge in the USA in the early 1930s. There they collaborated with the charismatic Hallie Flanagan and amongst other things helped to give shape to the Living Newspaper, a form of agit-prop theatre that was to be identified with the Federal Theatre Project. The fascination with Americana was definitely not a one-way street.[45]

The Federal Theatre Project (1935–39)

We live in a changing world: man is whispering through space, soaring to the stars, flinging miles of steel and glass into the air. Shall the theatre continue to huddle in the confines of a painted box set? … The stage too must experiment – with ideas, with psychological relationships of men and women, with speech and rhythm forms, with dance and movement, with color and light – or it must and should become a museum product.

In an age of terrific implications as to wealth and poverty, as to function of government, as to peace and war, as to the relation of an artist to all these forces, the theatre must grow up. The theatre must become conscious of the implications of the changing social order, or the changing social order will ignore, and rightly, the implications of the theatre.[46]

The above manifesto-style proclamation was not taken from a speech by the members of the Russian avant-garde, but from Hallie Flanagan's address to the regional and state directors of the Federal Theatre in Washington on 8 October 1935. As it was an inaugural speech, it had to outline the aims of the project and its more general aspirations. The threat of confinement to the museum, the call for a radical reworking of theatrical form, together with a reassessment of the role of theatre in society, all bear the indelible traces of the European avant-garde manifesto. This was a legacy that Hallie Flanagan had experienced directly.

In 1926 Hallie Flanagan, a professor of drama at Vassar College, was the first woman to receive a Guggenheim Foundation Grant for a tour of Europe to study theatre. She visited Yeats in Ireland, Craig in Italy and she went to the Soviet Union, where she met Meyerhold, Tairov and the Blue Blouse groups amongst others. These encounters were to prove decisive in determining Flanagan's own vision of a popular theatre for the USA. Flanagan herself was looking for models that she could apply to the American context. That specific context, as we have seen, was already very attractive to the European avant-garde. In the late twenties, that attraction was mutual. The crisis created by the Stock Market crash of 1929 was interpreted by many Americans as a failure of capitalism, and the experiments taking place in the Soviet Union appeared attractive to many intellectuals and artists in the USA. The kind of apocalypse that was experienced by the Russians through the Revolution was seen as analogous to the collapse of the US economy. Everything needed to be thought anew. And the theatre had a crucial role to play, as Flanagan states in her address.

The 'renaissance spring' of 1933 saw the arrival of the US government's New Deal, an attempt to address the crisis of 1929 through more direct intervention by the state. In the realm of the arts the Works Progress Administration sought to bring together amateurs and professionals in an attempt to utilise the skills of professionals and address unemployment. Such a venture, of course, brings into relief similar problems to those encountered by the avant-garde. The issues of autonomy and engagement are recast albeit within the liberal politics of the New Deal. The very nature of the work of art, as was the case with the European avant-garde, needed to be redefined. This was not the total immersion of art in the 'praxis of life' that the Soviets so desired, but in some ways it reads like a liberal, less radical version of the same problematic. Characteristically, Richard Lowe, one of the key figures of the Federal Theatre Project, expresses his concerns in a letter to Flanagan:

> I have reached an impasse. What should my standards be? Am I doing the workers an injustice to allow them to function in a profession for which they are unfitted? Are they unfitted for work in a provincial theatre? How much consideration should I give to the laudatory letters from high schools and clubs who get entertainment free of charge? ... Have I any justification for burdening the capables with the incapables? Should I make a perceptible cut in personnel immediately ... ? *Is this social work, or theatre?*[47]

This reads like a mild variation on the fundamental avant-garde question: is it art or is it politics? In the USSR the impasse reached was resolved through the operation of direct and brutal state power. In the USA, as the Works Progress Administration clearly shows, it appeared, at least initially, that this relationship was still negotiable. For the philo-Soviet strand of the Federal Theatre Project the specific USA context offered the possibility of realising the dream of the avant-garde in American Technicolor. The Stock Market crash had created the desired apocalyptic climate that required the restructuring and rebuilding of society; the USA had all the necessary technological advances coupled with a huge, now disaffected working class. The Moscow trials had not yet occurred to polarise communists, fellow travellers and liberals in equal measure. However, despite the politics of some of its members, the FTP never issued explicitly political manifestos in the style of *Lef*. As the rewriting of the debate shows ('social work or theatre', for instance), it remained firmly within the context of liberalism. Despite its total dependency on government funding, it always saw itself as independent, critical and democratic, which would create yet another impasse that was to help bring about its demise.

Before this demise actually occurred in 1939 the FTP proved, like the Blue Blouse, very successful and popular with audiences. The May 1937 issue of *Fortune* magazine claims that the FTP is 'a roaring success'. To mid-season that year sixteen million people had seen its productions. The play *It Can't Happen Here* by Sinclair Lewis, an exploration of the possibility of fascism in the USA, played to 275,000 people in four months in 1936. Productions would have simultaneous premieres in regional theatres all over the country. Living Newspaper productions, directly inspired by the Blue Blouse, were particularly popular. The Children's Theatre in New York was attended by over a quarter of a million people, while the New York Marionette Theatre attracted over one and a half million in its first two years. A Black FTP and a Yiddish FTP were founded as well.[48]

It was not only agit-prop, music theatre and vaudeville that proved successful. The first production of *Macbeth* to include an all-black cast, directed by Orson Welles in 1934 for the Negro People's Theatre, played for 144 performances and was seen by 120,000 people. Even Eliot's High-Anglican drama *Murder in the Cathedral* played to over 40,000 people. These were audience numbers that could only be rivalled by the parallel Soviet experiment. Its fusion of high art and popular forms of entertainment, its use of amateurs and professionals and its freedom from box-office constraints offered a particularly American inflection on the political efficacy of engaged theatre. At its peak the FTP presented itself as the only attempt to date to create a national theatre for the USA. It claimed to represent most aspects of American society and to make a vital contribution to the life of the nation. Furthermore, its reliance on liberal democracy, rather than the more radical politics of the European Continent, gave the impression that it would be immune from censorship and persecution. And this was to be its contribution to the impasse created by the conflation of arts and politics. The fundamentals of liberal democracy were seen as guarantors of the freedom of art to have a close positive relationship with the workings of the state and, at the same time, to remain apart from it, at a critical distance.

Both the European high-art legacy and the experiments of the avant-garde seemed to co-exist in the FTP without the usual tensions and theoretical complexity that similar approaches attracted in Europe. Indeed, the possibility offered by 'America' itself, as both historical and imaginative site, formed part of the uniqueness and the specificity of the project itself. This was the 'America' that so inspired the European, especially the Soviet, avant-garde. It was the place where tradition and modernity could meet without tearing each other apart. Here is how *Fortune* comments on the FTP repertoire and its reception:

> *Doctor Faustus* has admirers as intelligent and as devoted as any collected by the various Shakespearean revivals of the last New York season. And the Living Newspaper, applying to the stage the technique developed in the air and on the screen by the March of Time, has created as much excitement among playwrights as among Republicans who see its *Triple A Plowed Under* and its *Power* as government subsidized propaganda.[49]

The quotation first links the high European tradition (Marlowe's *Doctor Faustus*) with the popular tradition of the 'living newspaper'. The following link, however, adds a particularly American flavour. 'The technique developed in the air and on the screen by the *March of Time*', is, of course, montage-based, episodic and fragmentary; it relies on critical distance and abstraction rather than empathy and, crucially, it is seen to derive from the workings of the cinema. This transplanting of European experiment onto American soil is heavily inflected by the new medium of the cinema. Again, this has parallels, if not origins, in the experiments conducted by Sergei Eisenstein in the USSR.

By 1938, just three years after its founding, and despite its successes with audiences, demise was imminent for the FTP. The fusion of art and politics that it was proposing was beginning to confront some of the foundational aspects of US society, economy and overall culture. Indeed, the accusations levelled against the FTP intriguingly echo those against the Russian avant-garde. However, whereas the criticism against the Russians was mainly grounded on aesthetic criteria (the charge of formalism), the FTP was confronted because of its politics, which was seen as 'communistic'. In particular, the New Jersey Republican J. Parnell Thomas urged that the matter be assessed by the House Un-American Activities Committee (HUAC):

> It is apparent from the startling evidence received thus far that the Federal Theatre Project not only is serving a branch of the communistic organization but is also one more link in the vast and unparalleled New Deal propaganda machine.[50]

The above was part of J. Parnell Thomas's testimony to the HUAC, to which Hallie Flanagan was summoned. By 1939, after the successful machinations of the HUAC, the FTP was terminated, following accusations of 'communism' and 'anti-Americanism'. Indeed, Hallie Flanagan and Ellen S. Woodward, the assistant administrator of the WPA, were the first 'aggrieved persons accorded the privilege of testifying before the Dies [the chairperson] Committee'.[51] Furthermore, Flanagan was attacked as co-author of a play described by the *New Masses* as 'the best revolutionary play yet produced in America'.[52] In her defence she claimed that only ten per cent of the plays produced by the FTP were concerned with social and political issues. This, however, was not a matter of number crunching but primarily an issue of ideology. At times it seems like the accused and accusers spoke different languages, which of course further polarised the debates. A characteristic extract from the transcripts of those early interrogations:

> MRS WOODWARD: You know it seems to me the capitalistic press would certainly say so if we were doing that [spreading Communistic propaganda].
> THOMAS: What press did you say?
> STARNES: She said the capitalistic press.
> THOMAS: What do you mean by capitalistic press?
> DIES: That is a Communistic term.[53]

In their own crude way the committee members were also attacking the plays for their lack of 'cultural value'. They were mainly guided by their titles:

> I have one here – *A New Deal for Mary*, which is a grand title. Then there is *The Mayor and the Manicure* and *Mother Goose Goes to Town*. Also, *A New Kind of Love*. I wonder what that can be. It smacks somewhat of the Soviet. Then there is *Up in Mabel's Room*. There is an intriguing title for you … Now, if you want that kind of salacious tripe, very well, vote for it, but if anybody has an interest in decency on the stage, if anyone has an interest in real cultural values, you will not find it in this kind of junk.[54]

As Walter Goodman mentions in his study *The Committee*, 'a few minutes later, an amendment to save the Federal Theatre was voted down, 56 to 192'.[55] It is fascinating to note that the rhetoric and discourses of the Cold War are, in many ways, formulated as both a correction and a continuation of the debates about the avant-garde and political efficacy. In both cases the inter-vention of the state proved catastrophic; in the USSR the state itself decid-edly fills in the gap between aesthetics and politics, leaving no room for experiment, critique or subversion. In the USA the theatre severs its links to state power (and funding) and is once again 'thrown out into the cold', relegated back to the sphere of the aesthetic. In the former instance theatre is totally deprived of autonomy, in the latter it totally relies on the illusion of autonomy. Those two extremes are ready to be further polarised by the crystallisation of Cold War ideology. This is how the *New York Times* reported the demise of the FTP in June 1939:

> The Relief Bill for 1939–40, described by the *New York Post* as 'aimed at radicals', was reported to the House on June 15. While granting the full amount requested by the President, the bill called for sweeping changes in the relief program ... Other restrictive provisions stipulated that relief personnel employed on WPA projects for eighteen months or more be dismissed, and that a loyalty oath be required of new workers. Writers', Music and Art Projects were to be continued only if locally sponsored; the Theatre Project was to be abolished outright.[56]

So much for the liberal aspiration of making politically engaged theatre within the workings of democracy. Again, more than other art forms, and possibly due to its ability to *stand in* for and provide a model for another world, theatre becomes the target of the most vicious attacks. Where other Federal projects are simply monitored, the FTP is banned outright.

Almost a decade later in 1947 Brecht, in exile from Nazism, is summoned before the committee. By now J. Parnell Thomas, who in 1939 had testified against Hallie Flanagan and called for the dismantling of the FTP, has been promoted to the Chair of the 'Investigation into the Entertainment Industry'. Theatre probably suffered more than other artistic forms, for the same reasons it suffered in the USSR. The 'world-creating' powers of the performance event – the collective dream of the historical avant-garde – is seen as particularly threatening. However, this parallel reading does not intend to reduce the significant differences between the two cases, equating the totalitarian violence of Stalinism with the workings of the HUAC. It does aspire to stress that in both cases matters of political efficacy were crucial, in relation both to the audience and to state power.

Equally, both projects – historical avant-garde and the FTP – have a particular interest in matters of form and how they pertain to political relevance. Indeed, the term 'formalism' became anathema in 1930s USSR and the cause of much pain and violence. The same term, however, resurfaces in late 1930s USA, especially in the work of the US art critic Clement Greenberg, whose influential article 'Avant-Garde and Kitsch' appears in 1939.[57] Here the term is recuperated to connote aesthetic radicalism, but only once divorced from politics. Admittedly Greenberg is writing against the instrumental use of the avant-garde in the USSR and the mass culture of capitalism, both of which he terms as 'kitsch'.

25 Poster for the Federal Theatre Project production of the Living Newspaper *One Third of a Nation*, Adelphi Theatre, New York, 1938

However, As Susan Buck-Morss states in her recent revaluation of the Russian/Soviet avant-garde this total valorisation of form at the expense of *any* kind of politics was a position quickly appropriated by the discourses of the Cold War. She writes:

> This position [Greenberg's], which has been called 'apolitical politicism', became a weapon in the Cold War, when non-representational art came to be

26   *One Third of a Nation*, opening scene of the above production

equated with democratic societies as opposed to the representational realism of totalitarian regimes (the latter category did not differentiate between fascism and socialism). The Museum of Modern Art in New York became an institutional embodiment of this Cold War politics.[58]

Later in the 1950s this evolves into his passionate championing of any form of 'abstraction', culminating in the ultimate of forms for Greenberg, abstract expressionism. All of this, however, takes place in the shadow of the workings of the HUAC and later the Committee for Cultural Freedom during the Cold War. Berghaus writes of this period in the early 1950s:

> During the first ten years of the Cold War, hardly any artist driven by a genuine quest for the betterment of society could maintain a position on the West-European art market. The often messianic visions of Expressionists and Constructivists, who in their majority had belonged to the Left-wing, and often Communist, community of artists, gave way to a rather inane Utopian optimism and to works of austere minimalism, which bore no relation to any kind of experienceable reality.[59]

Of course, the avant-garde would experience other more politicised revivals in its American life, but during the 1940s and 50s political commitment is almost

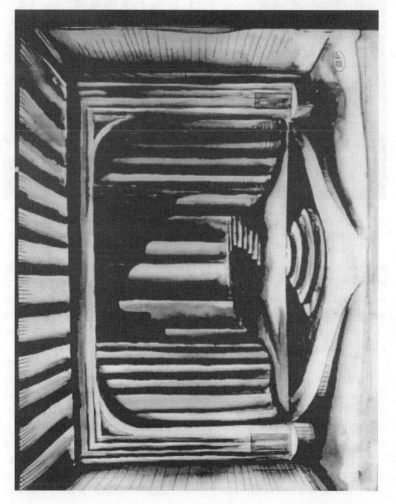

27 Design for *Dr Faustus*, directed by Orson Welles

28   From the production of T. S. Eliot, *Murder in the Cathedral*, directed by Halsted Welles, with Harry Irvine as the Archbishop

a taboo.[60] And although Greenberg had very little to say about theatre as such, his writings have had a huge impact on the 'de-politicisation' of the historical avant-garde; they are also crucial in the received perception of 'failure' that accompanies most later evaluations of the projects. From Adorno to Greenberg and more recently to Boris Groys (interestingly all at least one-time Marxists) the category of 'failure' looms large in most critical assessments.

It is beyond the scope of this study to assess the later critical/ philosophical receptions of the avant-garde, but it would be fair to say that the accusation of failure in most accounts results from the mingling of aesthetic experimentation and political aspiration. This political dimension, however, need not necessarily be read as instrumental (i.e. artists' collaboration with the Soviet state) but as in the more recent approach outlined by Susan Buck-Morss, could be seen as participating in a long and diverse history of utopian thought and practice. For an aesthetic immersed in catastrophe the concept of 'failure' is not in and of itself undesirable. Nor does the notion of imagined utopia teleologically lead to totalitarianism (as Groys would have it). Rather than viewing these experiments as failed/tragic attempts in reconciling politics and aesthetics, her study urges us to revisit these moments, particularly in their East/West encounters, as instances of hope. Making a case for the separation of the historical avant-garde from its instrumental use by state power, she writes:

> Is there cause to lament the passing of mass dreamworlds? They were compatible with terrifying assemblages of political power and economic power: world war machines, machines of mass terror, violent forms of labor extraction. But it was the structures of power, not the democratic, utopian idea, that produced these nightmare forms.
>
> [...]
>
> As long as the old structures of power remain intact [i.e. the Cold War], such imaginings will be dreamworlds, nothing more. They will be capable of producing phantasmagoric deceptions as well as critical illumination. But they are a cause for hope.[61]

This ability to provide critical illumination and hope, however, never solely relies on formal experiment nor on thematic context. The historical avant-garde, particularly in its performance dimensions, provides us with a quintessentially modern/ist way of renegotiating the two categories. This double movement within the historical avant-garde also needs to be read within its geo-political dimensions, folding over and in many ways helping to construct the discourses of the Cold War. The centrality of performance to these discourses (later reworked as the Brecht vs Beckett debate, for example) also merits further study.

This transatlantic model of reading the avant-garde sees the USA and 'Americana' not simply as a place where European artists seek refuge in their plight from fascism. Rather, the relationships with the USA and the imaginative space occupied by visions of a utopian America can be seen as formative of the avant-garde project itself. This fascination with an imagined America was to change drastically during the Cold War. However, the ideology of the Cold War, in this respect, might be read as a continuation of the debates articulated and experimented with by the historical avant-garde. This historical avant-garde, which we identify with the continent of Europe, in turn may have a strong American dimension, as the analysis of the case of the FTP tentatively gestures towards. The FTP also allows us to read the relationships between the Continental avant-garde and the USA as initiating prior to the arrival of the thousands of artists from war-torn Europe and totalitarian regimes. Indeed, the FTP equally draws on homegrown aesthetic and political legacies – such as the workers' theatre movement (particularly the Workers' Laboratory Theatre) and early New York Dada, underlining an already reciprocal relationship between the European and American avant-gardes. Formally innovative and experimental, it directly addressed and in many ways continued the experimentation of the historical avant-garde before the appearance of later US avant-garde schools such as the Black Mountain College and the Chicago Bauhaus of the 1950s.

The case of Brecht could contribute to such a transatlantic reading. By most critics of the avant-garde, from Bürger to Roland Barthes, the Brechtian project is seen as the culmination of the avant-garde experiment, which at once acknowledges its utopian aspirations *and* distils them into a working 'method'. Fredric Jameson's work on Brecht and the work of Tatlow in some ways act as correctives to the Marxist critical tradition (Lukács and Adorno) that in Bürger's words is 'incapable of understanding the most important materialist writer of our time'.[62]

Methods require models and Brecht offers such a model after his return to Berlin from the USA in 1947. His *Antigone-Model* can be read as such an attempt to distil the 'world-building' experiments of the avant-garde into a functional paradigm. As he clearly states, it is not a theory to be applied, copied or emulated Stanislavsky-style. Rather it is itself a type of *gestus* towards the theatre of the future. In Jameson's terms, and drawing on a tradition of German philosophy from Hölderlin to Benjamin, it is 'speculative'.[63] Characteristically it is a rewrite of a classical play – the very tradition that Brecht was defining his work against in his earlier period – and it reclaims an early European, German Romantic tradition for the purposes of a theatre after the catastrophes of two wars, the atomic bomb and his experience of the USA. Far from being a totalising document, the model itself as a work of art makes a very modest proposal for the artwork of the future. It contains designs by Caspar Neher and photographs of rehearsals and production by Ruth Berlau, focusing on the process rather than the end result. And most importantly it is not meant to be reproduced. This model is not a prototype, as it is itself a copy of sorts, and in Brecht's words poses a 'challenge to the artists of a period that applauds nothing but what is "original", "incomparable", "never been seen before", and demands what is "unique"'.[64] In other words, it is not a work of reconstruction in the sense articulated by the Soviet avant-garde; rather it presents itself as a work of critique and catastrophe. It emerges less as a manifesto and more as a piece of reflective, performative philosophy.

From the first production of *Ubu Roi* to Brecht's *Antigone-Model* the preponderance of notions of theatricality, with their theories of embodiment, critique and their sometimes world-building aspirations, have significantly determined what we understand as Modernism and modernity in its broader socio-political context. The separation of Modernism and the avant-garde into two distinct spheres, usually differentiated by their embracing or not of theatricality, has created a critical tradition that sees literary Modernism and the theatrical avant-garde as two distinct, often opposing negotiations of the modern. This book has charted some significant moments in the debates about theatricality, through which the notion of performance begins to appear as an emergent aesthetic notion, one created in many ways to address the critical gap between textuality and materiality, between text and stage, between the body of the actor and the written word. It also aspires to re-establish the binding link between what we understand as high, mainly Anglophone Modernism and the Continental avant-garde, adding a transatlantic inflection in the process. Hopefully this will allow us once more to speak of 'Modernism and the avant-garde' in the same critical breath, as it were, despite the 'post war settlements', as Raymond Williams called them, that helped create its canonisation by the academy and its partial appropriation by the discourses of the Cold War. The restoration of this linking word *and*, in constructivist manner, will bring out the similarities but also the differences, the contradictions and the rifts created by more than half a century of criticism that sees them as separate; the notion of performance is located on and enacts the paratactic quality of this *and*.

Notes

Notes to Chapter 1: Introduction: Savages, Gods, Robots and Revolutionaries: Modernist Performance

1 W. B. Yeats, 'The Tragic Generation' (1914) in *Autobiographies* (London: Macmillan (now Palgrave Macmillan), 1955), pp. 279–349, pp. 348–9.

2 The term 'historical avant-garde' is used throughout this study to refer to the Continental movements of Expressionism, Futurism, Dadaism, Constructivism and the Bauhaus, as these appeared in the first three decades of the twentieth century. This is adopting the use coined by Peter Bürger and more recently adopted by Günter Berghaus, in *Theatre, Performance, and the Historical Avant-Garde* (New York: Palgrave Macmillan, 2005).

3 Jean Cocteau, 'Preface' (1922) to *The Wedding on the Eiffel Tower* (1921), trans. Michael Benedikt, in *Modern French Plays: An Anthology from Jarry to Ionesco* (London: Faber and Faber, 1964), p. 96–7.

4 For a splendid study of the manifesto see Martin Puchner, *Poetry of the Revolution: Marx, Manifestos, and the Avant-Gardes* (Princeton, NJ: Princeton University Press, 2005).

5 See Jane Milling and Graham Ley, *Modern Theories of Performance* (Basingstoke and New York: Palgrave Macmillan, 2001), p. vi.

6 Viktor Shklovsky, *Zoo or Letters Not About Love*, trans. Richard Sheldon (Chicago: Dalkey Archive Press, 2001), Letter Twenty-Three, p. 84.

7 John E. Bowlt and Olga Matich (eds), *Laboratory of Dreams: The Russian Avant-Garde and Cultural Experiment* (Stanford, CA: Stanford University Press, 1996), pp. 9–10.

8 See David Bevington, *Medieval Drama* (Boston, MA: Houghton Mifflin, 1975); for an analysis of the Roman Empire's offical ban on theatre after the espousal of Christianity see, 'Liturgical Beginnings', pp. i–56.

9 Martin Puchner, *Stagefright: Modernism, Anti-theatricality and Drama* (Baltimore, MD and London: Johns Hopkins University Press, 2002).

10 See Penny Farfan, *Women, Modernism and Performance* (Cambridge: Cambridge University Press, 2004).

11 Yeats, *Autobiographies*, p. 321.

12 Martin Puchner here borrows a term with a long philological history – possibly dating back to Seneca, but certainly to much sixteenth-century Latin drama and notably *Samson Agonistes* – referring to plays not meant to be staged.

13 Quoted in Bowlt and Matich, *Laboratory of Dreams*, p. 243.

Notes to Chapter 2: Puppets and Actors

1 Heinrich von Kleist, *Über das Marionettentheater*, in *Berliner Abendlatter* (c.1810). The first English translation appears in Edward Gordon Craig's journal, *The Marionette*, No. 4 (Florence, 1918). Here trans. Idris Parry, in *Essays on Dolls* (London: Penguin, Syrens, 1994), p. 12.

2 For Plato's attack on mimesis see his dialogue *Ion*, where the process of enacting by imitation is seen as potentially corrupting for both the actor or the rhapsode and his audience. See D. A. Russell and M. Winterbottom (eds), *Classical Literary Criticism: Ion* (Oxford: Oxford University Press, 1972), pp. 1–13. In the *Republic* he further elaborates, writing that the imitative artist 'rouses and feeds this part of the [the non-rational] mind and by strengthening it destroys the rational part'. See *Classical Literary Criticism, Republic*, p. 47. Plato scornfully calls actors and rhapsodes 'interpreters of interpreters', *Ion*, p. 6.

3 See T. D. J. Chappell, *The Plato Reader* (Edinburgh: Edinburgh University Press, 1996): 'Then prisoners like these will think that the truth is nothing other than the shadows of dummies', 515c1, p. 231. The terms that Plato uses are *andriantas* and *skeuaston*. See *Platonis Respublica* (Oxford: Oxford University Press, 2003), 514–519, pp. 259–66.

4 See Victoria Nelson, *The Secret Life of Puppets* (Cambridge, MA: Harvard University Press, 2001).

5 Karel Čapek, *R.U.R. (Rossum's Universal Robots)*, trans. Claudia Novack-Jones, in *Toward the Radical Centre: A Karel Čapek Reader*, ed. Peter Kussi (Highland Park, NJ: Catbird Press, 1990), p. 109.

6 Although this work was written in the 1930s it was not published until 1965, as *Tvorchestvo Fransua Rable* (Moscow: Khudozhestvennia literatura, 1965), and translated from Russian by Hélène Iswolsky in 1968, rpt. Mikhail Bakhtin, *Rabelais and his World* (Bloomington, IN: Indiana University Press, 1984).

7 Harold B. Segel, *Pinocchio's Progeny: Puppets, Marionettes, Automatons, and Robots in Modernist and Avant-Garde Drama* (Baltimore, MD and London: Johns Hopkins University Press), p. 37.

8 Charles Baudelaire, 'The Philosophy of Toys', trans. Paul Keegan, in *Essays on Dolls* (London: Penguin, 1994), p. 18.

9 Rainer Maria Rilke, 'Dolls: On the Wax Dolls of Lotte Pritzel', trans. Idris Parry, in *Essays on Dolls*, p. 27.

10 Ibid., p. 37.

11 Edward Gordon Craig, *The Mask*, Vol. 5, No. 2 (Florence, 1912). This volume of the journal is completely devoted to the marionette.

12 Quoted in *The Mask*, Vol. 14 (Florence, 1928), p. 76. From a letter to R. B. Cunningham Graham, 6 December 1897, in Jean Aubry, *Joseph Conrad: Life and Letters* (London: Heinemann, 1927), p. 213.

13 Walter Pater, 'Another Estimate of the Actor's Character', rpt. in *The Mask*, Vol. 3, Nos. 10–12 (Florence, 1911), p. 174.

14   Rupert Hart-Davis (ed.), *The Letters of Oscar Wilde* (London: Harcourt, 1962), p. 311, from a letter to the editor of the *Daily Telegraph*, 19 February 1892.

15   Ibid., p. 311.

16   Arthur Symons, 'Apology for Puppets', *The Mask*, Vol. 5, No. 2 (Florence, 1912), p. 103.

17   Quoted in Segel, *Pinocchio's Progeny*, p. 83. From Maurice Bouchor, *Mystères bibliques et chrétiens* (Paris: Ernest Flammarion, n.d.), pp. 7–8.

18   Alfred Jarry, *The Ubu Plays: Ubu Rex*, trans. Cyril Connolly (London: Methuen Drama, 1994), p. 57.

19   W. B. Yeats, 'The Tragic Generation', in *Autobiographies* (London: Macmillan, 1955), p. 348.

20   Segel, *Pinocchio's Progeny*, p. 88.

21   Edward Braun, *The Director and the Stage* (London: Methuen, 1982), pp. 54–5.

22   See Olga Taxidou, *The Mask: A Periodical Performance by Edward Gordon Craig* (London: Harwood Academic Publishers, 1998, rpt. Routledge, 2000).

23   Edward Gordon Craig, *The Mask*, Vol. 1, No. 2 (Florence, 1908), p. 3.

24   Kleist, *Über das Marionettentheater*. Craig publishes the first English translation by Amedeo Forestiin, *The Marionette*, No. 4 (Florence, 1918).

25   Edward Gordon Graig, 'The Actor and the *Übermarionette*', in *The Mask*, Vol. 1 (Florence, 1908), p. 156.

26   Edward Gordon Craig, *The Marionette*, Vol. 1, No. 6 (Florence, 1908), p. 170.

27   Eleonora Duse, quoted in *The Mask*, Vol. 1 (Florence, 1908), p. 22.

28   Walter Gropius (ed.), *The Theatre of the Bauhaus*, trans. Arthur Wensinger (Baltimore, MD and London: Johns Hopkins University Press, 1996), p. 17.

29   Ibid., p. 54.

30   Wilhelm Worringer, *Abstraction and Empathy: A Contribution to the Psychology of Style* [1908], trans. Michael Bullock (New York: International Universities Press, 1967). This small but influential book was to become for the early decades for the twentieth century what Nietzsche's *The Birth of Tragedy* had been for the last decades of the nineteenth century. It proposed a universal *urge to abstraction* as a model for a transhistorical/transcendental type of modernism. The urge to empathy, according to Worringer, only produced representational art, which he considered to be of a lower order. Because of its proto-fascist undertones the impact of this study was for a long time underestimated.

31   Ibid., p. 24.

32   Oscar Schlemmer, *The Letters and Diaries of Oscar Schlemmer*, selected and edited by Tut Schlemmer, trans. Krishna Winston (Middletown, CT: Wesleyan University Press, 1972), September 1922, pp. 126–7.

33   See Robert Leach, *Vsevolod Meyerhold* (Cambridge: Cambridge University Press, 1989).

34   Fyodor Sologub, 'The Theatre of a Single Will', in Laurence Senelick (ed. and trans.), *Russian Dramatic Theory from Pushkin to the Symbolists: An Anthology* (Austin, TX: Univerity of Austin Press), pp. 132–48.

35 Quoted in Laurence Senelick, 'Moscow and Monodrama: The Meaning of the Craig-Stanislavsky Hamlet', in *Theatre Research International*, Vol. 6 (1981), pp. 109–24, p. 114.

36 Robert Leach, 'Vsevolod Emilevich Meyerhold', *Makers of Modern Theatre: An Introduction* (London and New York: Routledge, 2004), pp. 53–101, pp. 73–4.

37 Catriona Kelly, *Petrushka: The Russian Carnival Puppet Theatre* (Cambridge: Cambridge University Press, 1990), p. 147.

38 Segel, *Pinocchio's Progeny*, p. 233.

39 See *Petrushka: the Russian Carnival Puppet Theatre*, p. 150.

40 See Edward Braun (ed.), *Meyerhold on Theatre* (London: Methuen, 1969), p. 128.

41 Edward Gordon Craig as 'Tao', 'Women in the Theatre', *The Mask*, Vol. 3, No. 2 (Florence, 1910), p. 97.

42 Nelson, *The Secret Life of Puppets*, pp. 250–5.

43 Carlo Collodi [Carlo Lorenzini], *Pinocchio*, trans., M. A. Murray, Intro. Jack Zipes (London: Penguin, 2002).

44 Auguste Villiers de L'Isle-Adam, *L'Ève future* (1885–6), trans. Robert Martin Adams, *Tomorrow's Eve* (Urbana, IL: University of Illinois Press, 1982).

45 Segel, *Pinocchio's Progeny*, p. 40.

46 Carlo Collodi [Carlo Lorenzini], *The Adventures of Pinocchio: Story of a Puppet*, trans. Nicolas J. Perella (Berkeley and Los Angeles, CA: University of California Press, 1986), p. 461.

47 For an analysis of the sexual politics of this 'technology of woman', see Marie Lathers, *The Aesthetics of Artifice: Villiers's L'Ève future* (Chapel Hill, NC: University of North Carolina Press, 1996).

48 Quoted in Nelson, *The Secret Life of Puppets*, p. 253.

49 Ibid., p. 248.

50 Harold B. Segal, *Pinocchio's Progeny: Puppets, Maronettes, Automatons, and Robots in Modernist and Avant-Garde Drama* (Baltimore, MD: Johns Hopkins University Press, 1995), p. 262.

51 Duncan-Craig Collection, The Dance Collection, The Library for the Performing Arts at Lincoln Center, New York, Letters from Craig to Duncan, p. 272.

52 See Tony Howard, '"Why Are You Looking at Me Like That?": Raikh and Gonsharova – Two Actresses After the Revolution', in M Gale and V. Gardner (eds), *Women and Theatre, Occasional Papers* (University of Birmingham and Manchester, 1996/97), No. 3, pp. 140–55.

53 Ibid., p. 131.

54 For an insightful analysis of the sexual politics of the early period of the October Revolution see John Bowlt and Olga Matich (eds), *Laboratory of Dreams: The Russian Avant-Garde and Cultural Experiment* (Stanford, CA.: Stanford University Press, 1996).

55 Ibid., p. 131.

56 Djuna Barnes, 'When the Puppets Come to Town', *New York Morning Telegraph Sunday Magazine*, 8 July 1917. Reprinted and Introduced by Rebecca Loncraine in *Poetry Nation (PN) Review* (Manchester: Carcanet Press, 2003), no. 157.

57 Barnes, 'When the Puppets Come to Town', p. 48.

58 Ibid., p. 48.

59 Ibid., p. 50.

60 Ibid., p. 48.

Notes to Chapter 3: The Director, the Playwright and the Actress

1 Edward Gordon Craig, *The Art of the Theatre* (Edinburgh and London: William Heinemann, 1905), p. 138.

2 Ilya Ehrenburg, quoted in Edward Braun, *The Director and the Stage* (London: Methuen, 1982), p. 138.

3 Ibid., p. 138.

4 See Roger Savage and Matteo Sansone, '*Il Corago* and the staging of early opera: four chapters from an anonymous treatise *circa* 1630'. *Il Corago* is described as 'a functionary whose role had at least something in common with the modern director's, though he might have elements about him of the 20th-century impresario, movement coach, *dramaturg* and stage-manager as well', in *Early Music*, November 1989, p. 495; pp.495–511; also see Roger Savage, 'Staging an opera: Letters from a Cesarian poet'. 'It is clear that the Operatic Stage-Director both in function and name, is busily at work in mid-18th-century Vienna [referring to the librettist Metastasio], though the term – and to some folk the activity too – seems such a 20th-century one', in *Early Music*, November 1998, p. 590; pp. 583–95.

5 Theodor Adorno, *In Search of Wagner*, trans. Rodney Livingstone (Manchester: Manchester University Press, 1981), p. 91.

6 Craig, *The Art of the Theatre*, pp. 56–7.

7 Emile Zola, *La Naturalisme au théâtre* (Paris, 1881), quoted in Braun, *The Director and the Stage*, p. 24. Extracts in English in Eric Bentley ed., *The Theory of the Modern Stage* (London: Penguin, 1970).

8 Bertolt Brecht, 'Three Cheers for Shaw', in John Willett, *Brecht on Theatre* (London: Methuen, 1974), pp. 10–13.

9 Quoted in John Stokes, *Resistible Theatres* (London: Elek, 1972), p. 121.

10 Quoted in Roger Shattuck, *The Banquet Years* (London: 1959), p. 161.

11 Letter to Lugné-Poë, January 1896. Quoted in Braun, *The Director and the Stage*, p. 53.

12 Quoted in ibid., p. 55.

13 Quoted in ibid., p. 53.

14 August Strindberg, 'Preface to *Miss Julie*' (1888), extracts in Vassiliki Kolocotroni, Jane Goldman and Olga Taxidou, eds, *Modernism: An Anthology of Sources and Documents* (Edinburgh: Edinburgh University Press, 1998), p. 116.

15 Ibid., p. 116.

16 Quoted in *Ibsen: The Critical Heritage*, Michael Egan, ed. (London: Routledge and Kegan, 1972), p. 388.

17 Penny Farfan, *Women, Modernism & Performance* (Cambridge: Cambridge University Press, 2004), p. 1.

18 Quoted in ibid., p. 12.

19 Ibid., p. 32.

20 Gail Finney, 'Ibsen and Feminism', in James MacFarlane, ed., *The Cambridge Companion to Ibsen* (Cambridge: Cambridge University Press, 1994), pp. 89–105; pp. 95–6.

21 Isadora Duncan quoted in Deborah Jowitt, *Time and the Dancing Image* (Berkeley, CA: University of California Press, 1988), p. 81.

22 Virginia Woolf, 'Rachel', *Times Literary Supplement*, 20 April 1911, p.155; quoted in Farfan, *Women, Modernism & Performance*, p. 51.

23 See August Strindberg, *From an Occult Diary: Marriage with Harriet Bosse* (London: Secker and Warburg, 1965); Carl Waal, *Harriet Bosse: Strindberg's Muse and Interpreter* (Illinois: Southern Illinois University Press, 1990).

24 In the case of Brecht we also need to take into account the defining contributions made to his work by a number of significant women in his life. The most prominent were Elizabeth Hauptmann, Margarete Steffin and Ruth Berlau. See John Fuegi, *The Life and Lies of Bertolt Brecht* (London and New York: HarperCollins, 1994). For a critical review and analysis of the dangers of viewing all these women as victims of Brecht's 'evil genius and charm' see, Olga Taxidou, 'Crude Thinking: Brecht and Feminist Criticism', in *New Theatre Quarterly* (Cambridge: Cambridge University Press, August 1995).

25 Robert Leach, *Stanislavsky and Meyerhold* (Bern: Peter Lang, Stage and Screen Studies 3, 2003), pp. 41–2.

26 Quoted in Braun, *The Director and the Stage*, p. 60.

27 Vsevolod Meyerhold, 'The Reconstruction of the Theatre' (1929), extracts in Kolocotroni et. al., eds, *Modernism: An Anthology of Sources and Documents*, pp. 241–2.

28 Ibid., p. 242.

29 Quoted in Edward Braun, ed. and trans., *Meyerhold on Theatre* (London: Methuen, 1969), p. 206.

30 Leach, *Stanislavsky and Meyerhold*, pp. 169–70.

31 Sergei Mikhailovich Tretyakov, *I Want a Baby*, trans. Stephen Holland, ed. Robert Leach (Birmingham: Studies in Drama and Dance, University of Birmingham, 1995).

32 Leach, *Stanislavsky and Meyerhold*, p. 195.

33 See Laurence Senelick, 'Moscow and Monodrama: Meaning of the Craig-Stanislavsky Hamlet', in *Theatre Research International*, Vol. 6 (Glasgow, 1981), pp. 109–24.
34 Quoted in ibid., p. 114.
35 Edward Gordon Craig, *The Mask*, Vol. 10 (Florence, 1924), p. 188.

Notes to Chapter 4: '… as if the words themselves could sing and shine': Poetic Drama and Theatricality

1 Martin Puchner, *Stagefright: Modernism, Anti-theatricality and Drama* (Baltimore, MD and London: Johns Hopkins University Press, 2002), p. 25.
2 Ibid., pp. 5–7.
3 E. Martin Browne, 'The Poet and the Stage', *Penguin New Writing*, 31 (1947), pp. 82–3.
4 Gertrude Stein, 'Plays' (1934), in Bert Cardullo and Robert Knopf (eds), *Theatre of the Avant-garde, 1890–1950: A Critical Anthology* (New Haven, CT and London: Yale University Press, 2001), p. 454.
5 Ibid., p. 458.
6 Ibid., p. 463.
7 'The Play, The Player and the Scene', *Samhain* (1904), pp. 31–2; *Explorations* (London, 1962), pp. 177–9. Quoted in James W. Flannery, 'W. B. Yeats, Gordon Craig and the Visual Arts of the Theatre', in Robert O'Driscoll and Lorna Reynolds (eds), *Yeats and the Theatre* (London: Macmillan, 1975), p. 90.
8 For Yeats's experiments in lighting see O'Driscoll and Reynolds, *Yeats and the Theatre*, pp. 90–5.
9 Quoted in Joseph Hone, *W. B. Yeats: 1865–1939* (London: Macmillan, 1943), p. 252. Despite his concerns Yeats joined a group called 'The Society for the Theatre' in 1912 (members included Craig, Augustus John, William Poel, J. Martin Harvey, Konstantin Stanislavsky, Tomasso Salvini, Cecil Sharpe and Ezra Pound). The manifesto, probably written by Craig, stated that the group 'aims at creating a dramatic movement which shall appeal to the theatrical rather than to the literary aspects of drama. By "theatrical" is meant that form of stage production which makes an appeal to the senses through the imagination rather than to the intellect. The society has adopted the idea of Gordon Craig, and is formed to promote discussion of that idea, and to try to establish a School for the Art of the Theatre, with Gordon Craig as authoritative director.' See Allardyce Nicoll, *English Drama: 1900–1930* (Cambridge: Cambridge University Press, 1973), pp. 103–4. Although this society was not very active, Yeats wrote in a letter to Craig in 1913, 'Your work is always a great inspiration to me. Indeed I cannot imagine myself writing any play for the stage now, which I did not write for your screens.' See Gordon Craig Collection, Bibliothèque de l'Arsenal, Paris, 29 July 1913. Quoted in Denis Bablet, *Edward Gordon Craig* (London: Heinemann, 1966), p. 130.

10 Allan Wade (ed.), *The Letters of W. B. Yeats* (London: R. Hart-Davis, 1954), p. 579. This volume never appeared until *Plays and Controversies* (1923).

11 'It is only in his last play *Purgatory* that he solved his problem of speech in verse, and laid all his successors under obligation to him;' see T. S. Eliot, *Poetry and Drama* (London: Faber and Faber, 1950), p. 20.

12 Ibid., p. 22–3.

13 Ibid., p. 15.

14 See *Doctor Faustus Lights the Lights* in Cardullo and Knopf (eds), *Theatre of the Avant-garde, 1890–1950*, p. 443.

15 W. B. Yeats, *Explorations* (London: Macmillan, 1962), p. 263.

16 W. B. Yeats, *Autobiographies* (London: Macmillan, 1955), p. 416.

17 Joseph Holloway, *Joseph Holloway's Abbey Theatre*, eds Robert Hogan and Michael J. O'Neill (Carbondale, IL: Southern Illinois University Press, 1967), p. 8.

18 Yeats, *Explorations*, pp. 86–7.

19 *The Irish Times*, 13 January 1911, W. H. Henderson Press Clippings, National Library of Ireland, Ms 1734, p. 6. Quoted in *Yeats and the Theatre*, p. 102.

20 W. B. Yeats, *Four Plays for Dancers* (London: Macmillan, 1921), p. v.

21 Puchner, *Stagefright*, p. 130.

22 T. S. Eliot, *Poetry and Drama*, p. 20.

23 Ibid., p. 22.

24 Ibid., p. 27.

25 Ibid., p. 15.

26 Martha C. Carpentier, *Ritual, Myth and the Modernist Text: The Influence of Jane Ellen Harrison on Joyce, Eliot, and Woolf* (Amsterdam: Gordon and Breach, 1998), p. 102.

27 Hugh Kenner, *The Invisible Poet* (London: Routledge and Kegan Paul, 1959), p. 339.

28 Carpentier, *Ritual, Myth, and the Modernist Text*, p. 106.

29 Ibid., p. 108.

30 See Jane Ellen Harrison, *Themis: A Study of the Social Origins of Greek Religion* (Cambridge: Cambridge University Press, 1912). Also see Chapter 6 of this book.

31 Eliot, *Poetry and Drama*, p. 31.

32 *The Complete Poems and Plays of T. S. Eliot* (London: Faber and Faber, 1969), p. 39.

33 Quoted in E. Martin Browne, *The Making of T. S. Eliot's Plays* (Cambridge: Cambridge University Press, 1970), p. 247.

34 Eliot, *Poetry and Drama*, p. 34.

35 Gertrude Stein, *Last Plays and Operas*, ed. and intro. Bonnie Marranca (Baltimore, MD and London: Johns Hopkins University Press, 1995), p. xvii.

36 See Cardullo and Knopf (eds), *Theatre of the Avant-garde, 1890–1950*, p. 463.

37 Bonnie Marranca, 'Introduction' in Stein, *Last Plays and Operas*, p. x.

38 Quoted in Cardullo and Knopf (eds), *Theatre of the Avant-garde, 1890–1950*, p. 463.

39   The exception would be the extraordinary English Vorticist aritist, Wyndham
     Lewis, whose plays *Enemy of the Stars* (1914; 1932) and the brief *The Ideal
     Giant* (1914) blend discourses from the visual and textual arts with an
     emphatic philosophical imperative. *Enemy* first appears in Lewis's
     journal/manifesto *Blast* and according to Puchner, 'both its failure and its
     appeal are products of the collision between the literary form of drama and the
     genre of the manifesto'. See Martin Puchner, *Poetry of the Revolution: Marx,
     Manifestos, and the Avant-Gardes* (Princeton, NJ: Princeton University Press,
     2005), p. 120. As in Stein's 'plays' the 'painterly aesthetics' (p. 119) of Lewis
     helps create a theatrical form that defies allegory, metaphor and interpretation
     in general.
40   Ibid., pp. 435–6.
41   Ibid., p. 444.
42   Ibid., p. 445.
43   Ibid., 431– 2.
44   Puchner, *Stagefright*, p. 105.
45   Bertolt Brecht, *Poems, 1913–1956*, trans. and ed. J Willet and R. Manheim
     (London and New York: Methuen, 1976), p. 225.
46   *Brecht on Theatre*, trans. and ed. John Willet (London and New York: Methuen,
     1974), pp. 37–8.
47   Ibid., p. 156.
48   W. H. Auden, *The English Auden* (London: Faber and Faber, 1977), p. 233.
49   See John Willet, 'Auden and Brecht', in Ian Donaldson (ed.), *Transformations
     in Modern Drama* (London: Macmillan, 1983), pp. 162–76.
50   Christopher Isherwood, *Christopher and his Kind* (London: Methuen,
     1977), p. 180.
51   T. S. Eliot, *Selected Essays* (London: Faber and Faber, 1951), p. 46.
52   Ibid., p. 46.
53   Ramsay Burt, *The Male Dancer* (London and New York: Routledge, 1995).
54   Ibid., p. 3.
55   *The Mask*, Vol. 4 (Florence, 1911), p. 98. Craig had designed a ballet, *Psyche*,
     for Diaghilev in 1906–07, which was turned down. See Edward Gordon Craig,
     Designs for the Theatre (London: Heinemann, 1948), p. 8; p. 18.
56   See Sally Banes, *Dancing Women: Female Bodies on Stage* (London and New
     York: Routledge, 1998), pp. 5–7.
57   Igor Stravinsky and Robert Craft, *Expositions and Developments* (London:
     Faber and Faber, 1962), pp. 130–1.
58   Quoted in Sally Banes, *Dancing Women*, p. 119.
59   Quoted in Joan Acocella and Lynn Garafola (eds), *André Levinson on Dance*
     (Hanover, NH: Wesleyan University Press, 1991), p. 41.
60   See DVD, *The Firebird* and *Les Noces*, BBC, 2001.
61   See Sally Banes, *Dancing Women*, p. 120.
62   Jean Cocteau, 'Preface: 1922', to *The Wedding on the Eiffel Tower*, in Michael
     Benedikt and George E. Wellwarth (eds and trans.), *Modern French Plays: An
     Anthology from Jarry to Ionesco* (London: Faber and Faber, 1964), p. 97.

63 Ibid., p. 98.

64 Ibid., p. 99.

65 Jean Cocteau, *The Wedding on the Eiffel Tower*, in *Modern French Plays*, pp. 101–15, pp. 112–13.

66 Jean Cocteau, 'Preface: 1922', p. 99.

67 T. S. Eliot, *Poetry and Drama*, p. 20.

68 Ninette de Valois, *Come Dance with Me* (London: Faber and Faber, 1957), p. 88.

69 See Richard Taylor, *The Drama of W. B. Yeats: Irish Myth and the Japanese Noh* (New Haven, CT and London: Yale University Press, 1976), pp. 162–70.

70 Quoted in *The Drama of W. B. Yeats: Irish Myth and the Japanese Noh*, p. 170.

Notes to Chapter 5: Sada Yakko, Michio Ito and Mei Lan-fang: Orientalism, Interculturalism and the Performance Event

1 Edward Said, *Musical Elaborations* (London: Chatto and Windus, 1991); also see *Culture and Imperialism* (London: Chatto and Windus, 1993), where he writes, 'cultural identities exist not as essentialisations ... but as contrapuntal ensembles ... since no identity can ever exist by itself and without an array of opposites, negatives, oppositions', p. 60. As Hallward stresses, this is a constant theme throughout Said's work.

2 Aijaz Ahmad, *In Theory: Classes, Nations, Literatures* (London: Verso, 1992); 'The Politics of Literary Postcoloniality', in Padmini Mongia (ed.), *Contemporary Postcolonial Theory: A Reader* (London: Arnold, 1996), pp. 276–93.

3 Rustom Bharucha, *Theatre and the World: Performance and the Politics of Culture* (London and New York: Routledge, 1990).

4 Ibid., p. 15.

5 This line of analysis is dominant in the work of the more traditionalist theatre critics like Martin Esslin, but interestingly is also apparent in the more recent work of Peter Hallward. Hallward writes, dismissing Brecht together with the historical avant-garde, 'Nether politics nor art has anything to gain, today, from a general didactic coordination à la Brecht or Sembène – such coordination can be defended only in quite *specific* circumstances. After a sequence of ultimately unsustainable theoretical attempts to blend literature and politics in a single vanguardism (surrealism, existentialism, situationism, *Tel Quel* ...), it is time to recognise that the evaluation of literature is essentially indifferent to politics as such', Peter Hallward, *Absolutely Postcolonial: Writing Between the Singular and the Specific* (Manchester and New York: Manchester University Press, 2001), p. xx.

6 Ibid., pp. 42–3.

7 Alain Badiou, *L'Ethique: Essai sur la conscience du mal* (Paris: Hatier, 1993), p. 25; for an elaboration see *Saint Paul et la foundation de*

l'universalisme (Paris: PUF, 1997). Quoted here from trans. Hallward, *Absolutely Postcolonial*, p. xx.

8   Hallward, *Absolutely Postcolonial*, p. 45.

9   For an assessment of the impact of Artaud on the post-1960s schools of philosophy and theory, see Jane Milling and Graham Ley, *Modern Theories of Performance* (Basingstoke and New York: Palgrave Macmillan, 2001), pp. 89–93. 'What is striking is that Artaud's theatricality is, if anything, conservative. His insistence on the theatre as a radical cultural force is nostalgic in the immediate postwar years, when performance was an instrument of a larger disillusionment. Ironically, it has been this conservativism and nostalgia which have, to a great degree, ensured his later influence', p. 93.

10 Antony Tatlow, *Shakespeare, Brecht, and the Intercultural Sign* (Durham, NC and London: Duke University Press, 2001); Tatlow, *Brechts Ost Asien* (Berlin: Parthas, 1998); Tatlow and Tak-Wai Wong (eds), *Brecht and East Asian Theatre* (Hong Kong: Hong Kong University Press, 1982); Fredric Jameson, *Brecht and Method* (London: Verso, 1998); Also see Tatlow, 'For and Against Method: Jameson, Brecht, and the Dao', in *Colloquia Germanica*, vol. 34, no. 3/4, 2001, pp. 287–316.

11 See Said, *Culture and Imperialism*, 'the contrapuntal critic submits composite, hybrid identities to a negative dialectic which dissolves them into variously constructed components', p. 378.

12 Tatlow, *Shakespeare, Brecht, and the Intercultural Sign*; Tatlow, *Brechts Ost*; Tatlow and Tak-Wai Wong (eds), *Brecht and East Asian Theatre*.

13 Hallward, *Abolutely Postcolonial*, p. 14.

14 See Antony Tatlow (ed.), *Where Extremes Meet: Rereading Brecht and Beckett, The Brecht Yearbook 27* (Madison, WI: University of Wisconsin Press, 2002).

15 Tatlow, *Shakespeare, Brecht, and the Intercultural Sign*, p. 223.

16 Ibid., p. 73.

17 Gilles Deleuze, *Cinéma 2: L'Image-temps* (Paris: Minuit, 1985), trans. Hugh Tomlinson and Barbara Habberjam (Minneapolis, MN: University of Minnesota Press, 1989), quoted in Hallward, *Absolutely Postcolonial*, p. 342, n. 80.

18 Tatlow, *Shakespeare, Brecht and the Intercultural Sign*, p. 45.

19 Claude Schumacher (ed.), *Artaud on Theatre* (London: Methuen, 1989), pp. 89–90.

20 Ibid., pp. 125–6.

21 Quoted in L. C. Pronko, *Theatre East and West* (Berkeley, CA: University of California Press,1967), p. 120.

22 Quoted in Ibid., p. 120.

23 Edward Gordon Craig, 'Women in the Theatre', *The Mask*, Vol. 3, No. 2 (Florence, 1910), p. 96.

24 Ibid., p. 97.

25 See Olga Taxidou, *The Mask: A Periodical Performance by Edward Gordon Craig* (Amsterdam: Harwood Academic Publishers, 1998; London: Routledge, 2000), pp. 79–109.

26 This important book formed part of a growing interest in Japanese theatre in the Anglophone world, but it was not the first translation in English to appear: Marie Stopes, *Plays of Old Japan*, was published in 1910 and M. A. Hink's *The Art of Japanese Dancing* appeared in 1906.

27 W. B. Yeats, *Certain Noble Plays of Japan: From the Manuscript of Ernest Fenollosa, Chosen and Finished by Ezra Pound, with an Introduction by W. B. Yeats* (Churchtown Dundrum: Cuala Press, 1916), p. ii.

28 Ibid., p. xiv.

29 Liam Miller, *The Noble Drama of W. B. Yeats* (Dublin: Dolmen, 1977), pp. 223–5.

30 Yeats, *Certain Noble Plays of Japan*, p. vii.

31 Edward Gordon Craig, *The Mask*, Vol. 3 (Florence, 1910), pp. 90–1.

32 Yeats, *Certain Noble Plays of Japan*, p. viii.

33 *The Ten Principal Upanishads, Put into English by Shree Purohit Swami and W. B. Yeats* (London: Faber and Faber, 1937), p. ii.

34 Edward Gordon Craig, *The Mask*, Vol. 9 (Florence, 1919), p. 34.

35 See Brian Victoria, *Zen at War* (New York: Weatherhill, 1998).

36 Julia Kristeva quoted in Naomi Greene, '"All the Great Myths Are Dark": Artaud and Fascism', in Gene A. Plunka (ed.), *Antonin Artaud and the Modern Theatre* (Madison, NJ: Fairleigh Dickinson University Press, pp. 102–16, p. 104.

37 Ibid., pp. 104–5.

38 Jo Riley, *Chinese Theatre and the Actor in Performance* (Cambridge: Cambridge University Press, 1997), p. 9.

39 A. C. Scott, *Mei Lan-Fang: The Life and Times of a Peking Actor* (Hong Kong: Hong Kong University Press, 1959), pp. 116–17.

40 Ibid., p. 101.

41 Carol Martin, 'Brecht, Feminism, and Chinese Theatre', *The Drama Review*, Vol. 43. No. 4, 1999, pp. 77–85, p. 79.

42 Katherine Hui-ling Chou, 'Staging Revolution: Actresses, Realism, and the New Woman Movement in Chinese Spoken Drama & Film, 1919–1949', PhD thesis, New York University, quoted in Martin, ibid., p. 77.

43 Martin, ibid., p. 81.

44 Brecht, 'The Question of Criteria for Judging Acting' (notes to *Mann ist Mann*), in *Brecht on Theatre: The Development of an Aesthetic*, ed. and trans. John Willet (London: Methuen, 1964), pp 53–7, p. 55.

45 Riley, *The Chinese Theatre and the Actor in Performance*, p. 85.

46 Ibid., p. 315.

47 Ibid., p. 11.

48 Ibid., pp. 316–17.

49 Brecht, 'Alienation Effects in Chinese Acting', in *Brecht on Theatre*, pp. 91–9, p. 95.

50 Ibid., p. 96.

51 Riley, *The Chinese Theatre*.

Notes to Chapter 6: Greeks and Other Savages: Neo-Hellenism, Primitivism and Performance

1   Tom Kuhn and Steve Giles (eds), 'Conversation about Classics' (28 April 1929), in *Brecht on Art and Politics* (London: Methuen, 2003), p. 76.
2   D. D. Paige (ed.), 'Letter to Margaret C. Anderson' (January 1917), in *The Selected Letters of Ezra Pound 1907–1941* (London: Faber and Faber, 1950), p. 107.
3   See Robert Ackerman, *The Myth and Ritual School* (New York and London: Garland, 1991). For a full bibliography of the group's work see Arlen Shelley, *The Cambridge Ritualists: An Annotated Bibliography* (New Jersey and London: Scarecrow, 1990).
4   See Henry Francis Mallgrave, *Gottfried Semper: Architect of the Nineteenth Century* (New Haven, CT and London: Yale University Press, 1996).
5   Ibid., p. 8, pp. 251–67.
6   Ibid., p. 8.
7   Ulrich von Wilamowitz-Moellendorff (1848–1931), called the greatest classicist of his time, famously attacked the works of the Cambridge group, particularly Jane Ellen Harrison. See Ward W. Briggs and William M. Calder III, *Classical Scholarship: A Biographical Encyclopaedia* (New York: Garland, 1990).
8   Quoted in Richard J. Finneran, George Mills Harper and William M. Murphy (eds), *Letters to W. B. Yeats, Vol. 1* (London: Macmillan, 1977), p. 116.
9   Robert Crawford, *The Savage and the City in the Work of T. S. Eliot* (Oxford: Clarendon Press, 1990), pp. 108–9.
10 Ackerman, *The Myth and Ritual School*, p. vii.
11 Letter (1933) to Hallie Flanagan quoted in Crawford, *The Savage and the City*, p. 162.
12 Ibid., p. 162.
13 See Martha C. Carpentier, *Ritual, Myth and the Modernist Text: The Influence of Jane Ellen Harrison on Joyce, Eliot, and Woolf* (Amsterdam: Gordon and Breach, 1998).
14 Ibid., p. 106.
15 T. S. Eliot, *The Complete Poems and Plays* (London: Faber and Faber, 1971), p. 83.
16 For classical themes in the theatre of Yeats see Brian Arkins, *Builders of My Soul: Greek and Roman Themes in Yeats* (London: Rowan and Littlefield, 1990).
17 T. S. Eliot, 'Euripides and Professor Murray' (1920), in *Selected Essays* (London: Faber and Faber, 1932, rpt. 1951), p. 62.
18 Gilbert Murray's translations of Euripides had a huge impact on the British theatre at the time. See Fiona Macintosh, 'The Shavian Murray and the Euripidean Shaw: *Major Barbara* and the *Bacchae*', *Classics Ireland*, Vol. 5, 1998; Edith Hall and Fiona Macintosh, *Greek Tragedy and the British Theatre 1660–1914* (Oxford: Oxford University Press, 2005), pp. 488–554.

19 Quoted in Finneran et al. (eds), *Letters to W. B. Yeats, Vol. 1*, 27 January 1905, p. 146.

20 See Hall and MacIntosh, *Greek Tragedy and the British Theatre 1660–1914*, 'Greek Tragedy and the Cosmopolitan Ideal', pp. 521–54.

21 Quoted in J. L. Styan, *Max Reinhardt: Directors in Perspective* (Cambridge: Cambridge University Press, 1982), p. 81.

22 See Erika Fischer-Lichte, 'Between Text and Cultural Performance: Staging Greek Tragedies in Germany', *Theatre Survey*, Vol. 40, 1999, pp. 1–30.

23 Quoted in Finneran et al. (eds), *Letters to W. B. Yeats, Vol 1*, p. 146.

24 To Iris Barry, August 1916, *Selected Letters of Ezra Pound, 1907–1941*, p. 94.

25 See *Greek Tragedy and the British Theatre 1660–1914*, pp. 543–54.

26 Ibid., p. 540.

27 *Morning Post*, 20 January 1912, quoted in Styan, *Max Reinhardt*, p. 84.

28 Ibid., p. 84.

29 Ibid., p. 85.

30 For Count Kessler's contribution see L. M. Newman, 'Reinhardt and Craig?', in *Max Reinhardt: The Oxford Symposium* (Oxford: Oxford Polytechnic, 1986), pp. 6–15.

31 Craig edited *The Mask* and wrote most of it himself under no less than 65 pseudonyms. See Taxidou, *The Mask: A Periodical Performance by Edward Gordon Craig*, 'Authorship and Narrative in the Periodical', pp. 175–91.

32 Quoted in Newman, 'Reinhardt and Craig?', pp. 8–9.

33 J. Michael Walton, 'Gordon Craig and the Classical Revival', Getty Lecture, 20 March 2002, The Getty Centre, Los Angeles.

34 See Newman, 'Reinhardt and Craig?', p. 14.

35 Taxidou, *The Mask: A Periodical Performance by Edward Gordon Craig*, p. 71.

36 See Francis Steegmuller, *Your Isadora: The Love Story of Isadora Duncan and Gordon Craig* (New York: Random House, 1974). Also documented in the 'Craig-Duncan Collection', The Dance Collection, The Library for the Performing Arts, Lincoln Centre, New York.

37 Interestingly Craig did try to work with a fully fledged dance company, where these issues would have been explored. In 1911 he met with the composer Vaughan Williams and Diaghilev and Nijinsky from the Ballets Russes to discuss a production of a ballet on 'Cupid and Psyche'. Nothing came of it. See Ursula Vaughan Williams, *R.V.W.: A Biography of Ralph Vaughan Williams* (Oxford: Clarendon Press, 1988), pp. 93–4. ('"Let me have the music," said Craig, "and I'll fit in the story." "Impossible," said Ralph, "you must let me have the scenario and I will write music for it." "Impossible," said Craig, "just send the music" – and so they parted. Neither sent anything to the other and the projected ballet became another might-have-been.'), p. 94.

38 Sophocles, *Women of Trachis, A Version by Ezra Pound* (London: Faber and Faber, 1956), p. ii.

39 Ibid., p. 39.

40   Ezra Pound, 'A Retrospect' (1918), in Vassiliki Kolocotroni, Jane Goldman and
     Olga Taxidou (eds), *Modernism: An Anthology of Sources and Documents*
     (Edinburgh: Edinburgh University Press, 1998), p. 374.
41   Ibid., p. 387.
42   Pound, '*Ulysses*, Order, and Myth' (1923), in ibid., pp. 371–3.
43   Eileen Gregory, *H.D. and Hellenism* (Cambridge: Cambridge University Press,
     1997), p. 3.
44   See Susan Stanford Friedman, *Penelope's Web: Gender, Modernity, H.D.'s
     Fiction* (Cambridge: Cambridge University Press, 1990); and *Psyche Reborn:
     The Emergence of H.D.* (Bloomington, IN: Indiana University Press, 1981).
45   See Gregory, *H.D. and Hellenism*, p. 118.
46   Quoted in ibid., p. 207.
47   H.D. (Hilda Doolittle), *Helen in Egypt* (Manchester: Carcanet, 1961). She
     writes in Book 2: '*Lethe, as we all know, is the river of forgetfulness for the
     shadows, passing from life to death. But Helen, mysteriously transposed to
     Egypt, does not want to forget. She is both phantom and reality*', p. 3.
48   Walter Mehring, *Simply Classical! An Oresteia With a Happy Ending*, trans.
     Henry Marx, in Mel Gordon (ed.), *Dada Performance* (New York: PAJ
     Publications, 1987), pp. 67–79; p. 70.
49   Ibid., p. 71.
50   'Texts by Brecht' on 'The *Antigone* of Sophocles', in Tom Kuhn and David
     Constantine (eds), *Brecht, Collected Plays, Vol. 8: The Antigone of Sophocles*,
     trans. David Constantine (London: Methuen, 2003), p. 205.
51   Ibid., p. 204.
52   Theodor Adorno, 'Commitment', in *Aesthetics and Politics*, trans. Francis
     McDonagh (London and New York: Verso, 1980), pp. 177–95, p. 188.
53   'Texts by Brecht' on 'The *Antigone* of Sophocles', p. xii.
54   *Hölderlin's Sophocles' Oedipus and Antigone*, trans. and intro. David
     Constantine (Highgreen: Bloodaxe Books, 2001), pp. 11–12.
55   He writes in a letter, 16 December 1947, 'On Cas's [Caspar Neher] advice I am
     using the Hölderlin translation, which is seldom or never performed because it is
     considered too obscure. I come across Swabian accents and grammar-school
     Latin constructions and feel quite at home. And there is some Hegel in there too.
     It is presumably the return to the German-speaking world which is forcing me
     into this enterprise', 'Texts by Brecht' on 'The *Antigone of Sophocles*', p. 197.
56   Ibid., p. 217.
57   Ibid., pp. 199.
58   Ibid., pp. 198–9.
59   For a discussion of the philosophical dimension of the translations of *deinon*
     from Hölderlin to Heidegger, see Stathis Gourgouris, *Does Literature Think?
     Literature as Theory for an Antimythical Era* (Stanford, CA: Stanford
     University Press, 2003), pp. 134–5.
60   See 'Texts by Brecht' on 'The *Antigone* of Sophocles', p. 18.
61   Ibid., p. 217.

62 Ibid., p. 203.

63 *Brecht on Theatre*, ed. and trans. John Willett (London: Methuen, 1990), p. 75.

64 For the impact of Aristotelianism on German Idealism, see Riccardo Pozzo, *The Impact of Aristotelianism on Modern Philosophy* (Studies in Philosophy and the History of Philosophy) (New York: Catholic University of America Press, 2003); For the different schools of interpretation of Aristotle, see R.W. Sharples, *Whose Aristotle? Whose Aristotelianism?* (London: Ashgate, 2001).

65 Ibid., pp. 37–8.

Notes to Chapter 7: 'The Revolution said to the theatre ...': Performance and Engagement

1 A. V. Lunacharsky, the first Narkom (People's Commissar), quoted in Konstantin Rudnitsky, *Russian and Soviet Theatre: Tradition and the Avant-Garde* (London: Thames and Hudson, 1988), p. 41.

2 See Ernst Bloch, Georg Lukács, Bertolt Brecht, Walter Benjamin and Theodor Adorno, *Aesthetics and Politics*, trans. and ed. Ronald Taylor, Afterword by Fredric Jameson (London: Verso, 1980).

3 See the very influential Peter Bürger, *Theory of the Avant-Garde*, trans. Michael Shaw (Minneapolis, MN: University of Minnesota Press, 1984); for critical responses to Bürger, see Richard Murphy, *Theorising the Avant-Garde: Modernism, Expressionism, and the Problems of Postmodernity* (Cambridge: Cambridge University Press, 1999), and Dietrich Scheunemann (ed.), *European Avant-Garde: New Perspectives* (Amsterdam: Rodopi, 2000); for an account of the Russian avant-garde see Boris Groys, *The Total Art of Stalinism*, trans. Charles Rougle (Princeton, NJ: Princeton University Press, 1992), originally published in German as *Gesamtkunstwerk Stalin* (Vienna: Carl Halser, 1988).

4 See Groys, *The Total Art of Stalinism*.

5 See Bürger, *Theory of the Avant-Garde*, p. 41.

6 Günter Berghaus, *Theatre, Performance, and the Historical Avant-garde* (Basingstoke and New York: Palgrave Macmillan, 2005), p. 41.

7 Ibid., p. 41.

8 See Theodor Adorno, 'Reconciliation under Duress', trans. Rodney Livingstone, in *Aesthetics and Politics*, pp. 151–76, p. 160.

9 For an illuminating account of the apocalyptic strand in modernist and avant-garde aesthetics see Jane Goldman, *Modernism, 1910–1945: Image to Apocalypse* (Basingstoke and New York: Palgrave Macmillan, 2004), 'Introduction: "Make It New"', pp. 1–30.

10 Berghaus, *Theatre, Performance and the Historical Avant-garde*, p. 102.

11 Ibid., p. 42.

12   Walter Benjamin, 'The Work of Art in the Age of Mechanical Reproduction', in Vassiliki Kolocotroni, Jane Goldman and Olga Taxidou (eds), *Modernism: An Anthology of Sources and Documents* (Edinburgh: Edinburgh University Press, 1998), pp. 570–6.

13   Ibid., p. 576.

14   See Günter Berghaus (ed.), *Fascism and Theatre* (Oxford: Berghahn Books, 1996).

15   Berghaus, *Theatre, Performance and the Historical Avant-garde*, p. 113.

16   In Umbro Apollonio (ed.), *Futurist Manifestos* (London: Thames and Hudson, 1973, pp. 197–200.

17   For a detailed account and documentation of Berlin Dada see Hanne Bergius, '*Dada Triumphs!' Dada Berlin, 1917–1923: Artistry of Polarities, Montages, Metamechanics, Manifestations*, Brigitte Pichon, trans. (New Haven, CT: Thomson Gale, 2003).

18   Ibid., p. 26.

19   Ibid., p. 263.

20   See Goldman, *Modernism, 1910–1945*, p. 253.

21   See Bergius, '*Dada Triumphs!*', p. 263.

22   See Bürger, *Theory of the Avant-Garde*, p. 49.

23   See Bergius, '*Dada Triumphs!*', pp. 278–9.

24   See speech by Adolf Hitler inaugurating the 'Great Exhibition of Modern Art', Munich 1937, in Kolocotroni, Goldman and Taxidou (eds), *Modernism: An Anthology of Sources and Documents*, pp. 560–3.

25   This is an extended version of Benjamin's essay (1936–39), unpublished in his lifetime (first published in Volume 7 of Benjamin's *Gesammelte Schriften*, 1989), in Walter Benjamin, *Selected Writings: Volume 4, 1938–1940* (Cambridge, MA: Harvard University Press, 2006).

26   Eduardo Cadava, *Words of Light: Thesis on the Photography of History* (Princeton, NJ: Princeton University Press, 1997), 'Reproducibility', pp. 42–4.

27   For an analysis of the ways in which 'liveness' and 'reproducibility' become central to the theatres of Modernism, see Philip Auslander, *Liveness: Performance in a Mediatized Culture* (London and New York: Routledge, 1999).

28   There was a very influential Russian émigré community in Berlin in the 1920s. Some were exiles from the Tsarist regime, others from the Soviet Union, others still were representing the Soviet Union. Berlin became the crossroads for the Continental and Russian avant-gardes just before the Stalinist purges began and before the infamous Moscow trials of the 1930s. For a wonderfully insightful fictional account see Viktor Shklovsky, *Zoo or Letters Not About Love*, trans. Richard Sheldon (Chicago: Dalkey Archive Press, 2001). Ilya Ehrenburg writes in his memoirs, 'There existed a place in Berlin reminiscent of Noah's Ark, where the clean and the unclean met peaceably; it was called the House of Arts. Russian writers congregated in the ordinary German café on Fridays. Tolstoy, Remizov, Lidin, Pilnyak, Sokolv-Mitikov read their stories, Mayakovsky performed. Esenin, Marina Tsvetaeva, Andrei Bely, Pasternak, Khodasevich

recited their poetry. Once I caught sight of Igor Severyanin, who had come from Estonia; he was full of self-admiration as ever and read the same "poesies". A storm broke out at a lecture by the painter Puni, which Archipenko, Mayakovsky, Sterberg, Gabo, Lissitzky and I enjoyed furiously', in Ilya Ehrenburg, *Memoirs: 1921–1941* (Cleveland, OH and New York, 1963), p. 20.

29 From 'Die Blockade Russlands geht ihrem Ends entegegen' (The Blockade of Russia Is Coming to an End), 1922, quoted in Bergius, *'Dada Triumphs!'*, p. 81.

30 Groys, *The Total Art of Stalinism*, p. 20.

31 Ibid., p. 20.

32 Ibid., p. 22.

33 Ibid., p. 25.

34 Quoted in Frantisek Deak, 'Blue Blouse: 1923–28', in *The Drama Review: TDR*, Vol. 17, No.1, Russian Issue (March, 1971), pp. 35–46; p. 36.

35 Sergei Eisenstein, 'The Montage of Attractions', in Lars Kleberg, *Theatre as Action* (Houndmills, Basingstoke: MacMillan, 1993), pp. 78–80; p. 79.

36 Quoted in Frantisek Deak, 'Blue Blouse: 1923–28', p. 39.

37 For an analysis of the 'laboratory' analogy in all fields of cultural production see John E. Bowlt and Olga Matich, eds, *Laboratory of Dream: The Russian Avant-Garde and Cultural Experiment* (Stanford, CA.: Stanford University Press, 1996).

38 Quoted in Frantisek Deak, 'Blue Blouse: 1923–28', p. 38.

39 Quoted in Groys, *The Total Art of Stalinism*, p. 55.

40 Meyerhold explains how he was forced to 'confess' on the charges of Trotskyism and espionage, 'They laid me face down on the floor and beat the soles of my feet and my back with a rubber truncheon. When I was seated on a chair they used the same truncheon to beat my legs from above with great force, from my knees to the upper parts of my legs. And in the days that followed, when my legs were bleeding from internal haemorrhaging, they used the rubber truncheon to beat me on the red, blue and yellow bruises. The pain was so great that it was like boiling water being poured on the tenderest parts of my legs (I screamed and wept with pain)', quoted in Edward Braun, 'Vsevolod Meyerhold: the Final Act', in Katherine Bliss Eaton, ed., *Enemies of the People* (Evanston: Northwestern University Press, 2002), pp. 154–5. Robert Leach reports that after a series of pleas to Molotov, Stalin's Prime Minister, he was again tortured, brought to 'trial' on 1 February 1939 and shot the following day: 'His body was burned, and the ashes tipped into "Common Grave Number One" in the Don Monastery cemetery', see Robert Leach, *Makers of Modern Theatre* (London and New York: Routledge, 2004), p. 69.

41 Groys, *The Total Art of Stalinism*, p. 54.

42 Ibid., p. 50.

43 See Robert Leach, *Revolutionary Theatre* (London and New York: Routledge, 1994), p. 169.

44 See Stuart Cosgrove, *The Living Newspaper: History, Production and Form*, unpublished PhD dissertation, University of Hull, 1982, p. 26.

45 After watching a performance of the Blue Blouse in Moscow, Hallie Flanagan commented, 'these actors/acrobats take possession of Russia's free, high stage, they leap upon the bare boards or upon the machines. They need no curtain to separate them from the audience for they have no illusion to maintain. They never pretend to be imagined characters, they remain members of the society which they illustrate on the stage', quoted in Flanagan, 'The Soviet Theatrical Olympiad', *Theatre Guild Magazine* (September, 1930), p. 10. Also see Lynn Mally, 'Exporting Soviet Culture: The Case of Agitprop Theatre', *Slavic Review* 62(2) (Summer, 2003), pp. 324–42, where she traces the links between the Workers Laboratory Theatre of New York and the Blue Blouse. She mentions extensive correspondence between the parties where the Blue Blouses are asked to explicate their methods. She also traces links between the editors of the journal *New Masses* and the Moscow Blue Blouse in 1930.

46 Hallie Flanagan, 'Address to Regional and State Directors of the Federal Theatre', Washington, 8 October 1935, quoted in Jane DeHart Matthews, *The Federal Theatre* (Princeton, NJ: Princeton University Press, 1967), p. 42.

47 Lowe to Flanagan, 18 January, 1936, quoted in DeHart Matthews, *The Federal Theatre*, p. 82.

48 See Rena Fraden, *Blueprints for a Black Federal Theatre, 1935–9* (Cambridge: Cambridge University Press, 1996).

49 'Unemployed Arts', *Fortune*, XV, May 1937. Quoted in DeHart Matthews, *The Federal Theatre*.

50 New Jersey Republican, J. Parnell Thomas, The House Un-American Activities Committee, 26 July 1938, quoted in De Hart Matthews, *The Federal Theatre*, p. 125.

51 Walter Goodman, *The Committee: The Extraordinary Career of the House Committee on Un-American Activities* (London: Secker and Warburg, 1969), p. 44.

52 Quoted in ibid., p. 44.

53 Quoted in ibid., p. 44.

54 Ibid., p. 46.

55 Ibid., p. 46.

56 *The New York Times*, 13 June 1939, quoted in DeHart Matthews, *The Federal Theatre*.

57 Clement Greenberg, 'Avant-Garde and Kitsch', *The Partisan Review*, Vol. VI, No. 5, Fall 1939.

58 Susan Buck-Morss, *Dreamworld and Catastrophe: The Passing of Mass Utopia in East and West* (Cambridge, MA and London: MIT Press, 2002), p. 89.

59 Berghaus, *Theatre, Performance and the Historical Avant-garde*, p. 236.

60 Berghaus quotes the influential performance artist of this period Allan Kaprow, 'The modern artist is apolitical … Political expertise belongs to the politician. As with art, only the full-time career can yield results,' in *Theatre, Performance and the Historical Avant-garde*, p. 236.

61 See Buck-Morss, *Dreamworld and Catastrophe*, pp. 276–8.

62 Bürger, *Theory of the Avant-garde*, pp. 87–8.

63 Fredric Jameson, *Brecht and Method* (London and New York: Verso, 1998), pp. 168–9.

64 Bertolt Brecht, 'Masterful Treatment of a Model (Foreword to the *Antigone-Model*)', in *Brecht: Collected Plays: Eight* (London: Methuen, 2003), p. 205.

Name Index

Page numbers referring to illustrations are in italics.

Ackerman, Robert, 153
Adorno, Theodor W., 4, 7, 45, 122, 172, 181, 184, 210, 212
Aeschylus, 10, 88, 138, 156, 167, 170–1
  Oresteia, 88, 116, 155, 160, 168–71
Ahmad, Aijaz, *In Theory*, 120
Anderson, Margaret C., 148
Antheil, George, 116
Antoine, André, 44, 48–9, 51–2, 57–8
Apollinaire, Guillaume, 7–8
Aristotle, 2–3, 11, 72, 145–6, 149
  Poetics, 176, 182
Arp, Hans, 187
Artaud, Antonin, 7, 118–19, 120–7, 135–6, 143, 146, 171–2
Auden, W. H., 3, 7, 69, 70, 80, 101–4, 117
  Ascent of F6, The (with Isherwood), 103
  Dance of Death, The (with Isherwood), 102, 103–4
  Dog Beneath the Skin, The (with Isherwood), 78, 103
  On the Frontier (with Isherwood), 103
Auric, Georges, 110–11

Baader, Johannes, 188–90, 191
Bachofen, Johann Jakob, 154
  Mother Rite, 106
Badiou, Alain, 122, 123
Bakhtin, Mikhail, 59
  Rabelais and his World, 14
Bakst, Léon, 104–5

Balla, Giacomo, *Futurist Reconstruction of the Universe* (with Depero), 186–7
Banes, Sally, 105–9
Barba, Eugenio, 120
Barnes, Djuna, 'When the Puppets Come to Town', 40–3
Barthes, Roland, 212
Baudelaire, Charles, 40–1
  'The Philosophy of Toys', 15
Bausch, Pina, 109
Beckett, Samuel, 69, 85, 125, 133, 211
  Waiting for Godot, 155
Belyi, Andrei, 194
Benjamin, Walter, 7, 15, 103, 121, 122, 144, 171, 176, 181, 182, 192–3, 212
  'The Work of Art in the Age of Mechanical Reproduction', 13, 186
Benois, Aleksandr, 31, 65–6
Bentley, Richard, 158
Bergius, Hanne, 187–9, 191
Bergson, Henri, 52
Berlau, Ruth, 172, 212
Bernhardt, Sarah, 39, 55, 62, 96, 128
Bhabha, Homi, 119–20
Bharucha, Rustom, *Theatre and the World*, 120
Bloch, Ernst, 7, 181
Blok, Aleksandr, *Fairground Booth, The*, 31
Bohn, John, 201
Bonnard, Pierre, 49
Bosse, Harriet, 57

Bouchor, Maurice, 18–19
Bowlt, John E., 4
Brecht, Bertolt, 1–8, 70–3, 99–103,
    120–7, 138–51, 171–9
    'Alienation Effects in Chinese
        Acting', 118
    Antigone-Model, 3, 171–6, *177, 178,
        179*, 212
    'Bad Time for Poetry', 100
    Caucasian Chalk Circle, The, 72
    'Conversation about Classics', 148
    He Who Said No, 141
    He Who Said Yes, 141
    Mann ist Mann, 141–2
    Short Organum for the Theatre, 3,
        149, 172, 176
    'Solely because of the increasing
        disorder' (poem), 99–100
    The Lindberg Flight (opera), 8
    'Three Cheers for Shaw', 47
    Threepenny Opera, The, 102
    Wort, Das, edited by (periodical), 4
Britten, Benjamin, 103
Brook, Peter, 120
Browne, Martin, 73–4, 90
Buck-Morss, Susan, 207–8, 210–11
Burchard, Otto, 190–1
Bürger, Peter, 182–3, 189–90, 212
Burt, Ramsay, *Male Dancer, The*, 105

Capek, Karel, *R.U.R. (Rossum's
    Universal Robots)*, 13, 26, 37
Cadava, Eduardo, 192–3
Carpentier, Martha C., *Ritual, Myth
    and the Modernist Text*, 88–9, 154
Cavafy, C. P., 167
Chekhov, Anton, 52, 58–9, 63, 91
    Seagull, The, 59
Chou, Katherine Hui-ling, 140
Clurman, Harold, 39
Cocteau, Jean, 3, 71, 104
    *mariés de la Tour Eiffel, Les (The
        Marriage on the Eiffel Tower)*,
        70, 109–15
Collodi, Carlo *see* Lorenzini, Carlo

Conrad, Joseph, 16–17, 40–1
Constantine, David, 173
Cook, Arthur Bernard, 150
Cornford, F. M., 150, 152, 155
    Origins of Attic Comedy, The, 153,
        154
Craig, Edward Gordon, 3, 5, 7, 12, 17,
    22–32, 35, 37–40, 43–6, 55, 57,
    64–8, 70, 71, 75–6, 82–4, 94, 107,
    118, 120, 121, 129–35, 159–64,
    166, 170, 201
    'Actor and the Übermarionette, The',
        23–5
    Art of the Theatre, The, 23, 160
    'First Dialogue on the Art of the
        Theatre', 66
    'Kleptomania, or The Russian
        Ballet', 106
    Mask, The, edited by (periodical),
        23–4, 66, 131, 160, 161–2
    Page, The, edited by (periodical), 23
Craig, Edith, 155
Crommelynck, Fernand, *Magnanimous
    Cuckold, The*, *32, 33*
cummings, e. e., 7–8

Darwin, Charles, 150
de Chavannes, Puvis, 1
de L'Isle-Adam, Auguste Villiers,
    Future Eve, The, 35
de Maré, Rolf, 111
de Valois, Ninette, Dame, 115–16
    Come Dance with Me, 116
Deleuze, Gilles, 121–2, 124, 125–6, 145
Depero, Fortunato, *Futurist
    Reconstruction of the Universe*
    (with Balla), 187
Derrida, Jacques, 122
Diaghilev, Sergei, 5, 70–1, 102, 104–5,
    111
Doone, Rupert, 102, 103–4
Drew, David, 108–9
Dulac, Edmund, 131–4, 135
Duncan, Isadora, 5, 23, 39, 55–8, 64,
    66, 71, 105–7, 162–3, 166

Dumas *fils*, Alexander, *La dame aux camélias* (*The Lady of the Camellias*), 39–40, 61–3, 96–7
Durkheim, Émile, 152
Duse, Eleanora, 5, 23, 25, 39, 55, 57, 62, 96, 161–4

Ehrenburg, Ilya, 43, 44, 193
  History of the Fall of Europe, 44
  Object, edited by (with Lissitzky, journal), 193
Eisenstein, Sergei, 30, 138–9, 198, 204
  Battleship Potemkin, The (film), 138
  'Montage of Attractions, The', 30, 198
Eliot, T. S., 3, 4, 6, 7, 69–78, 80, 85, 86–92, 100–5, 109, 111, 115, 116, 117, 135, 150, 152–6, 166, 167, 203
  'Beating of a Drum, The', 154
  Cocktail Party, The, 77, 87, 88, 90–1, 92, 154
  Confidential Clerk, The, 92
  'Dialogue on Dramatic Poetry', 104
  Elder Statesman, The, 92
  'Euripides and Professor Murray', 156
  Family Reunion, The, 77, 87, 88–9, 90, 154
  Murder in the Cathedral, 71–2, 76–7, 86, 103–4, 203, *210*
  Poetry and Drama, 76, 90, 91–2
  Sweeney Agonistes, 88, 102, 153, 154–5
  Waste Land, The, 86
Engels, Friedrich, 57, 154
Esslin, Martin, 101
Euripides, 90, 92, 152, 156, 157, 158, 167
  Alcestis, 90
  Hippolytus, 152, 156, 167
  Medea, 156

Evreinov, Nikolai, 30

Farfan, Penny, *Women, Modernism and Performance*, 54–5
Faulikner, Fanny, 57
Fenollosa, Ernest, *'Noh' or Accomplishment, A Study of the Classical Stage in Japan*, 84, 131–2
Finney, Gail, 55
Fokine, Michel, 31, 104–5
Frazer, Sir James, *Golden Bough, The*, 135, 150–1

Gan, Aleksei, 195
Gémier, Firmin, 21–22, 50
George II of Saxe-Meiningen, 44
Goncharova, Natalia, 107, *110*
Goodman, Walter, *Committee, The*, 205–6
Granville-Barker, Harley, 57, 156
Greenberg, Clement, 'Avant-Garde and Kitsch', 206–10
Greene, Naomi, 136
Gregory, Augusta, Lady, 80, 116
Gregory, Eileen, *H.D. and Hellenism*, 167
Gregory, Robert, 75–6
Gribble, Francis Henry, *Rachel: Her Stage Life and her Real Life*, 56
Grosz, George, 187, 188, 190–2
  Gesicht der herrschenden Klasse, Der (*The Face of the Ruling Class*, drawings), 192
Groys, Boris, 182–4, 186, 190, 194, 199–200, 210
  Total Art of Stalinism, The, 183
Guthrie, Tyrone, 102

H.D. (Hilda Doolittle), 154, 166–8
  Helen in Egypt (poem), 167
  Hippolytus Temorizes (poem), 167
Hall, Edith, 158
Hallward, Peter, 121, 122, 124
Harrison, Jane Ellen, 88–90, 150, 152–5, 167

Hauptmann, Elizabeth, 141
Hecht, Ben, 187
Hink, M. A., *Art of Japanese Dancing, The*, 133
Hölderlin, Friedrich, 149, 172–7, 212
Hollaender, Friedrich, 168, 170
Homer, *Odyssey*, 148, 150–1
Honegger, Arthur, 110–11
Housmann, Raoul, *qngE*, edited by (with Lissitzky, journal), 193
Hulme, T. E., 119

Ibsen, Henrik, 47–55, 57, 58, 91, 106, 138, 152
   Doll's House, A, 53, 54, 69–70
   Ghosts, 48, 53
   Hedda Gabler, 53, 54
   Lady from the Sea, The, 48
Ihering, Herbert, *Reinhardt, Jessner, Piscator or the Death of the Classics*, 149
Irving, Henry, 25, 27, 128
Isherwood, Christopher, 3, 7, 69, 70, 78, 80, 101–3, 117
   Ascent of F6, The (with Auden), 103
   Dance of Death, The (with Auden), 102, 103–4
   Dog Beneath the Skin, The (with Auden), 78, 103
   On the Frontier (with Auden), 103
Ito, Michio, 70, 76, 84, 115, 118, 123–7, 129, 131–3, *134*, 135, 137, 164, 166

James, William, 93
Jameson, Fredric, 7, 123, 212
Jarry, Alfred, *Ubu Roi*, 1–3, 19–23, 40, 48–52, 116, 185, 212
Johnson, Ben, 35
Joyce, James, *Ulysses*, 53, 107, 166

Kandinsky, Wassily, 14, 195
Kelly, Catriona, 31
Kenner, Hugh, 88

Kessler, Count Harry, 23, 159–60
Kipper, Olga, 57
Kleist, Heinrich von, 5, 10–13, 16, 26, 28, 30, 32, 40
   'On the Marionette Theatre', 5, 10–11, 24

Lan-fang, Mei, 118, 119, 123–4, 127, 137–47
Lang, Fritz, *Metropolis*, 36–8
Leach, Robert, 30, 58–9, 63–4, 66–7, 200
Leeming, Glenda, 90
Lessing, Gotthold Ephraim, *Laoköon*, 151
Levinson, André, 108, 109
Lewis, Sinclair,
   It Can't Happen Here, 203
Lissitzky, El
   Object, edited by (with Lissitzky, journal), 193
   qngE, edited by (with Housmann, journal), 193
Loncraine, Rebecca, 41–2
Lorenzini, Carlo,
   Adventures of Pinocchio: Story of a Puppet, 35–6
Løvborg, Eilert, 55
Lowe, Richard, 202
Lugné-Poë, Aurélien, 2, 3, 19, 23, 44, 48, 49, 50, 51, 57, 59, 185
Lukács, Georg, 144, 181, 184, 212
Lunacharsky, A. V., 65–6, 181

MacIntosh, Fiona, 158
Maeterlinck, Maurice, 19, 31, 48, 69
Maholy-Nagy, László, 27
Mallarmé, Stéphane, 1, 69
Mallgrave, Henry Francis, 151
Mallory, George, 103
Marinetti, F. T., 3, 5
   donna è mobile, La (Woman is Fickle), 37–8
   Electric Puppets, 37–8, 185

Marinetti, F. T. – *continued*
　Foundation and Manifesto of
　　Futurism, 184–5
　Roi Bombance, Le, 185
　Variety Theatre, The, 198
Marlowe, Christopher, *Doctor Faustus*, 204
Marranca, Bonnie, 93, 94
Marshall, Norman, 115–16
Martin, Carol, 140–1
Matich, Olga, 4
Mayakovsky, Vladimir, 73, 80, 101, 136, 193
　Bedbug, The, 62
　Mystery Bouffe, 60
McCarthy, Lillah, 57, 158
Mehring, Walter, 191
　Simply Classical!, 113, 168–71
Meyerhold, Vsevolod, 3, 5, 13, 22, 25, 29–34, 39–40, 44, 46, 51, 55, 57–66, 73, 81, 97, 108, 119, 124, 127, 129, 138, 139, 195, 199, 201
　'Balagan', 31
Milhaud, Darius, 110–11
Miller, Liam, *Noble Drama of W. B. Yeats, The*, 131–2
Moreau, Gustave, 1
Murray, Gilbert, 89, 150, 152, 154–9, 162
Mussolini, Benito, 37, 135

Neher, Caspar, 100, 172, 174, *177, 178, 179*, 212
Nelson, Victoria, 35
Newman, L. M., 161
Nietzsche, Friedrich, 15, 16, 23, 51, 119, 124, 145, 149, 151
Nijinska, Bronislava, 107–12
Nijinsky, Vaslav, 105–7

Pater, Walter, 16, 17, 92, 119
Picasso, Pablo, 14, 92
Pico della Mirandola, Giovanni Francesco, *De Dignitate (On the Dignity of Man)*, 148, 150

Pinter, Harold, 69
Plato, 6–7, 11–12, 17, 24, 30, 34, 41, 70–3, 82, 92, 97, 99, 145, 147
　Republic, 11
Poulenc, Francis, 110–11
Pound, Ezra, 4, 75, 131–3, 135, 148–53, 156, 158, 159, 164–7
Pritzel, Lotte, 15
Propp, Vladimir, 108
Puchner, Martin, 5, 6, 71, 72, 84, 98–9, 101

Reikh, Zinaida, *65*
Reinhardt, Max, 23, 76, 149, 157–62, 168, 170
Ricketts, Charles, 40–1, 132–4
Riley, Jo, 137–8, 141–2,145
Rilke, Rainer Maria, 15–16
Robins, Elizabeth
　'Ibsen and the Actress', 54–5
　Votes for Women, 54, 55
Rodchenko, Aleksandr, *63*, 193, 195
Rodius, Apollonius, *Argonautica*, 58

Said, Edward, 118–20, 123
　Orientalism, 118
Sano, Seki, 200–1
Schklovsky, Victor, 32
Schlemmer, Oskar, 'Theatre of the Bauhaus, The', 26–9
Schwitters, Kurt, 189
Scott, A. C., 137–9
Segel, Harold B., 14, 21–2, 31, 35, 37
Selvinsky, I. L., *Second Commander, The*, 65
Semper, Gottfried, 151, 153
Shakespeare, William, 76, 137–8, 204
　Hamlet, 64, 66, 67, 160
　King Lear, 159–60
　Macbeth, 20, 160, 203
　Tempest, The, 18, 160
Shaw, George Bernard, 41, 46, 47
　Caesar and Cleopatra, 159–60
Shelley, Mary, *Frankenstein*, 36

Sologub, Fyodor, 29, 30, 34
   'Theatre of the Single Will, The', 29,
     111
Sontag, Susan, 120
Sophocles, 156–9, 164, 167
   Antigone, 149, 171–6
   Elektra, 161, 164–5
   Oedipus at Colonus, 92
   Oedipus Rex, 157, 158–9, 160
   Women of Trachis, 164, 166
Spivak, Gayatri Chakavorty, 119–20
Stalin, Joseph, 7, 8, 39, 43, 60, 115,
     124, 183, 200, 206
Stanislavsky, Konstantin, 23, 25, 46,
     52, 57–67, 160, 161, 199–200,
     212
   My Life in Art, 66
Stein, Gertrude, 3, 7–8, 70–5, 78–80,
     92–9, 117
   Doctor Faustus Lights the Lights,
     72, 78–9, 92, 93, 94–9
   Four Saints in Three Acts, 72, 74–5,
     93, 94
   It Happened, a Play, 92
   'Plays', 74, 93
   Yes Is for a Very Young Man, 92
Stravinsky, Igor, 31, 114
   Firebird, The (ballet), 105, 109
   Noces, Les (*The Wedding*, ballet),
     105, 107–12
   Rite of Spring, The (ballet), 105,
     109
Strindberg, August, 47, 48, 57, 58, 85,
     106
   Miss Julie, 48, 51–3
Swami, Shree Purohit, *Ten Principal
   Upanishads*, translation of (with
   Yeats), 135
Symons, Arthur, 16, 18, 49, 119,
     155–6

Tailleferre, Germaine, 110–11
Tatlin, Vladimir, 188, 195
Tatlow, Antony, 7, 123–6, 130, 141,
     212

Terry, Ellen, 23, 54, 55, 57, 128
Thomas, J. Parnell, 204–6
Thomson, Virgil, *Four Saints in Three
   Acts* (opera, with Stein), 74–5, 94
Thorwaldsen, Bertel, 151
Toller, Ernst, 102
Toulouse-Lautrec, Henri de, 49
Tretyakov, Pavel
   I Want a Baby, 63–4
   Roar, China!, 138, 139
Trotsky, Leon, 39
Tzara, Tristan, 187

Verlaine, Paul, 1
von Hofmannsthal, Hugo, 157
Vuillard, Édouard, 49

Wagner, Richard, 13, 43, 45–6, 67,
     100–1, 115, 149, 151, 153, 157,
     176–7
Waley, Arthur
   Certain Noble Plays of Japan,
     135–6
   Noh Plays of Japan, The, 135–6
Walton, Michael, 161, 162
Weigel, Helene, 55, 57
Weill, Kurt, 100
Welles, Orson, 203, *209*
Wilde, Oscar, 16, 17, 18, 41
   Salomé, 6, 84–6
Williams, Raymond, 57, 58, 213
Woodward, Ellen S., 205
Woolf, Leonard, 54
Woolf, Virginia, 54, 56, 154, 155,
     167
Worringer, Wilhelm, *Abstraction and
   Empathy*, 27–8, 119
Wrangel, Siri, 57

Yakko, Sada, 118, 123, 127–31, 133,
     137
Yeats, W. B., 1–7, 20–1, 25, 40, 41, 50,
     69–87, 99, 115–21, 124, 130–5,
     151–6, 164, 167, 201
   Cat and the Moon, The, 84, 85

Yeats, W. B. – *continued*
  Cathleen Ni Houlihan, 80
  Certain Noble Plays of Japan, 131,
    133
  Countess Cathleen, The, 80–2
  Deirdre, 80
  Fighting the Waves, 115, 116
  Full Moon in March, A, 84
  At the Hawk's Well, *132*, 153
  Hour Glass, The, 75, 82, *83*, 84,
    161, 166
  King of the Great Clock Tower, The,
    84
  Land of Heart's Desire, The, 152
  On Baile's Strand, 115
  Only Jealousy of Emer, The, 115,
    116
  Plays and Controversies, 69
  Plays for Dancers, 5, 77, 82–3, 84,
    115, 116, 131, 166
  Purgatory, 72, 76, 77–8, 85, 115,
    116, 155
  'Tragic Generation, The', 1–2, 5–6,
    50
  Ten Principal Upanishads, transla-
    tion of (with Swami), 135
Yuzhanin, S., 198–9

Zola, Émile, *La Naturalisme au
    théâtre*, 46–7

Subject Index

Page numbers referring to illustrations are in italics.

A-effect, 144–5
Abbey Theatre, Dublin, 70, 75, 80, 82,
    85, 115–16, 130–1
acting, theories of
    and actors' bodies, 5, 26–7, 32–4,
        40, 52, 56–8, 66, 70, 72, 76,
        81–2, 86, 87, 89, 91, 92, 104,
        105, 123–7, 133, 139, 142–3,
        145–7, 169, 197–8
    in the Blue Blouse movement, 197–9
    the actor-tribune, 61–4
    Craig's theories, 160–4
    and dance, 70–1, 104–7, 111, 197
    and directors, 9, 24–5, 29, 44–6,
        57–8, 64, 138
    importance to modernist experimen-
        tation, 9, 10–11
    influence of technology, 12–13, 27–8
    man/marionette debate, 2, 10–12,
        16–17, 20–42, 50, 142, 162
    Meyerhold's dialectical actor, 34, 40,
        61, 127, 142
    and Naturalism, 51–8, 67, 104
    and Orientalism, 104–5, 123–47, 164
    in poetic drama, 70–4, 76, 77, 86–8,
        100–1
    and playwrights, 10, 29, 44, 48, 56,
        73–5, 81–2, 106, 138
    and ritual, 126
    Yeats's theories, 75–6, 81–2
    see also actresses, female imperson-
        ators
actresses
    and female bodies, 34–40, 56, 89,
        128, 133
    and Naturalism, 52–8
    and Orientalism, 35, 104–5, 124,
        128–30, 139–41
    and puppet theatre, 34–40
    relationship with directors, 39, 106–7
    and robots, 36–7, 38
    and technology, 5, 37–40, 95–6
    see also female impersonators, femi-
        nism, 'woman question',
        women
'aestheticisation thesis', 182–3, 186,
    191, 210–11
aestheticism, 16–18, 24, 28, 40–1, 43,
    45, 86, 92, 119, 133, 182–3, 186,
    190, 191, 198
agit-prop theatre, 55, 197, 198, 201, 203
Alexandria, Egypt, 148, 150–1, 166–7
America see United States of America
Americana, 8, 187, 191, 201, 211
anthropomorphism, 5, 10, 12, 50, 119,
    146
anti-theatricalism
    and actors' bodies, 71–2, 98–9,
        133–4
    in the Platonic tradition, 6, 7, 11–12,
        24, 72, 147
    in poetic drama, 73, 79–80, 85, 99,
        101
    in puppet theatre, 11–12, 24–5
    and the Übermarionette, 24–5, 30
'Art as Action', 185
Arts and Crafts movement, 23, 161
Athenian theatre, 2, 4, 149–50, 156,
    157, 160–1, 166, 171–82
athleticism, 110, 111, 115, 127

audiences
  engagement of, 51, 60
  and the Epic Theatre, 30, 50, 177
  and Naturalism, 48, 51
  and Orientalism, 127–8, 131, 137,
    141, 143
  and poetic drama, 77, 80, 86–7, 91,
    101
  relationship with performers, 183–4,
    186, 188, 189
  see also spectators
authors, *see* playwrights
avant-garde, the
  attachment to the word, 3–4, 97,
    117, 213
  bridging of manual, aesthetic and
    intellectual labour, 60
  destruction and rebuilding, 184,
    188–90, 192–204, 212
  and estrangement, 12, 50, 57
  'failure'of, 184, 200, 209–10
  fascination with theory, 4
  fascination with the USA, 7–8,
    200–4, 211
  and Hellenism, 168, 181–2
  and the human body, 5, 117, 213
  and literary Modernism, 3, 7–9,
    212–13
  and Naturalism, 47–8, 55, 58, 62
  and poetic drama, 69, 70, 75, 78,
    102–3, 116
  and 'popular' theatre, 197–8
  radical politics of, 7, 8, 12, 108, 148,
    181–4, 186, 195–7, 202, 204–9
  and technology, 29, 47, 169–70
  theatricality of, 69, 75

Balinese dance, 118–19, 120, 126
Ballet Russes, 5, 70, 71, 76, 102,
  104–10, 115–16
Bauhaus, 3, 12, 13, 26–7, 40, 199, 211
Berliner Ensemble, 3
biomechanics, 5, 13, 25, 29, 30, 32, 39,
  55, 61, 73, 108
Blue Blouse, 184, 193–201, 203

'Book Beautiful', 23
bourgeoisie, 37, 39, 48, 57, 62, 183,
  185, 186, 189–90, 199
Buddhism, 124, 125, 136
Bunraku theatre, 26, 118

Cabaret Voltaire, Zürich, 18, 187
Cambridge Ritualists, 7, 88, 106, 135,
  150–6, 157, 162, 164, 166, 167,
  178–80
capitalism, 62, 97, 102, 108, 183, 202,
  205, 206
Celtic Twilight, 80, 155
children, 14, 15, 16, 35, 49, 129, 203
Children's Theatre, New York, 203
Chinese theatre, 4, 118, 123–8,
  137–47
Christianity
  and actors' bodies, 72, 89
  and the Cambridge Ritualists, 135,
    150
  and Eliot, 6, 71, 72, 76–7, 88–92,
    100–2, 135, 150, 155
  and Hellenism, 4, 7, 155
  and Orientalism, 4, 135
  and the representation of women,
    88–9
  and Stein, 72, 93–5
Christian Science Monitor
  (newspaper), 197
circuses, 27, 157, 197–8
Classicism, 148–59, 162–76
  and Brecht, 171–80, 212
  and Craig's designs for the stage,
    162–4, 170
  in Jarry's *Ubu Roi*, 19–20, 185
  in Mehring's *Simply Classical!*,
    168–71
  and Orientalism, 5, 119, 125, 153
  and Pound's New Hellenism, 151–2,
    165–6
  and tragedy, 79, 85
  and the representation of women, 5,
    56, 88–9, 97, 106, 154–5
closet drama, 6, 71

Cold War, 8, 205–8, 211, 213
Colonial Exhibition, Paris (1931),
    118–19
Commedia dell'Arte, 13–14, 26, 31,
    33, 35
communism, 102–3, 185–9, 195, 202,
    204–5, 208
constructivism, 13, 108, 111, 187, 188,
    189, 193–4, 213
Costanzi Theatre, Rome, 18
cubism, 73, 74, 93

Dadaism, 13, 14–15, 19–20, 73–4,
    211
    Blue Blouse reaction to, 194, 197,
        200
    First Dada International Fair, Berlin
        (1920), 184, 187–94
    and Mehring's *Simply Classical!*,
        168–71
Dalcroze School, 132
dance, 103–17
    in Auden and Isherwood's *The
        Dance of Death*, 50, 102,
        103–4
    and the Blue Blouse, 197
    and Duncan, 39, 56, 57, 71, 106–7
    female dancers, 105–7
    and Hellenism, 151, 154, 156, 162–6
    influence on theories of acting,
        70–1, 104–7, 111, 197
    and Orientalism, 70, 104–5, 115–16,
        128–33
    in Wilde's *Salomé*, 6, 85, 104
    in Yeats's *Plays for Dancers*, 5–6,
        50, 70, 80, 82, 84–5, 115–17
    see also Ballet Russes
Degenerate Art exhibition, Munich
    (1937), 192, 193
democratic traditions in theatre, 18, 37,
    40, 43, 47, 60, 73, 79, 83, 133–4,
    203, 211
dialectical actors, 34, 40, 61, 127, 142
dialectical materialism, 72, 100, 124–5,
    143, 174, 200

directors
    changing role of, in Modernism, 3,
        9, 24–6, 43–6, 52–3, 55, 67–8,
        75, 83, 106
    control of puppets, 14, 24–6, 34,
        39–40
    and Naturalism, 45, 47–8, 51
    relationship with actors, 9, 24–5, 29,
        44–6, 57–8, 64, 138
    relationship with actresses, 39, 106–7
    relationship with playwrights, 24–5,
        29–30, 43–8, 58, 75, 160, 163
'Dynamic Plastic Complexes', 187

electricity, 13, 36, 37–8, 45, 47, 126
Enlightenment, the
    and gender, 56, 79
    and modernist attitudes to human-
        ism, 5, 14, 52, 119, 129, 149,
        158, 159
    and Naturalism, 47
    and Orientalism, 119
    and theories of light, 79, 169
Epic Theatre
    and Athenian tragedy, 149, 171, 176
    and Benjamin, 7, 192
    engagement of audience, 30, 50, 177
    and estrangement, 50, 51
    and Hellenism, 149, 171, 176, 177
    in Jarry's *Ubu Roi*, 3
    and Lan-fang, 141–4, 146
    and Naturalism, 51, 52, 58, 67–6
    and poetic drama, 76, 99–102
    and the representation of women, 62,
        97
    and Wagnerian totality, 176–7
estrangement
    and Brecht, 1, 28, 51, 57, 172
    in Jarry's *Ubu Roi*, 1, 50–5
    in puppet theatre, 10, 12, 15, 27–2,
        30
    and the Russian Revolution (1917),
        194
    use of shock, 57, 61
    and the 'woman question', 57–8

expressionism, 7, 22, 47, 94, 157, 181, 208

fascism, 7, 8, 43, 79, 121, 135, 176, 186, 203, 208, 211
  of Artaud, 121, 136
  of Craig, 29, 37, 121, 135
Federal Theatre Project (FTP), 8, 184, 201–6, *207*, *208*
female impersonators, 5, 35, 128–9, 139–40, 145
feminism, 34, 39, 53–4, 64, 92–3, 95, 108, 155
  see also actresses, women
First Dada International Fair, Berlin (1920), 184, 187–94
First World War, 149, 151, 167–8, 171, 177, 188
Florence, Italy
  Arena Goldoni, 23
  School for the Art of the Theatre, 75
Formalism, 32, 64, 66, 141, 144, 172, 195–7, 199, 204, 206
  and estrangement, 1, 28, 30, 194
Fortune (magazine), 204
Frankfurt School, 125
'friendly group', 111–12, 115
Futurism
  and the democratisation of the stage, 79
  Futurist robots, 5, 13, 27, 37–9
  Futurist *serate*, 184–7
  influence of Craig, 29, 65–6
  love of technology, 13, 27, 37–9, 169–70, 185, 187
  and the mechanics of production, 13, 186
  in poetic drama, 73–4, 79–80
  in puppet theatre, 12, 185
  and the representation of women, 37–9

'generative violence', 185
German theatre

and the A-effect, 144
and abstraction, 27
and the Blue Blouse, 200–1
and Dadaism, 188, 190–1
and Hellenism, 149–51, 153, 157–8, 172, 212
production of *The Threepenny Opera*, 102
and the Romantic tradition, 172–3, 212
see also Berliner Ensemble, First Dada International Fair, Frankfurt School, Munich
Gesamtkunstwerk, 13, 45, 151, 176
gestus, 2, 57, 61, 62, 101, 125–7, 141, 144, 174, 183, 190, 212
Greek theatre, 89, 90, 148–80
  see also Hellenism

Hellenism, 148–180
  and Christianity, 4, 7, 155
  and dance, 151, 154, 156, 162–6
  and humanism, 148, 149, 158, 159, 165, 174
  and poetic drama, 152, 156, 165, 169
  and primitivism, 4, 152–6, 159, 162, 164–6, 175
  and ritual, 4, 88–9, 152–9, 164–6, 175–7
  and 'totality', 149, 160–1, 163–4, 177–8
  see also Greek theatre
'high' traditions in art, 10, 20, 29, 152–3, 182, 203–4
high Modernism
  fascination for theory, 4
  in poetic drama, 79, 100
  in puppet theatre, 40
  theatricality, of 70
House Un-American Activities Committee (HUAC), 8, 191, 204–6

humanism
   and actors' bodies, 5, 134–5, 146,
      162–3, 169, 189
   Brecht's reworking of, 52, 174–6
   and the Cambridge Realists, 153
   and the Enlightenment, 5, 14, 52,
      119, 129, 149, 158, 159
   and Hellenism, 148, 149, 158, 159,
      165, 174
   in Jarry's *Ubu Roi*, 2, 20, 50–2
   Meyerhold's modernist concept of,
      34
   and Naturalism, 51–2, 58, 67
   and Orientalism, 119, 125, 129
   in puppet theatre, 10, 12, 13–14, 20,
      22–3, 34, 50
   and radical politics, 12
   and the Soviet avant-garde, 200

interculturalism, 118–47
Irish theatre, 6, 72, 80–1, 82, 84, 135,
      155 *see also* Abbey Theatre
Irish Times, The (newspaper), 82–3
Italian theatre
   attitude towards technology, 27,
      37–9
   attitude towards women, 37–9
   and the Futurist *serate*, 185–6
   influence of Athenian theatre, 149
   and poetic drama, 79–80
   and puppet theatre, 12, 35, 37–9
   see also Florence, Rome

Japanese theatre
   influence on Artaud, 5, 120, 135–6,
      146
   influence on Brecht, 5, 118–19, 141,
      146
   influence on Pound, 131, 135, 164
   influence on Yeats, 70, 82–3, 115,
      118, 120, 131, 133, 135
   tour of the Blue Blouse, 200–1
   tour of Ito, 70, 115, 118–19, 127,
      131–5
   tour of Yakko, 127–30
   see also Noh theatre

Karaziogis (marionette), 13–14

landscape plays, 74, 78, 92–9
Lef (journal), 194–5
literary Modernism
   and the avant-garde, 3–4, 7–9,
      212–13
   and poetic drama, 69–70, 79
   and puppet theatre, 17, 25, 27, 42
   theatricality of, 3–4, 70, 79
little magazine movement, 23, 193
Little Review, The, 148
living newspaper productions, 197,
      201, 203–4, *207*, *208*
Luo diagrams, 142–3

marionettes, 1, 10–40, 66, 82, 203
   man/marionette debate, 2, 10–12,
      16–17, 20–42, 50, 142, 162
   see also puppet theatre
Marxism 39, 107, 108, 120, 209, 212
   of Brecht, 71, 121, 124–5, 143, 146,
      200
   of Meyerhold, 29, 60
Mask, The (periodical), 23–4, 66, 131,
      160, 161–2
Masquers Society, 155–6
Mechanized Eccentric, the, 27, 28, 29,
      199
Mizuki Dancing School, Tokyo, 132
Modernism
   aestheticising the political, 182, 186
   and the avant-garde, 3, 8–9, 12, 70,
      182, 211–13
   and the changing role of directors, 3,
      9, 24–6, 43–6, 52–3, 55, 67–8,
      75, 83, 106
   and Christianity, 4, 72, 100–1
   and dance, 104–6, 116–17
   debates about theatricality, 6, 12, 72,
      147

Modernism – *continued*
  fascination with technology, 29, 38,
    45
  and Hellenism, 148–9, 156, 159,
    162–4, 177–81
  and Orientalism, 4, 118–19, 138,
    146
  and puppet theatre, 10–12, 16, 22,
    35, 40–2
  relationship between the word
    and the body, 5, 56, 70, 75,
    117
  and the representation of women, 5,
    39, 56–7, 88–9, 97, 106, 128,
    154
  and the Romantic tradition, 25, 30
  see also high Modernism, literary
    Modernism
Morning Post, The (newspaper), 158
Moscophoros (sculpture), 148, 150–1
Moscow, Soviet Union
  and the Blue Blouse movement, 197,
    199, 202
  Moscow Art Theatre, 59, 64
  Stanislavsky's production of *Hamlet*,
    64, 67, 160, 161
  visit of Brecht, 138–9, 142–6
  visit of Craig, 65–7, 160, 161
  visit of Lan-fang, 119, 137–48
  Writers' Conference (1935), 119
Munich, Germany, 15, 148, 151,
    157–8, 192

Naturalism, 45–68
  of Brecht, 47, 51, 52, 76, 101
  of Chekhov, 52, 59
  influence of Craig, 25–6, 30, 64
  and dance, 104, 107
  and Eliot, 87–8, 101, 104
  and poetic drama, 76, 101
  and puppet theatre, 22–3, 27
  and the representation of women,
    25–6, 53–8, 62
  role of directors, 45, 47–8, 51

  role of playwrights, 47–8, 51
  use of technology, 47–8
Nazism, 172, 183, 191, 206
Negro People's Theatre, 203
New Deal, 202, 204
New Masses, The (periodical), 205
New Statesman, The (periodical),91
Nation and Athenaeum (journal), 154
'new woman', the, 53–5, 57, 140
New York Marionette Theatre, 203
New York Morning Telegraph, The
    (newspaper), 40
New York Post, The (newspaper), 206
New York Times, The (newspaper),
    206
Noces, Les (*The Wedding*, ballet), 105,
    107–12
Noh theatre, 72, 75–6, 82–5, 118,
    120, 130–6, 141, 153, 155, 164,
    166
Novji Lef (journal), 194

Object (*Weshtsch – Object –
    Gegenstand*) (journal), 193
October Revolution, *see* Russian
    Revolution (1917)
One Third of a Nation (Living
    Newspaper), *207, 208*
opera, 8, 18, 44, 45, 62, 74–5, 94, 100,
    103
oral traditions in art, 4, 13–14, 16, 29,
    37, 60, 72, 80–1, 98, 155, 197
Orientalism, 4, 81, 115, 118–47, 159,
    164, 173
  and actors, 104–5, 123–47, 164
  and dance, 70, 104–5, 115–16,
    128–33
  in puppet theatre, 118, 133, 137
  and the representation of women,
    35, 104–5, 124, 128–30,
    139–41
  and ritual, 122–3, 126, 133, 135,
    153, 164
otherness, 118–24, 128, 137

Page, The (periodical), 23
Paris, France
 Colonial Exhibition (1931), 118
 International Exposition (1900), 128
 Petit Théâtre des Marionettes, 18
 Théâtre de l'Oeuvre, *22*, 185
 Théâtre de la Gaîté-Lyrique, 107
 Théâtre du Châtelet, 31
 Théâtre Libre, 48
 see also Ballet Russes
performance, 1–9, 180–93, 211–13
 and actors' bodies, 5, 81, 148–9, 162
 and Dadaism, 168, 187–8, 191–3
 debates about theatricality, 6, 85,
  148, 212–13
 and Futurism, 185–7
 and Hellenism, 4, 7, 148, 152–4,
  156, 161, 178–80
 language of performance, 1–9, 12,
  70
 and manifestos, 181
 and modern dance, 104, 107, 116–17
 and Orientalism, 118–19, 143, 146
 relationship between language and
  the stage, 2, 44–5
 relationship between the political
  and the aesthetic, 181–4
 use of shock, 1–2
Petrushka
 ballet, 31
 marionette, 13–14, 31
playwrights
 and actresses, 53, 56, 58, 106
 authorship through the actor's body,
  56, 81–2, 86, 106
 control of puppets, 10, 12, 17–18,
  24–5, 160
 development of Naturalism, 47–8,
  51
 and Oriental actors, 138
 and poetic drama, 73, 75, 78–82, 86,
  89, 103
 and the role of directors, 24–5,
  29–30, 43–8, 58, 75, 160, 163

poetic drama, 69–117
 anti-theatricality of, 73, 79–80, 85,
  99, 101
 and Futurism, 73–4, 79–80
 and Hellenism, 152, 156, 165, 169
 and literary Modernism, 3, 69–70,
  79
 and Naturalism, 76, 101
 and theories of acting, 70–4, 76, 77,
  86–8, 100–1
 'popular' traditions in theatre, 4,
  13–14, 31–2, 34–5, 37, 39, 42, 52,
  60, 61, 80–1, 98, 102, 197–9, 201,
  203
postmodernism, 4, 118
primitivism
 and Hellenism, 4, 152–6, 159, 162,
  164–6, 175
 in Jarry's *Ubu Roi*, 2
 and Orientalism, 164
 and the representation of women,
  105, 106, 154–5
psychoanalysis, 51, 58, 97, 136, 167
Punch and Judy, 13, 20
puppet theatre
 and actors, 2, 10–12, 16–17, 20–42,
  49, 50, 52, 66, 142, 162
 and directors, 14, 24–6, 34, 39–40
 and Futurism, 12, 185
 and humanism, 10, 12, 13–14, 20,
  22–3, 34, 50
 and Naturalism, 22–3, 27
 and Orientalism, 118, 133, 137
 and the representation of women,
  34–40
 and technology, 12–13, 16, 26–7,
  30–1, 37–8, 185
 as total theatre, 29
 see also marionettes, robots

qngE (journal), 193

realism, 67, 76, 149, 172, 181, 195, 208
 see also Socialist Realism

Renaissance, the, 19, 20, 76, 150
ritual
    and Christianity, 4, 72, 90, 93, 135,
        155
    and Eliot, 88, 89, 152, 153–4
    and Hellenism, 4, 88–9, 152–9,
        164–6, 175–7
    of marriage and death, 109, 114
    and Orientalism, 122–3, 126, 133,
        135, 153, 164
    in poetic drama, 89
    see also Cambridge Ritualists
robots, 5, 9, 10, 13, 26–7, 36–8
Romanticism, 11, 13, 14, 24–6, 30–1,
    37, 52–3, 101, 136, 151, 172–3,
    212
Rome, Italy, 18
Russia, *see* Soviet Union
Russian Revolution (1917), 39, 59–60,
    107, 108, 193–4, 199, 202

sameness, 121–4
'Savage God', the, 1, 6, 20, 25, 50,
    116, 159
savages, 2, 9, 148, 152, 155, 159, 162,
    166
Second World War, 136, 149, 171, 184
socialism, 60, 150, 188, 208
Socialist Realism, 183, 186, 199
somatophobia, 73, 133
Soviet theatre
    and the democratisation of the stage,
        79
    and estrangement 1, 28, 30
    fascination with the USA, 8, 200–4
    folklore and 'popular' traditions,
        79–82
    politics of, 183, 186–8, 190, 195,
        207–8
    and puppet theatre, 12, 13–14, 31,
        33
    representation of women, 39–40,
        64
    and technology, 29

    and 'total' theatre, 182–4, 186, 194,
        197, 198, 200, 202
    visit of Craig, 30, 60–8
    visit of Lan-fang, 138–42
    see also Blue Blouse, Moscow,
        Russian Revolution (1917)
spectators, 27, 29–30, 60–1, 78, 102,
    127, 142, 143, 145, 176, 188, 198,
    199
    see also audiences
Stock Market Crash (1929), 201–2
Superdada, 188–90
Symbolism, 4, 6, 16–19, 27, 29, 30, 31,
    65, 111
synaesthesia, 2, 13, 18, 44, 100

technology
    and biomechanics, 29, 61
    and Dadaism, 169
    democratisation of the stage, 60–1,
        134, 169
    and Futurism, 13, 27, 37–8, 169–70,
        185, 187
    and the mechanics of production,
        12–13, 16, 31, 113, 200
    and Naturalism, 47–8
    and puppet theatre, 12–13, 16, 26–7,
        30–1, 37–8, 185
    and the representation of women, 5,
        37–40, 95–6
    in Stein's *Doctor Faustus Lights the
        Lights*, 93–6
    and theories of light, 169
    see also technophobia
technophobia, 5, 7, 13, 26–7, 37, 93,
    133, 170
Third Programme (BBC radio chan-
    nel), 164
totality
    and aestheticism, 45, 183
    and the Ballet Russes, 104–5
    and the Blue Blouse, 198, 200
    and Dadaism, 170–1, 187, 190, 192,
        197

totality – *continued*
and fascism, 121, 135–6
and Hellenism, 149, 160–1, 163–4,
177–8
and Orientalism, 164
in poetic drama, 115
and puppet theatre, 13, 18, 24, 37
and the Russian avant-garde, 182–4,
186, 194, 197, 198, 200, 202
and technology, 13, 28, 45
and Wagner, 45, 67–8, 100, 101,
115, 149, 151, 176, 177

Übermarionette, the, 17, 23–6, 28,
30–3, 35
United States of America, 8, 37,
106, 131, 153, 164, 200–5,
208–9, 211
exile of Brecht to, 8, 102, 191
influence on Stein, 7–8, 69
see also Americana, Federal Theatre
Project, House Un-American
Activities Committee, Negro
People's Theatre
'universal athlete', 110–11, 115
Utopia
and the 'aestheticisation theses',
183, 186, 210–11
and Brecht, 6–7, 8, 34, 143, 146,
182, 212
fascination with the USA, 8, 211
and Hellenism, 163, 177

and Marxism, 29, 107, 143, 146, 183
and Meyerhold, 29, 34, 60
and the Russian Revolution (1917),
60, 108
and technology, 13, 29, 38

ventriloquism, 70, 86, 87, 89, 97
Verfremdungseffect, 1, 40

Wayang theatre, 26, 118
'woman question', the, 5, 39–40, 53,
54–8, 62–6, 107, 108
women
attitude of Craig, 25, 38, 39, 64–6,
129–30, 133, 162
attitude of Eliot, 88–9
and Classicism, 5, 56, 88–9, 97, 106,
154–5
in Dumas' *La Dame aux camélias*,
96–7
the 'female principle', 88, 154–5
and Futurism, 37–9
and marriage, 107–9
and modern dance, 105–7
in Stein's *Doctor Faustus Lights the
Lights*, 96–8
and technology, 5, 37–40, 95–6
see also actresses, female impersonators, feminism, 'new woman',
'woman question'
working classes, 43, 59, 86, 202
Wort, Das (periodical), 4